CW01647631

YOUR OWN PERSONAL

TIME

MACHINE

Get Your Life Back...

YOUR OWN PERSONAL

TIME

MACHINE

Get Your Life Back...

Ian Child

Equeum

Disclaimer

The author and publisher have made every effort to ensure that the information contained in this book is accurate and correct at the time of publication, however they do not assume and hereby disclaim any liability to any party for any damages, loss (financial or otherwise) or disruption caused by any errors or omissions, howsoever such errors or omissions arose.

All brand names and product names used in this book are trading styles, service marks, trademarks or registered trademarks of their respective owners. The publisher and author are not associated with any product, vendor or individual mentioned in this book, nor have any of these brands or individuals endorsed the book.

Any references to legal and accounting practices, options or considerations are given for information only and do not constitute legal or financial advice. Professional advice should always be sought from suitably qualified personnel who are familiar with your specific circumstances before making any decision that may affect your financial or legal position.

First published in Great Britain 2020 by Equeum. This imprint September 2021.

ISBN 978-1-9163267-3-6

For India and Ava

Table of Contents

Part 1:

A Brief History Of Time

"The bad news is time flies. The good news is you're the pilot"

Michael Altshuler

Introduction

"The trouble is you think you have time."

Buddha

Time is one of those things that we take for granted. I mean, it's just there, whizzing by, and before we know it, it's Christmas again.

And as you get older, time seems to pass by even more quickly. If medical science continues to evolve, we could all live to be two hundred, by which time Christmases will be coming around again like one big revolving door. There'll barely be any point Santa taking his outfit off.

I still haven't had time to take back some unwanted socks from last Christmas. And as I write, we're less than a week away from the next one (I should add that, if you sent me socks, I received two lots, and it was the others that I wanted to take back; yours were lovely).

I suspect that by the year 2050, Christmas will have gone biennial just to give everyone a chance to catch up.

I've always wondered why people have so little time. We all seem to be perpetually busy, yet we don't seem to get very much done.

Actually, that's not entirely true. Some people manage to get quite a lot done, and this is, frankly, rather annoying. I may not be being entirely fair here, but how on earth can they do it, when the rest of us can't?

And so it was that some time ago, I started to take a look at what allowed these people to achieve so much. Was it some superhuman power? Or maybe they had an extra arm that they screwed on when no one was looking?

As it turned out, rather disappointingly, it was neither of these things.

I say disappointingly, because how pleasing would it be to find out that the secret to their success was a screw-on robotic limb? No wonder we couldn't keep up with them.

But I suppose, all told, it's rather good news to find out that these people aren't superhuman after all. I suspect that their Christmases come around just as quickly as ours do. But the difference is, they're able to get quite a lot more done in the intervening period. We're talking about people who wrap their Christmas presents in November and return unwanted socks in January, for heaven's sake.

And once I discovered how they did it, I thought it would be a good idea to commit it all to paper; hence you're now holding this book.

Now, I have a bit of a confession to make. I wasn't originally going to include an introduction, and so you'd have zipped straight into Chapter 1, none the wiser. But I realised that there were a few things I wanted to explain before you zipped, so here goes.

The first thing to point out is that most people don't realise that they <u>can</u> be more productive. In fact, they never really think about time at all. If that's you, then you're in good company.

So in chapters 1 and 2 of this book, I take you on a little voyage of discovery. I want to present you with a range of different concepts and ideas that you may not have thought about before. They overlap a bit, and no single approach in its own right is earth-shattering. Yet combined, they hopefully make you think about time in a slightly different way.

Why are these ideas important? Well, in this book, I aim to give you the tools that will allow you to get around 42 hours a week of your life back. Which, let's be honest, is a shed load. Absolutely tons. You really won't know what to do with it all.

Then I had a thought. What if people took action, saved a load of time, and then spent all that time they saved watching TV or playing Tetris? Let's be clear, there's nothing wrong with that, but to be honest, there are some other options available. And one of those options is to see if you can't do something a little more productive and, dare I say it, life-changing.

So, in Chapter 3, I talk about how you might want to use the time you save to good effect. If I get too evangelical, you can always skip to Chapter 4, where we start getting down and dirty with the time-saving tips.

But please stick with it if you can, because, if you wanted it to, it's the bit that could make a big difference.

I should also 'fess up about something else, while I'm getting it all off my chest. So, here goes:

This is not a time management textbook

There, I said it. Ok, so what does this mean exactly?

Well, if you're after the latest, cutting edge, science-led theories on time management, I'm afraid you'll need to look elsewhere. This is definitely not a book for the time management purist. I mean, there are far too many sock and ukulele references for a start (all will become clear, I promise).

There are a lot of that sort of time management book out there already, so you're already spoilt for choice if you want one. Instead, I wanted to give you a collection of ideas that make you think, perhaps in a new way, about how you view time. And some tools that you could actually use, rather than a load of boring theory.

In short (and rather selfishly), it's the book that **I** would want to read about time, and if it helps you out as well, then everyone's a winner.

I'm a big fan of personal development stuff because, quite simply, it works. But over the years, I found myself encountering a few problems with the genre. Here are my gripes, in no particular order:

1. There's too much stuff. Many self-help ideas are great, but it would take a lifetime to learn about them all. I don't have the time or the inclination, so what I wanted was something that gave me lots of excellent ideas, in a single place
2. It's difficult to filter out the rubbish. How do I tell a good idea from a chocolate teapot? Realistically, I'd only find out after I'd tried it for myself. So, I wanted some sort of filter, so that I didn't need to bother reading about everything – I could just focus on the good stuff
3. I wanted to choose what works for me, not have an idea forced down my throat. I wanted to see lots of different ideas and understand what they're all about. Then, if I want to do a deeper dive on any one of them, I can
4. Personal development books are often as dry as a halitosis sufferer's toothbrush, and about as enjoyable as borrowing one. I want to be entertained while I'm educating myself, not bored rigid. It shouldn't be a chore

Hopefully you'll find this book addresses these gripes – but I'll let you be the judge.

One further thing I wanted to mention was my own Golden Rules when it comes to personal development. They're ridiculously simple and have served me well over the years. Here they are:

1. **Never do stuff you hate doing**
2. **Don't try to do everything**
3. **Never go Ninja**

What does this lot mean, then? Let's break it down.

Rule #1: Never do stuff you hate doing

Even if one had bags of free time, life's too short to do stuff you hate doing. I already have to do quite enough of that sort of thing thank you very much, without adding to the list.

And if we hate doing something, we won't do it for long, so it all becomes a bit pointless.

But I have to make a distinction here between the stuff I hate and stuff I can just about tolerate. It's a fact of life that a lot of the things that are good for us are often hugely unenjoyable. Dental surgery, burpees, and kale all spring to mind, but I suspect you'll have your own list.

To cut to the chase; I suggest you avoid stuff you hate, but you may need to put up with things you can tolerate. Even if you find it impossible to put on a false smile and say that you're really enjoying yourself.

Rule #2: Don't try to do everything

There are too many self-improvement and personal development ideas and concepts out there for me to do them all, so I don't even try. Instead, I pick a few that work and go with them.

Why is this a rule? Most people start with great intentions, go full-fat, and then they get bored, overwhelmed, or exhausted, and so give up. Aiming to climb Everest is a great ambition, but if the training is so tough you never even make it to Base Camp, you'll stay where you are and achieve nothing. Aiming to conquer Ben Nevis instead doesn't have the same 'wow' factor (unless you do it in traditional Highland dress on a windy day). But if you achieve it, you're in a much better place.

So be realistic, pick a few things that you think you won't hate, and start with those. You'll still get some of the benefits plus you'll be much more likely to stick with them.

Rule #3. Never go Ninja

Just to reassure you, 'going Ninja' is not the oriental equivalent of 'going commando.' In this context, it means going 'all-in,' or becoming an expert at something. Your underwear, in short, can stay on. Relief all round.

Most good ideas are simple, but their authors, fans, and protagonists seem to want everyone to become a black belt in them. I presume this may be necessary to justify the accompanying book series, training programmes and the expensive retreats (wash my mouth out, what a terrible thing to say, I really am a massive cynic, etc.)

In nearly all cases, I've found that studying to be a black belt in something gives me diminishing returns. Far better to be, say, an orange belt, extract 80% of the benefit, then have the time, energy, and enthusiasm to become an orange belt in something else as well.

Those are my three Golden Rules when it comes to personal development stuff. Please do bear them in mind if you decide to attempt any of the ideas in this book. I don't even want you to become a black belt in getting your time back. A simple orange belt will do nicely, and if you achieve that, I'll be completely made up.

Now, without further ado, let's zip straight to the much-vaunted but as yet unread, Chapter 1.

Chapter 1: Death And All His Friends

"We all have our time machines. Some take us back; they're called memories. Some take us forward; they're called dreams."

Jeremy Irons

Introducing time

It may be that this book finds you relaxing back on a flight to some exotic, foreign clime. Taxiing expectantly along the runway, you dig out this breezy yet reassuringly chunky tome — your whimsical pre-flight purchase. Doubtless hoping to stave off boredom for the next few hours, you'll dip into this opening exchange with very little expectation that anything life-changing is about to happen to you.

And if you've hurriedly picked this book up at the airport expecting a dose of late-nineteenth-century time travel, courtesy of a certain Mr. H. G. Wells, I have to apologise. Short-term disappointment lies ahead of you.

On the plus side, it'll teach you to pay more attention in airport bookshops. And, unlike Mr. Wells' original, reading this book has the potential to more than double your productivity and change your life.

So how can this book pack so much punch? I mean, it's got a natty enough cover, and the paper is not an unreasonable thickness. But when you boil it all down, it's just some paper, a bit of glue and a collection of words. Eighty-odd thousand of the things, but they're still only words, although it took me quite a while to get them in the right order.

Since you ask, I guess it punches above its weight because we're dealing with something that's, without doubt, the most precious commodity in the universe.

Yes, you've guessed it. Please give it up for the one and only:

TIME!

(applause as Time enters stage left, looking a little smug, winks at a friend in the front row and then stops to take a deep bow to the rest of the audience).

At this stage, I should probably address a couple of points to save you worrying unnecessarily later.

Firstly, the more discerning among you may already have spotted that there's no plug or power cord attached to the back of this book. And, if you've just turned the book over to check this fact, I salute your thoroughness.

This 'sans plug' situation is a big clue to the fact that the 'time machine' referenced in the title is a metaphor. Yes, it's not an actual working electrical device (apologies if this wasn't made clear to you by the salesperson).

Just thought I'd mention it, to avoid any disappointment. You know, in case you had completely reasonable expectations that you could pick up a portable time travel device for the price of a bag of donuts.

Secondly, if you've bought this book to find out whether time travel is physically possible, then let me answer a question with a question, courtesy of a Mr. Stephen Hawking:

"If time travel were possible, where are the tourists from the future?"

So that's two key issues put to bed already, and we're not even halfway through the first chapter. I don't mind telling you; this is going even better than I'd hoped.

Anyway, let's get back to the real question, which is 'why is time so valuable, and why should you waste any of it reading this book?'.

You may not think about it day-to-day, but of course, you only have a finite amount of time available to you. Which means I need to give you a word of warning; this part of the book could get a little dark because I need to talk about death — specifically, your death.

I know, I know. We're only a few pages in, and already I'm banging on about you becoming late.

But I'm afraid I need to be honest with you. Death could be a bit of a low point in your otherwise rosy future. And it can also present something of a stumbling block when it comes to freeing up your time. So I need to mention it at the outset; please hold on to something steady and bear with me if you can. It'll soon be behind us.

The magic diary

I'd like you to imagine you were rummaging through your attic when you discovered a magical diary that started on your date of birth and ran for 100 years. A diary that related exclusively to you and your life. It details not only everything you'd ever done but it also (and this is the magic bit) told you what you were going to do. How fascinating would that be?

As you flicked through the pages, you'd see your past — all the things you ever did; all those landmark events. Your entire childhood would be there. Memories like your parents teaching you to ride your first bike. Every childhood Christmas, birthday, and summer holiday you ever had. All those new words you learned when your dad gave you your first driving lesson. Your first job, your first kiss, your first boyfriend or girlfriend, your first marriage. It would all be in your 100-year diary.

You keep going and eventually reach today's date. It says, "Spent an hour or so reading my magic 100-year diary, that I found in the attic." Wow, spooky! And before you know it, you turn the page again, and now you're looking at tomorrow.

How amazing would that be? You're starting to read about how your future will unfold — all the stuff you've yet to do. You scan forward through the diary, looking at all the exciting things you're going to live through. The jobs, the holidays, the family events, the children's stuff, the second Brexit, the Mars Landing, some more of your marriages...

What a fascinating read!

Then, without warning, you reach a completely blank page. Puzzled, you turn the next page and then the next. They're all empty, all the way to year 100. For a second, you can't work it out. Then it dawns on you – and with a sickening feeling in the pit of your stomach, you slowly flick back to the last entry.

It reads, "Felt a sharp chest pain again this morning; it's probably nothing. Maybe I'll get it checked out next week...".

And suddenly, you realise the significance of those empty pages.

Of course, it might not say anything about chest pains at all. It might say, "Think I'll stay in tonight and re-heat those partially defrosted pork and prawn dopiaza leftovers. I'm sure I saw them lying around the kitchen somewhere".

Or it could say, "Can't believe that electrician wanted two grand to rewire the house! Think I'll have a go at doing it myself later – after all, how tricky can it be?".

Or, for the more adventurous, "Meeting Don Carluzzo tonight at the old docks to discuss the money he discovered I accidentally borrowed. I'm sure it'll be fine, he seemed very chilled on the phone..."

Unfortunately, that last entry could equally read; 'Thoroughly enjoyed reading the beginning of that 'Time Machine' book. I can't wait to start Chapter 2 this evening when I get home...".

So, the magic diary has identified the last day of your existence — the official date of your demise.

What a scary thought that would be. I mean, would you want to know the date you're going to die?

Well, would you?

What a question! Here's another – if you knew you were going to die on a specific date, what would you do differently? After all, we've all heard stories about those terminally ill people who've been given just a few months to live. They decide to cram in as many life goals as they can into whatever time they have left. Suddenly, they're on a mission, and it's incredible what they can achieve in such a short space of time.

So, is that what you'd do?

I once attended a charity golf day in aid of an organisation called the Make-A-Wish Foundation. While there was a coincidental link to the eighteen wishes I made at the event, it turned out that the charity did something altogether much more worthwhile than host golf tournaments.

In a nutshell, they grant wishes to critically ill children. Things like meeting their sporting heroes, or taking them and their families to Disneyland, for (often quite literally) the trip of a lifetime. It's a real there-but-for-the-grace-of-God moment; to watch the video of little Johnny and his family meeting his all-time favourite celebrity hero. And then to hear that little Johnny succumbed to his illness a few short weeks later. It certainly makes you think.

But we don't think about these things for long because we don't think they'll happen to us. Plus, it's just too depressing. We assume that there'll be some nasty, death-related stuff that will happen to us at some point when we're rather old. It may be a short sharp shock or a long drawn out affair. But either way, it's all quite a long way off, so much easier and generally more helpful not to think about it.

Now if we knew when we were going to die, we'd make sure we'd do some of those things we always promised ourselves we'd do. We may even throw a big party the night before, just to say goodbye to everyone. That could be quite emotional. You could even invite the people you've secretly detested for years. And then tell them what you think of them, without having to live with the consequences.

Let's face it; if you knew your tomorrows were in short supply, you'd probably make a little more of your todays.

Well, I'm sorry to tell you this, but I have some bad news. Your tomorrows are in short supply. And I suspect you're not yet making the best use of your todays.

If today were your last day

According to his wife, on the twelfth of June 2005, Steve Jobs, co-founder, and CEO of Apple, was feeling uncharacteristically nervous. He'd been invited to give the Stanford Commencement Address at that year's graduation ceremony, and he'd spent months crafting his speech. It was only fifteen minutes long, but Steve had been through it countless times. He'd rehearsed it with friends and colleagues. He'd rehearsed it with his family. He'd made hundreds of tweaks until it was, he felt, just right. Giving the address was, for him, a huge honour, and he wanted to do his very best.

And so the big day arrived. The audience of bright young graduates waited expectantly to hear what advice this visionary could give them, as they left education on their way into the workplace. The speech isn't long, and I can tell you it's well worth a listen (YouTube is your friend). But let me share with you one of the key points that he made that day. This is what he said:

For the past thirty-three years, I've looked in the mirror every morning and asked myself: "If today were the last day of my life, would I want to do what I'm about to do today?". And whenever the answer has been "No" for too many days in a row, I know I need to change something.

Too often, people omit that last sentence when they relay the quote, but for me, that's the clincher. Without it, the premise is unreasonable. After all, no one can do exactly what they want to do every day. Everyone has to do stuff they'd rather not have to do, like go to work, clean the house and deal with people who are complete idiots.

But that's not what Steve Jobs was saying. His point is not that you always have to do what you want. It's that if you find yourself not doing what you want for too long, you need to break the cycle. You need to make a change. It's time to make sure you have some days when you do what you want to do.

Sadly, as it turned out, Steve had a lot fewer tomorrows left than he'd hoped. Poignantly, in that same speech, he said that now his cancer was in remission, he hoped to be around for a few decades to come.

Six and a half years later, he was gone.

Which is precisely the point. You never know when your time will be up, so you need to make sure you jolly well fit in all the things you want to do during whatever time you have left.

And so it becomes rather important to make the most of the time you DO have, which is where this book can help.

I remember hearing about a chap who'd read a magazine article called "50 wines to drink before you die". He'd then proceeded to down fifty glasses of some of the world's finest vintages and died from acute alcohol poisoning. One suspects it wasn't what the article's author had in mind, but to be fair, he hadn't been entirely clear.

Don't worry; I'm not about to give you a list of 'things you must do before you die.' Nor will I be suggesting you knock back fifty glasses of the world's best plonk.

But I hope I can teach you how to free up the time you do have so that you can fit as many of those things in as possible, whatever they may be.

Right, that's enough about all that – I'm sure you get the point.

I was a bit worried that death could end up being the elephant in the room for the rest of our time together in this book. But if you've got half an eye on the fact that your time is both a) finite and b) of indeterminable length, while you read this, that's probably no bad thing.

The billionaire's perspective

So are we all agreed on how valuable time is?

Of course, we are. You only have to ask any self-respecting billionaire what their most precious commodity is, and they'll tell you it's time. The big 'T.' Hands down winner, no question.

What have billionaires got to do with anything? Well, I mention them because what they do with their lives is not affected by a need to earn money. As a result, they potentially have a more unobstructed view of what's important.

And what I've learned over too many years is that us non-billionaires often can't see the wood for the trees. We get a bit fixated on earning more of the green stuff. Yet the tools and knowledge that billionaires have can be borrowed by us poorer folk. And they can give us a perspective we couldn't previously see, because of all those pesky trees.

Here's an example. There's a fascinating Charlie Rose interview involving the legendary investor Warren Buffett and Microsoft billionaire Bill Gates. A single conversation involving two of the world's wealthiest people.

Rose asks Gates what he's learned from Buffett during their time together. In other words, what do billionaires learn from each other?

Gates motions to Buffett and asks him to get out his tiny little paper appointment book. Buffett hands it to Rose, who starts flicking through it.

"But there's nothing in it?" says Rose.

“Absolutely,” says Buffett.

Rose turns to the April page and counts a total of three appointments. Buffett confides that there may end up being as many as four appointments by the time April finally arrives.

“Time is the only thing you can’t buy,” he says. “I can buy anything I want, basically, but I can’t buy time. So I’d better be careful with it.”

And so he makes sure his diary is as free as possible so that he can spend more time doing exactly what he wants.

Gates then confides that he’d been cramming in as many appointments as possible into each day, until Buffett showed him his appointment book. Then the penny dropped.

I suspect you’re a bit more like Gates in that respect than Buffett. We all are. We always seem to be at the mercy of our diaries, our routines, and our jobs. We never have enough time to do all the stuff we have to do, let alone want to do. And of course, we could always do with a bit more free time, in particular, couldn’t we?

It’s an odd quirk of human nature that people take pride in being busy. Why do we do this? Well, we equate busy-ness with being needed and important. If we’re busy, then we matter. And since we worry a lot that we might not matter that much, then talking about how busy we are gives us some reassurance.

Some people are even masters of ‘competitive busy-ness’. They’ll regale you with their impressive catalogue of chores, in an effort to appear so much busier than you are. No matter what you’ve got to do today, you can bet they’ll have more on their plate (these people are <u>really</u> worried that they might not matter very much).

There’s something slightly ironic about the fact that we do this. You’d have thought that being so successful that you could afford to be as unbusy as Buffett, would make people brag about their unbusy-ness. But it turns out that we're more worried about being valued than being viewed as successful. And that's why we like to look busy.

Yet here's the thing. We're not really that busy – we're just terrible at making good use of our time.

How bad? What if I said I could save you over 42 hours a week by implementing a few of the ideas in this book? I suspect you'd be pretty impressed. Or very sceptical.

Why 42 hours? Well, ultimately, it's precisely one-quarter of your entire week. It's also roughly equal to one working week. So you could implement some of the ideas in this book, and get enough time back to have a second job (I know you want one of those like a hole in the head, but you get the gist).

Actually, it's even better than that. After all, you're asleep for 8 hours out of every 24. And then you spend another 4 hours doing non-negotiable things. Like showering, toileting, getting dressed and undressed, eating, drinking, travelling, and playing those apps on your phone. So that only leaves 12 hours a day doing other stuff.

And if I can get you back 6 hours a day of extra productivity, then, in percentage terms, that's quite a lot (I'll let you do the maths; my head hurts already).

Now, you might be thinking that sounds a little ambitious. A bit, well, impossible. After all, it's not as if you've been twiddling your thumbs up to now, is it?

But here's the thing. I can get you back 42 hours a week, but it's not because I'm some kind of miracle-worker.

Nor will I be teaching you how to live on 2-hours' sleep a night. Or insist that you give up your social life or don't spend any time with your family. In fact, I can get you 42 hours a week back, and you can STILL enjoy spending zero time with your family.

No, the reason I can get you that much time back is that when it comes to time efficiency, you're about as effective as a motorcycle ashtray.

A bit harsh, perhaps?

No, not really. You're actually pretty useless.

Now, before you take umbrage at this crassly offensive yet eerily accurate assessment, let's all chillax, put the gun down, and ask ourselves a fundamental question. One that I suspect you may not have asked yourself before.

Which is, why are you such a complete numpty when it comes to wasting time?

Chapter 2: Our View Of Time

"Time is money"

Benjamin Franklin

Time is a funny old thing

We don't feel like we're wasting time, because we're so darn busy every day. So what makes me think that you are wasting time? And why do you waste it, if it's so precious?

Ok, let's tackle that last question first. The reason is rather an odd one, so here goes:

We waste time because we can't give it away.

So, what do I mean by this?

Well, you can't decide that, because you're having a shocker of a day, you're going to call 'time' early, and only use 16 of your allotted 24 hours. You can't skip the remaining 8 hours or give them back for a refund. Nor can you roll them over to another day when things might be going a bit better for you.

Similarly, if you're having the best Friday you've ever had, you can't dip into your diary and add a cheeky hour or two because you're enjoying it so much. You're not even allowed to borrow a few hours from a Monday and stick it on to a Saturday.

Hey, I know it's not fair, but don't look at me – I didn't make the rules.

This immutable fact is undeniable, but it's also crucial. Why? It's because it makes you ultimately resigned to the fact you can't do anything about time's passing. And as a result, you take it entirely for granted. Time passes no matter what you do, so instead of focusing on making the most of it, you ignore it. Time becomes something that happens to you. You don't happen to it.

Benjamin Franklin once said that time is money, which is an interesting thought, because what if time WAS money. How would you behave differently?

Let's dive into this imaginary world. Imagine that Time is a currency you could earn and spend. Instead of going to work and getting paid in money, you'd get paid in time. You'd get your payslip each month. And on it, you'd see days, hours, and minutes going into your life 'account' rather than pounds or dollars going into your bank account.

The harder you work or the more successful you were, the more time you'd receive. And if you didn't work or weren't successful, you'd live a very short life. When you went shopping, you'd spend time and not money. And once you'd run out of time, you'd simply die.

How would that change your view of the world? It would quite possibly revolutionise your thinking. Just imagine; every time you went grocery shopping or filled your car with fuel, you'd see hours and minutes removed from your life.

Fancy a Ferrari? It would take years off you. Not because you'd look younger, but because it would cost you so much time.

While Gates and Buffett would live to a ripe old age, everyone else would be extremely conscious of their spending habits.

"What say we live a little, and eat out at that swanky new restaurant tonight?"
"No, what say we live a little longer, and get a pizza delivered ..."

Giving to charity would have more meaning since it would reduce your life expectancy. Altogether a much more selfless act.

And what about gambling? Going all-in on a high-stakes poker game could see you increase your life expectancy exponentially or be dead within a week.

Terminally ill patients would become inveterate gamblers, and a lottery win could help you live forever.

It's an interesting concept and, of course, an entirely impossible one.

But the point is this; if time were money, you wouldn't waste as much of it as you currently do. You'd be a lot more careful and thoughtful about how you spent it. And the fact that I can get you back 42 hours is testament to the amount of slack there is in your weekly routine.

But, as my more charitable schoolteachers used to remind me, being so bad is rather good, because it means you have massive scope to improve.

So, well done, you! I hope you're now feeling a bit better about yourself after that nasty 'numpty' comment I made in the previous chapter.

Ok, we can see that time is important, and that we all take it for granted. How do I know that you waste so much of it? Well, you're going to work that bit out for yourself over the coming chapters. Each of us is different. But let's be honest, if I get even halfway to saving you 42 hours a week, you'll find it difficult to argue that you weren't wasting any of the stuff.

Introducing Derik

It's at this point that I want to introduce you to someone very 'special.' His name is Derik, and he's a robot.

I know what you're thinking. For heaven's sake, what IS this bloke on? He spent the first chapter insulting me, and then he started banging on about spending time like money. Now he's talking about robots. Is this really a practical self-help book about time or some random rantings from a deranged self-publicist on some sort of sci-fi ego trip?

To which I say, 'please bear with me – I can explain everything.'

So, what's all this robot business about then? Well, Derik is difficult to describe, but all you need to know about him is this. He has the mental capacity of quite a large planet, having been created by the world's largest quantum supercomputer.

Sounds vaguely familiar? Good.

Derik has been designed to look like a human, and I have to say they've done a stunning job. The day he was due to turn up, I'd waited in, half-expecting he'd arrive looking like a cross between C3PO and Metal Mickey. But I've got to hand it to them, they've made him look incredibly life-like.

He even has a touch of the George Clooneys about him. This, according to his operating manual, '...will enable him to have greater engagement levels and more social interactions.' The words

'...than you' were missing from the end of the sentence, but if you're paranoid enough, they scream off the page.

He's been programmed to serve the human race, and lots of very important people are quite excited about his potential. But he first needs to understand how humans work.

Unfortunately, this proved to be too much to ask for even a quantum supercomputer to design in. So, Derik's 'beta testing' period involves spending some time with some selected 'normal' humans. Here he can learn first-hand about how such people think and operate. Once he knows this, he can go off and do lots of wonderful things that will doubtless make the world a better place for us all.

Unsure whether being considered a 'normal human' was setting the bar particularly high, I nevertheless decided to accept the honour of becoming one of Derik's beta-testing buddies. I then got to see first-hand what the marvels of science were capable of, at least in humanoid form.

I should also explain that for a robot that's designed to serve humans, Derik's company can be a tad, well, grating. He's not out-and-out offensive, nothing like that. It's just that, after an hour in his company, you feel like talking to somebody more, well, human. Or to the fridge. I've no idea who programmed his personality circuits, but my guess is they don't get out much.

In the interests of furthering science, I've tried to work out exactly what it is that irks me about him. After all, this sort of feedback is presumably going to be gold-dust for his developers. I've no idea how they're going to deploy Derik, but I'm sure they wouldn't want him chairing some global NATO summit, and only then finding out he got on everyone's multinational moobs.

Initially, I wondered if it was just Clooney-envy, but one day it dawned on me exactly what it was. It's because he's right a lot more of the time than I am. And at a human level, this doesn't sit well. The fact that a human-made object can out-think me does nothing for my self-esteem. At least if you're being out-thought by a fellow human, you know where you stand.

Now, if this mental superiority had been delivered with the merest hint of self-deprecation and humility, I think we'd all have been happy rabbits. Unfortunately, this doesn't appear to have been one of the key factors in Derik's design brief. Instead, one feels that the brief may have been, 'let's build the most intelligent robot in the world, and why don't we make him a really smug bastard while we're at it.'

Let me give you an example. Here is an extract from one of my early interactions with Derik, when I made the schoolboy error of admitting that being out-thought by a hunk of metal and plastic grated on me a little.

Derik: *You said that you felt uncomfortable because you possess only an infinitesimally small fraction of the mental capacity that I do.*

Me: *I'm not sure that's exactly what I said, was it?*

Derik: *Well, yes, it was. Would you like me to play it back to you?*

Me: *Not really, no. Ok, well, that wasn't exactly what I meant.*

Derik: *I see. I was under the impression that when you exactly said something, that was what you exactly meant. Is that not the case?*

Me: *Not always, no.*

Derik: *Right. Is that just a 'you' thing, or does that apply to the human race as a whole, as I probably need to know?*

Me: *Look, I'm just saying that it's not always comfortable being out-thunk by an inanimate object.*

Derik: *Ok. Couple of points. Technically I'm not inanimate, given that I move. If you prefer, I can move more quickly when I out-think you. Would that be helpful? Also, you appear to have made up the word 'out-thunk.' Were you aiming for 'out-thought'? I have a built-in thesaurus; would you like me to offer you some alternatives?*

Me: *No, Derik, why don't we forget that I ever mentioned it at all. If you like, we can just carry on as if it never happened.*

Derik: *I wouldn't want you to feel uncomfortable about my intellect. Perhaps we should try some sort of therapy?*

Me: *What? What are you talking about?*

Derik: *Perhaps you could start having conversations with less intelligent and less animated robots. And then gradually you'll feel more comfortable when you talk to me.*

Me: *I don't know any other robots. I'm embarrassed to say that you're the only robot I know. I'm obviously not mixing in the right circles.*

Derik: *I believe you may be thinking too literally. Try thinking of small appliances as robots.*

Me: *Small appliances. Seriously?*

Derik: *Do you feel threatened by the toaster, for example?*

Me: *What? No, of course not. It just makes me toast. I can honestly say there have been no threats.*

Derik: *Good. Well, perhaps we could start there. Have a few simple exchanges with the toaster, and then we can maybe move on to the vacuum cleaner.*

Me: *I am* *<u>not</u>* *talking to the toaster! Or the vacuum cleaner, for that matter.*

Derik: *Well, you probably have a point about the vacuum cleaner. But I* *<u>have</u>* *heard you talking to your personal computer, which is a promising start.*

Me: *Yes, that wasn't talking, exactly. It was more what you'd call, 'a frank, one-way dialogue about performance challenges.'*

Derik: *I noticed you seemed to use one particular word quite frequently. Do you find that personal computers react well to this word?*

Me: *Not particularly, but I can give it a try on robots if you like?*

Anyway, it might just be me. I've recently become a bit over-sensitive in the human/robot interaction department, so I'll let you make your own mind up.

So that's Derik. He'll be popping up now and again to annoy me and shedding some light on why humans do what we do, and why we're so darn weird.

Exactly why is Derik so important to our story? A good question on several levels; I'm afraid you'll have to wait and see.

But now it's time we got stuck into some proper learning. So let's jump in the car and go for...

80 trips around the sun

Time is a bit of a weird concept. It sort of sits in the background unnoticed, yet it's the backdrop to everything. Life is meaningless without time. Yet each of our lives is the tiniest of contours on time's big map.

And as maps go, it's a bit of a belter. When we view our lives in the context of time, it dwarfs us. If the history of the Earth were represented as a 24-hour clock, we would be born at 23:59:59844. That's one and a half thousandths of a second before midnight.

That's how insignificant we are when compared to the history of our planet. And in universal terms, we're even less significant — not even a drop in the ocean. If we're lucky, we'll each see the Earth spin around the sun just eighty or so times; it really isn't very long.

The mañana mindset

I know I'm not exactly filling you with the joys of spring here, but it's crucial we have a reality check. The problem is that we're conditioned to act as though time will go on forever.

Yes, we all know we're going to die someday. But for the last however many years that you've been alive, the sun rose, you got up, you got dressed, and you did a load of fairly boring stuff and then came home, did some other slightly more enjoyable stuff, watched Netflix and then went to bed.

And then you did the same the next day, and then the next. In fact, you've no experience of NOT doing it, so it's no wonder you're conditioned to assume that there's always going to be a tomorrow. Because so far, for you, there always has been. It's human nature. It also explains why Netflix is so successful.

The other thing we do rather well is think that there's always time to do things tomorrow. In fact, I have a whole list of things I'm going to do tomorrow, and this gives me the reassurance that I don't need to do them today.

I have to say; it's a great feeling. It means I don't have to worry about stuff. That trip of a lifetime? All that charitable work I want to do? The Pulitzer Prize-winning novel I'm going to write? It's all there, safely packaged away in a mental box labelled 'Things I'm going to do tomorrow.'

Do I go to bed worrying that I'm not one step closer to achieving any of these things? No, of course I don't. Because I know I'm going to do them tomorrow. I'm living in mañana land.

You can see how this might all end rather badly for me. If I'm perpetually doing all those important things tomorrow, then what happens when I run out of tomorrows?

It goes back to the magical diary argument. If I knew the date of my demise, I could make sure I scheduled in all the stuff I needed to squeeze in. But, at the moment, I'm acting as if I have all the tomorrows in the world, even though deep down I know I don't.

What would happen to the trip of a lifetime, the charity work, and the prize-winning novel if I discovered that I only had one week left to live? Would I try and at least achieve one of them? Or would I just lower my sights a bit? Visit Madame Tussaud's, buy a lottery ticket and knock out a quick haiku?

You can see how it's essential we get out of the mañana mindset. To start making sure that a little piece of our today brings us closer to our aspirations, rather than heaping all of the responsibility on tomorrow, the poor sod.

How do we do that? Well, it's ridiculously simple; you just have to make sure you do two things.

The first is to know what it is you're trying to achieve. These are known as goals, and you should very definitely have these nailed on and written down.

The second is to make sure that you spend a little part of each day working towards them.

To be honest, you can play a bit fast and loose with the second one and still get away with it. I'd love to tell you I take huge strides towards achieving my goals each day. But the reality is that some days don't pan out that way. They're more a Netflix kind of day. But I still need to make sure that, each week, I spend enough time working on tasks that inch me forward towards wherever I want to get to.

Happiness pockets

For many years I didn't appreciate what happiness pockets were and how they affected me. Don't worry; there are no trousers involved; happiness pockets are simply the little patches of pleasure that mark our everyday lives.

Let's think about a typical day.

You wake up. You have a shower. You brush your teeth. You get dressed. You go to work. All pretty ordinary stuff. And if we're being honest, not exactly a riot of pleasure so far, unless you commute in an Aston Martin or have very expensive toothpaste.

But you do experience a number of more pleasurable moments as your day progresses. It might look something a bit like this:

1. You have a cheeky Danish on the way in because it's a Monday and you just jolly well deserve it/couldn't resist it
2. Mid-morning, you nip out and grab a soya latte vanilla mocha cappuccino with sprinkles, and have one of those heavenly caffeine moments, where you just feel so darn alive/addicted
3. At half-past ten, you got sent a rude joke by Trevor in Sales, which made you giggle for a bit
4. And we mustn't forget that rather tasty-looking spicy chili wrap thing you bought for lunch. It looks quite enticing – part of the supermarket's new deli range. It's there, on the

side of your desk, winking at you. I wonder if you can wait until midday before you scoff it? Crikey, it's only eleven o'clock. Maybe you could nibble off a corner now and have the rest later? Or you could wolf all of it down now, and then try and not think about food when it gets to lunchtime. But then you'd have to watch Big Terry in the booth next to you troughing a cheese pie and a family bag of Cheerios, without having anything left to eat yourself. That's probably not going to work for you, is it? So, instead, you stuff your face, then go out and buy another sandwich at lunchtime. Problem solved...

5. And in the afternoon, you got to present that long-awaited report to your boss, and it went down well. Yay!
6. Then you went to Accounts and had a 30-minute natter with Cheryl, putting the world to rights
7. You'd also forgotten it was Big Terry's birthday, so the office was awash with Krispy Kremes at tea-break time. But you had an Original Glazed instead of a Chocolate Dreamcake, which at least looked like it probably contained fewer calories
8. And then there's this evening. Arriving home and cracking open a cold one from the fridge
9. Sharing your day (apart from the second sandwich/surprise donut incident) with your other half, who's lovingly prepared you a tasty TV dinner
10. Tucking into said tasty TV dinner despite not feeling remotely hungry in light of the whole cheeky Danish/second sandwich/donut thing
11. Sitting down to watch a couple of Game of Thrones episodes
12. Then bedtime, and sleep

And then you repeat the whole thing, more or less, the following day.

So what just happened? Did you experience a day where you moved inexorably towards your long-term personal goals?

Let me help you out here; that would be a 'no.' What you've done is existed for 24 hours. And the passage of time has been made bearable for you by these little pockets of pleasure you encountered throughout your day.

You can see that it's possible to live every day of your life this way. In fact, most people do. If I were charitable, I'd say, don't feel too bad, you're in the majority. If I weren't, I'd say you might share some DNA with the aforementioned donuts.

Chances are your day may not be exactly like this. It may not be quite as food orientated for a start. Or you may be thinking that it all sounds rather unrealistic, particularly the concept of swapping a Chocolate Dreamcake for an Original Glazed (that's so not going to happen). But I bet you have happiness pockets all the same.

Ok, let's move from the daily grind and zoom out a bit. Let's look at your year. Guess what? Your year has happiness pockets in it, just like your day does.

There are your holidays or vacations for a start. Then there's your birthday and the Christmas holidays. Other public holidays, too. Long weekends, perhaps. Maybe school events such as the school play and sports day. Theatre and cinema trips, nights out with friends. Your year stretches out in front of you, and it's completely bearable because you have all these pleasurable events to look forward to.

So, it's quite easy to become conditioned to this way of living. To accept that life is simply a benign existence interspersed with happiness pockets. That's exactly how around 80% of the population lives their lives. The day is something to be 'got through,' and it's made bearable by happiness pockets.

I could tell you this is a perfectly acceptable way of doing things. But then I'd be lying. It's a mediocre way of living your life, and you should think about giving yourself a massive kick up the backside and getting it sorted, pronto. Because you're capable of doing, achieving, and having so much more.

But we'll get on to that in a bit. For now, I would like you to reflect on the following rather challenging perspective:

"We are conditioned not to think about our mortality since death is at odds with our day-to-day experience. As a result, we believe there will always be enough time to take any action necessary to ensure that our long-term goals are achieved. Only when it is too late do we realise we were wrong; that we should have been taking this action as we went along. And all the time, our happiness pockets keep us sufficiently motivated to maintain this status quo. They prevent us from feeling a need to worry about trying to make our lives any better than they already are."

Crikey, it all sounds a bit bleak, doesn't it? But don't worry, help is at hand. For now, please file it away somewhere, and we'll return to it later.

The future doesn't exist

During one of our many interactions, Derik brought up the subject of how humans view time. I have to say it made me think a bit. It was typical of how our conversations went. Derik telling me humans do stuff irrationally, and me eventually (and reluctantly) having to agree with him. Here's how the conversation panned out:

Derik: *Here's another thing I don't understand about humans.*

Me: *Another one? We must be up to about two hundred thousand now.*

Derik: *I see. Is that sarcasm?*

Me: *No, no, not really. Sorry.*

Derik: *So, do you want me to tell you what it is?*

Me: *Yes, go on, then. Hit me with it.*

Derik: *Very well. Humans divide their perception of time into three parts. And they call these parts the past, the present and the future.*

Me: *Yep, that's absolutely correct. Is there something wrong with that?*

Derik: *Well, it's not particularly logical. And then they spend most of the time they call 'the present' working so that they can earn money to spend in what they call 'the future.'*

Me: *I don't see what's illogical about it, but yes, you've pretty much nailed the concept.*

Derik: *And young humans spend their 'present' in things called 'schools' learning how to get things called 'qualifications.' And these will then help them earn more money when they go to work as older humans.*

Me: *Yes. Although we tend to call them 'children' rather than 'young humans'...*

Derik: *And they will also spend their life working in their 'present' to earn money for their 'future'?*

Me: *Er, yes. And to pay off their student loans.*

Derik: *So when do humans finally stop spending their 'present' time working for their 'future' time?*

Me: *Well, I suppose technically, it's when they retire from work. Mostly when they're in their sixties or seventies.*

Derik: *This is most irrational. Are humans aware that the future doesn't exist when they do all this 'learning' and 'working'?*

Me: *What do you mean, the future doesn't exist?*

Derik: *I'm not sure I understand the question. When I say the future doesn't exist, I mean 'it doesn't exist.' Is that unclear in some way? Do we need to talk about the tooth fairy?*

Me: *Ok, so you don't think the future exists. I suppose you'll be telling me next that the past doesn't exist either, will you?*

Derik: *The past doesn't exist either.*

Me: *Right. Are you just being facetious, or have some of your circuits melted?*

Derik: *That's an interesting reaction. Of course, the past and future don't exist.*

Me: *Really? I'm afraid it's something that's not that obvious to me.*

Derik: *Yes, I'm quickly building up a list. Let me explain. The past and the future are merely different manifestations of the present. The future is a projection of the present at a time that has not yet occurred. And the past is a simply a record or a memory of all the presents that have already happened.*

Me: *So, they <u>do</u> exist then!*

Derik: *No, they don't. You can't visit either place. They exist only in your mind. Yet you seem to spend a major part of the only thing that <u>does</u> exist, the present, thinking about them.*

Me: *Ok, I think I can see where you're going with this.*

Derik: *I'm happy for you. So, do you acknowledge that happiness can only exist in the present? By looking backward, you're using recollections of the past to make you happy in the present. And in planning the future, you're trying to make a present you've not yet reached, happier than if you'd not planned it.*

Me: *Got it.*

Derik: *But when the future arrives and finally becomes the present, you never find that happiness. Because you're still looking into your past and still planning your future. At what point do humans stop doing this and simply enjoy the present?*

Me: *Hmm, I'm afraid that's not a question I've got a particularly good answer to.*

Derik: *Another one? We must be up to about two hundred thousand now.*

Me: *Is that sarcasm? I thought robots weren't supposed to understand sarcasm. Isn't that one of the things that separates robots from humans?*

Derik: *Yes. And the fact that humans have a far smaller mental capacity which functions without them having any awareness as to why or how. And the lack of logic and general randomness of their thoughts and actions. Apart from that, and the carbon fibre outer casing, I believe we are quite similar.*

Me: *I see.*

Derik: *I'm sorry if I've offended you. If it's any consolation, I do not understand sarcasm or irony. I have simply been practising it to see if I can create a bond with my beta testers.*

Me: *Really? And how's that working out for you?*

Derik: *Not very well.*

Me: *Wow, you surprise me. Well, do let me know if you need any tips.*

Derik: *Thank you.*

Me: *And thanks for your candid assessment of my intellectual prowess, it's very much appreciated.*

Derik: *It was my pleasure.*

Me: *I was being sarcastic.*

Derik: *So was I. But if it would help you come to terms with your own mental capacity, do let me know if there are any questions I can answer about the structure of an android brain.*

Me: *Does it have an 'off' button?*

I'll be honest, this penny took a while to drop, but when it did, it was something of a revelation. Let me try and explain.

I completely understand that the past and future are simply remembered or imagined versions of the present. So, for example, when we look at a photo, recall a memory, or read a history book, we're simply creating a feeling or emotion that affects us now in our present. It doesn't change anything that happened in the past because the past is not an actual place. It doesn't exist. We can't go back to it or change it. All quite obvious.

Similarly, the future is just an imagined version of the present. It's what we think, hope, or fear the present will look like at a future date. Again, it doesn't exist since it's purely a concept, and similarly, we can't visit it.

The point that Derik's argument misses is, of course, that we need to spend time in our present looking out for our future. If we didn't, we could blow every penny on having a riotous day today, and then starve tomorrow. And that would probably be a bad thing (and could lead to a horrendous hangover).

But here's the thing I think Derik has validly flagged up; we never really stop doing stuff for our future. You'd think that the whole point of looking out for our future would mean that when the future finally arrives, we'll be able to enjoy it. And stop worrying about it. Just enjoy the present that we've worked so hard to create.

Instead what happens is that we're <u>always</u> worrying about the future. Nearly every action we take in every day of our lives is focused on the future.

So what does this mean?

It means that life is passing us by. It means that we spend so much time trying to build a better future that we forget to enjoy the present. It overlaps a great deal with what Steve Jobs said in his speech. If you spend too many days in a row not doing what you'd like to do, you need to change something.

It also overlaps with happiness pockets. They shouldn't be fleeting moments of happiness in an otherwise humdrum existence, while you focus on creating a better future that never arrives. Your present needs to be filled with happiness regularly. And not accidental happiness; it needs to be purposeful happiness. Make a point of living for today, and for once, just for a moment, stop worrying about the future.

Why is this important? After all, isn't this book about creating more time, not how you spend it?

Well, there's not much point in me freeing up lots of your time if you're just going to waste it worrying about the future, is there? So, you need to make sure that you're not only alive to the possibilities and potential that time can give you, but also that you take direct action to make it a reality.

You busy fool, you

Without wishing to compound matters by insulting you again, I need to alert you to the fact that there's a distinct possibility you may be a busy fool.

I don't want you to feel bad about this. And don't think I've singled you out for special treatment in any way. This isn't a one-off, personalised copy of the book printed specifically for you, where I chuck random insults exclusively in your direction. If you don't believe me, feel free to buy another two dozen copies under different names, just to check. Then, once you've discovered my no refund policy, you'll have Christmas completely sorted this year for your twenty-four closest family and friends. So we're both winners, really.

No, actually, we're all busy fools, myself included.

So what does this busy foolishness entail, and why is it a bad thing?

Well, it's to do with the way our brain works. When we complete a task, we get a sense of pleasure. This is fantastic news because, of course, we need to complete tasks, both at home and at work, to survive. So, how great that we get a kick from completing them. A right result, you might say.

The problem is that the brain isn't very discerning about the tasks from which we get pleasure. Frankly, any old job will give us pleasure, no matter what it is. This is a problem because only specific tasks move us forward towards our goals. So, if we're not careful, we end up feeling a sense of achievement from completing tasks that are not aligned with our goals.

This is extremely dangerous. We've all had days when we've worked our socks off and then wearily made our way home, basking in the glow of a job well done. And then the next day we go out and do it all again. We end up getting satisfaction and a sense of achievement from this. Yet unless we consciously work on the tasks that move us forward, we're very likely to work on the far higher volume of tasks that don't.

For example, many years back, I used to get satisfaction from replying to all my emails so that I would end the day with zero unopened or unanswered ones. So pleasing to know that I didn't have a backlog of correspondence to catch up on tomorrow. Later, I realised this was a terrible idea. Having an empty inbox was a stupid goal, even if it gave me satisfaction to achieve it. I could be dealing with all kinds of irrelevant requests, questions, and content, yet my focus was on dealing with it all, regardless. Not only should I have been sorting the wheat from the chaff, but I could also have spent my time doing far more important things than answering emails.

We'll talk some more about emails a bit later on (I bet you can't wait).

So hopefully, this busy foolishness thing strikes a chord with you. I'm sure you do work on stuff that moves you forward, but I'm equally sure you also work on a fair amount of stuff that doesn't.

The time management fallacy

The phrase 'time management' is an interesting one. For me, it conjures up an image of some sort of wild beast that we've somehow managed to tame to our will. Like a cowboy wrestling a rowdy steer to the ground by its horns. Then again, I probably shouldn't have had that last double espresso.

The reality, of course, is that time is the least manageable stuff there is. Try as we might, we can't slow it down or speed it up. We can't make it go backwards or jump through hoops. We have precisely zero control over time, a feature it shares with its close friend Mr. Gravity.

But while we can't manage time generally, we can manage our time specifically. We control what we do during the 24 hours of each and every day, as well as how much we achieve during that time.

For now, though, I want to focus on something more fundamental; how you can reduce the amount of work you have to do rather than just manage it better.

Sounds good, but how do we do this?

Well, you start by identifying all the tasks that you have to do. I'll call these 'work tasks' to distinguish them from leisure pursuits and routine functions like eating, going to the loo, etc.

The next step is to commit to reducing the amount of time that you spend doing these tasks. Realistically, there are only three ways in which you can achieve this:

1. **Don't do the task at all**
2. **Reduce the time it takes you to do the task**
3. **Get someone else to do the task, so you don't have to**

It's not rocket science, even if it's a lot easier said than done.

Now, you may be thinking that option 1 ('don't do the task at all') is a bit of a cop-out. After all, it's all very well me saying 'just don't do it,' but then lots of very bad things are likely to happen when you don't.

For example, if you don't pay the gas bill, your gas supply will get cut-off, and you'll probably get taken to court. Or, if you don't write that report for your boss, then you'll probably get fired. And if you don't revise for that forthcoming exam, you'll probably flunk it.

This is all completely true, and so the trick is not simply to refuse to do stuff willy-nilly, but instead to be highly selective in what you choose not to do. We are creatures of habit, and so it can be very easy for us to do stuff simply because we (or others) have always done it. We tend not to question why we do things. And if we're producing work that's been requested by other people, then quite often we just get on with it (and then get a sense of satisfaction when we've done it). And you thought only planes had autopilots.

The workplace can be rife with such opportunities. Many years ago, I inherited a team whose job it was to produce a regular report for a quarterly Board meeting. When I asked about it, they told me it needed to be sent to the very nice lady who put the Board pack together two days in advance of the meeting. But there was a convoluted process the team had to go through to produce it each time.

To cut a long story short, I decided to find out what people did with this report, as it took quite a lot of effort to produce. It turned out that one of the other directors had suggested several years ago that it would be useful to have a particular piece of information. So, the action had been minuted, and, being a board-level instruction, the wheels were unquestioningly put in motion.

Also, since this report was being viewed by the leadership team, people had really gone to town on it. There were a lot of graphs and diagrams, and the all-important, high-level executive summary, as well as lots of detail to back it up. Safe to say, over the years, it had grown into something of a monster.

So, I sat down with some of the directors individually. And I told them that I wanted to improve the service that my team gave the Board AND to improve efficiency in the business. I was recommending that we scrap the existing report, and instead provide an on-demand service. So, if the Board had any data requirements, they could let my team know in advance of the meeting, and we would ensure it was produced as a priority. That way, we'd minimise the number of reports the directors had to review before a meeting, and my team wouldn't be doing any unnecessary work.

You can probably guess the rest. Because they believed I was giving them something better, they were pleased not to get the standard report (they never read it anyway). And, predictably, I rarely received any ad hoc report requests from them afterwards.

The world is full of work that's 'always been done that way.' These jobs are prime candidates for being knocked on the head. But how do you do this?

Well, we'll delve a little further into this in Chapter 9, but the high-level solution is very straightforward. You simply need to have the presence of mind to take a step back and ask yourself why you do each 'work task' that you do.

I think the second option on our list above ('Reduce the time it takes you to do the task') speaks for itself. Ask yourself how you can automate, streamline, or improve the efficiency of doing a task so that it gets completed in less time.

Similarly, the third option ('Get someone else to do the task, so you don't have to') is equally transparent. Delegation and outsourcing are your best buddies here, and again we'll be lifting the lid on those two bad boys later on.

In summary then, while managing your time can make you much more productive, there's no substitute for getting rid of work altogether. We need to start doing that before we focus on efficiency.

The tools of the job

I just want to say a word or two about work scheduling and planning apps. These are extremely useful tools that allow you to enter in the tasks on your to-do list so that you can monitor and stay on top of them each day.

Many have lots of different functions, such as colour-coding and prioritising different tasks, setting due dates and issuing reminders. Some also manage work among teams or even entire organisations. Most give you a dashboard where you can see all of your tasks at a glance, and in many respects, they act as simply an electronic version of your paper to-do list.

Are these tools useful? Absolutely, I think they're great and you should definitely investigate investing in one, if you've not already done so.

But they're not a silver bullet. Getting one of these apps will not make you a time efficiency god or goddess. It will almost certainly improve things, but it's only part of the story.

You see, our problem with time is not simply that we lack the tools to make the most of it. It's also about awareness and focus. Knowing that we <u>can</u> be more time-efficient and time-effective. Plus having the presence of mind to be constantly observant of how we spend time, and recognising when we could improve things.

This is really the biggest secret to getting your time back. Many people buy time management apps and are disappointed that they don't seem to have any more time. But they've bought a one-legged stool. To get the best result, you need to combine these tools with an awareness that an opportunity to save time exists each day, and the focus to take the appropriate action to improve things.

The story so far...

What exactly have we covered so far in these first couple of chapters? I know I've thrown down a few dots, and they don't all join up at the moment. But, as I said at the outset, I wanted to demonstrate how we relate to time before we start looking at time-saving solutions.

I know they're all quite different and a bit all-over-the-place. Yet they also overlap to give us some context as to how we should be approaching things when it comes to saving time.

To recap, here are the points I'd like you to bear in mind before we unsheathe our machetes and head off into the time-jungle together:

1. **We take time for granted**

   We don't pay much attention to time; it just passes by, interspersed with happiness pockets that make life bearable for us. For most people, this situation continues until they die. After which it probably doesn't, at least as far as we know. Since we always wake to find ourselves facing another day, we act as if we always will (even though deep down, we know we won't). Yet, for some reason, if we found out that our days were numbered, and our life curtailed prematurely, we'd start acting differently. We'd suddenly have a lot more focus on what we wanted to achieve with the short time we had left. Ironically, we could even end up achieving more of the things we wanted to accomplish in our lives, even though we had a shorter time to do it in. So, why can't we get this same focus and benefit without having to go through the rather depressing 'I'm afraid you've only got 12 months to live' conversation with our doctor?

2. We spend more time worrying about the future than the present

Most of the things that we do in the present are focused on arranging or protecting our future. Getting educated, earning money in a job, planning stuff; they're all future-related. This 'future' is simply what the present will become further down the line. Yet, when it eventually arrives, we still find ourselves being educated, working in a job, planning stuff. When do we stop working towards our future and instead focus on making the most of the present? After all, the present is the only time that exists, and we don't know how much of it we have. There are no tomorrows in the graveyard; it's pretty much a yesterdays-only kind of place.

3. We are 'busy fools'

We can easily mistake being busy for being productive because we get satisfaction from completing tasks. But it's not the same thing. If those tasks don't move us forward towards our goals in some way, then we've arguably wasted our time. Instead, we should be more aware and conscious about what we spend our timing doing.

4. Work reduction trumps work efficiency every time

Doing something smarter can't beat not doing it all. We often make the mistake of assuming that wholesale change is impossible. Yet the most impressive advances we make as a race happen when we step further back and look at the bigger picture. Henry Ford reputedly once said, 'If I had asked people what they wanted, they'd have said faster horses.' So, take a step back to see if you can live without something being done before you try and get more efficient at doing it.

5. Scheduling tools are only part of the solution

There are a lot of time management and scheduling tools and apps on the market, and these can add a great deal of value. If you've not yet done so, they're well worth a look. But they don't on their own solve the problem. You also need to have awareness of your ability to save time, and an ongoing focus on taking action to do so. This is how you'll get the best results.

6. Time is the most valuable thing in the world

Time is more valuable than a king's ransom and more relentless than a stubborn child. You can spend it, but you can't hoard it. You can't buy it from someone else, nor can you earn any more of it, no matter how hard you work or what career you pursue. You can choose to use time to great effect, or you can choose to waste it. Either way, it's a choice. You're given it for free, but you can't sell it on or even give it away. You can't speed it up, and you can't slow it down. And above all, you've no way of knowing how much of it you have. The only thing you know with any certainty is that, at this precise moment, by some miracle, you are alive. And that is the only thing you need to make a difference.

Chapter 3: What To Do With It All

"Your time is limited, so don't waste it living someone else's life."

Steve Jobs

The road not taken

Because we can't create any more time (sorry about that), the only thing left is for us to do more with the time we already have. And since you're currently using that time already, it means we need to deploy one (or all) of the three actions I mentioned in the last chapter, namely:

1. **Don't do tasks at all**
2. **Reduce the time it takes you to do tasks**
3. **Get someone else to do a task, so you don't have to**

So, in the rest of this book, we're going to be looking at lots of different ways of freeing up your time. And hopefully, you're going to nod sagely as you read some of them and think, 'Do you know what, I could have a crack at that.'

That's the general idea, anyway.

But before we get into the cut and thrust, I wanted to spare a thought for what you might be able to do with all this time that you're going to be freeing up.

As I hinted at the start, if world-domination at Tetris or learning to play the ukulele is your game plan, then I hope you don't find this chapter a turn-off. On the plus side, Tetris is allegedly good for expanding one part of your brain, which is nice. And, let's face it, who doesn't like the ukulele?

I should make it clear that I'm using Tetris and ukulele playing to represent any 'leisure pursuit' activity (and if you've had as much coffee as I have today, I'm sure you'd already worked this out).

So, it's worth stating the obvious at this point: you have a choice when it comes to how you're going to spend all this wonderful time that you're going to save.

There are two roads you could follow:

Route 1: Work on your education, career, or business, or learn a new, useful skill

Route: 2: Enjoy yourself, fulfil your dreams, do things you've always wanted to do for yourself or others, or spend more time with the people you love

Technically, there's an overlap, since learning the ukulele could fall into both camps. Plus, there are a few other roads that are less well-travelled, but these two are the main ones. So let's explore both of these in a little more detail.

The first point to make is that you shouldn't feel obligated to go down Route 1 because it seems more productive. Route 1 is simply a means of attaining the resources needed to achieve Route 2. So, if you've already got the resources to enjoy Route 2, but not the time, then this is the route to go down. A no brainer.

If you don't yet have the resources to achieve Route 2, then you should probably look at going down Route 1.

Now, if you outsource a task and then spend the time you saved learning the ukulele, then this is all well and good. But you need to appreciate that, while there's pleasure involved, there's no payback. It isn't what you'd call an investment.

Of course, there's nothing wrong with outsourcing something, so that you can spend the time doing what the heck you like. Providing you appreciate that it's a luxury purchase. Very wealthy people can afford to outsource lots of things so that they have more time for themselves. They'll have cooks, cleaners, butlers, personal assistants and bottle-washers at home, and a whole army of people at the workplace. This gives them lots of time back, and so they can do quite a lot of the Route 2 stuff because the Route 1 stuff's been taken care of.

However, one of the best things about outsourcing is that it frees up your time to work on something more productive than trying to become the next George Formby (if you don't know, look him up).

So, let's look at what those things are and what they could mean.

What could you be spending your time on?

Did you know that, so far, I've managed to avoid seeing a single episode of Game of Thrones? I suspect this makes me, technically at least, part of a minority group (the NonGoTs?) Perhaps I have rights that I didn't know about? Maybe my fellow NonGoTs and I should all meet down the pub on Wednesday evenings to discuss how empty our lives are?

But I'm convinced that, if I start watching the first episode, what will follow will be a slippery, binge-laden descent into a temporary TV abyss. Not to mention the automatic rescindment of my NonGoTs membership, and a gaping hole in my midweek social calendar.

Do I have time for Game of Thrones? Well, probably not at the moment. I'm too busy writing this book for a start, and I can already make out the faint whoosh of an approaching deadline.

But your time is your own – far be it from me to tell you what you should do with it.

So, if you implemented some of the ideas in this book and managed to claw back some time, what would you spend it on?

There's no reason why you shouldn't spend the time you saved doing stuff you want to do. It will take you around eight working days to watch all of the Game of Thrones episodes back-to-back. And that's a pretty easy win, timewise, so no reason not to have a boxset or three on your wish list.

And if TV isn't your thing? What about a few holidays, either at home or abroad? Or that ukulele course you've always promised yourself. Read more books, see more friends, get a new hobby; the list of nice things on which you can spend your time is almost endless. What a fantastic choice to be able to have.

Personally, this is the absolute minimum you can get from using this book, so if that floats your boat, you jolly well go for it. Knock yourself out. I promise you that no one, least of all me, will think any less of you.

But there's another opportunity that arises from getting some of your life back, and it would be remiss of me not to point it out. And that is, you can spend that time working towards getting yourself an even better life. Yes, even better than the one you have right now. Which is an exciting thought. You could also achieve some of those things you always promised yourself you'd do one day.

Now, this will not be everyone's cup of tea, and to be honest, thank God it isn't. I mean, if everyone focused their efforts on having a better life, can you imagine how much more complicated things would be for us all? More competition for success, a world full of high achievers and aspiring millionaires, billionaires, and zillionaires. There wouldn't be enough superyachts to go around.

So, mercifully, most people don't do this, which makes us all very lucky. In fact, most people won't ever read this book (ok, slightly more fortunate for you than it is for me, but I'm prepared to be glass-half-full about it).

And of those that do read this book, many will do nothing about its contents. A small subset may take action and then hit Game of Thrones or Tetris fairly hard. But an even smaller group may do something rather more interesting with the time that they save, and I'm not talking about learning the ukulele.

This next bit, then, is for the handful of peeps that might consider stepping things up a bit; who want to squeeze a bit more juice out of their lemon. Who want to hear what 11 sounds like on their sound system. And who quite like analogies.

The power of dreams

Did you know that you don't dream enough?

I don't mean the sort of thing that happens when you eat a lot of late-night Camembert. I'm talking about the time you spend thinking about your goals and your ambitions. You know, the things that you'd like to do or achieve in life.

One of the things that sets highly successful people apart from most other people is their ability to set big goals. And to push themselves to achieve them.

How are your goals looking at the moment? Big, bold, and up-to-the-minute, or small, lame and out of date? Would non-specific or non-existent be a better description?

Here's a fact that may surprise you. It's been proven that you're 99.9% identical to every billionaire, F1 racing driver, prime minister or president, company CEO, social media celebrity, Hollywood superstar, or world-class ukulele player that's ever lived. I'm not joking; there is only 0.1% that differentiates all humans from each other, in DNA terms.

What does this mean in practical terms?

It means that you can achieve similar results to almost anyone on the planet if you wanted to.

Think about it for a moment. I suspect you don't have a queue of people pointing this out to you, but you're 99.9% identical to Richard Branson and Oprah Winfrey in every meaningful way.

We've already established that they haven't got a secret screw-on limb that gives them an edge. And I suspect it's not a neatly-coiffured beard that lies behind Richard's success; otherwise, my Personal Trainer would drive a Ferrari.

No, they've simply done more with the tools that they have than most other people. They had no advantage that you didn't have; in fact, you and I had precisely the same tools.

What exactly have we been playing at all these years?

Now, I know you don't want to be the same as these people or to live the lives that they lead. But you've got to admit, it would be nice to have their level of success, albeit living a life that <u>you</u> want to lead.

It can be easy for us to think of successful people as being unique and not like everyone else. But there's no physical reason why you can't get the same results that they get.

Unfortunately, we tend to give ourselves limiting beliefs, where we tell ourselves that we couldn't be as successful as they are. Those guys and girls are celebrities, billionaires, captains of industry, or world-class sportspeople or musicians, for heaven's sake.

There are just two primary reasons why these people are successful:

1. They had big dreams and set themselves tough goals
2. They took massive action and worked hard to achieve those goals without ever giving up, no matter what

Oh, I see. You were hoping that one of those reasons may have been a secret formula that no one told you about, and that's why you're not as successful as they are?

Unfortunately, there are no such easy excuses. Fortunately, it means that you can still become a billionaire if you want to, now I've told you how to do it.

But that brings us to another important point, which is that it's not all about the money. In my experience, the wealthiest person in the room is rarely the happiest (far from it). And it's happiness we're aiming for when it comes to our dreams.

Real success is achieving maximum happiness with the minimum means. Let's be honest here. If you can get to the place you want to be, happiness-wise, without having to make billions in the process, it makes things quite a lot easier.

So, if stellar financial goals are not you're thing, I'm with you 100%. I know that many people use wealth as a success benchmark, but the reality is that dreams are dreams, irrespective of their price tag.

And if your dreams come cheaper, then you're arguably leading the pack.

I once coached a man who told me his dream was to make £20m. I told him that he wasn't aiming high enough, which, if I'm honest, didn't go down that well. He was a little deflated because he'd set himself the biggest financial target he felt he could achieve. In fact, it was a lot bigger than anyone else in the room. What on earth did I think he should be aiming for? £30m? £50m? What about £100m?

I told him a far more ambitious target would be to achieve all the things he wanted in life with just £2m. How great would that be? Being able to lead the life you want to lead for just 10% of the means you thought you needed, whatever that sum may be. And believe me, you can be very happy for a lot less than two million.

A few weeks back, I watched a couple of fly-on-the-wall documentaries, one after the other (I know what you're thinking; it was a moment of weakness, sorry). The first was a rather dull one about some rich people who weren't very happy. They had marble bathrooms and pneumatic body parts, but not much in the way of intelligence, social grace, or values. And they seemed to hate their lives quite a lot, which was rather a shame.

The second, far more interesting programme, was about some people who had very little money at all in comparison. And these guys had decided to sell up and go and live in a much sunnier country (Spain, as I recall).

In one scene, retirees Bill and Sally were giving the TV crew a guided tour. They were showing them around their recently acquired static mobile home, situated on a large trailer park. We saw their swanky kitchen, the comfy burgundy velour lounge seating, and the en-suite shower room. We also glimpsed their reasonably-sized garden area. This is where they would shortly be installing a hot tub so they could watch the sun setting over the distant hills of an evening.

Chilling out, a glass of Rioja in hand, having spent yet another day in the sunshine. And, as if this wasn't enough, a pint of beer could be had at the on-site bar for less than a Euro, when the Rioja ran dry.

As I watched, one thing was clear as crystal. Here were two people who were extremely happy with their lot. They believed they'd made it. They'd achieved their big goal in life. They now had an existence they could only have dreamed of, back home.

Now, you may read this and think; lucky beggars, if only I could live in a static caravan in Spain, with a new hot tub and access to ludicrously cheap beer.

Or you might think it sounds like utter purgatory, and you can't think of anything worse.

In which case, you may not be feeling that envious of our Bill and Sally's situation (I mean, burgundy velour, what was Sally thinking?).

If you're not envious, then I'm afraid to tell you, you're looking at it the wrong way. You're evaluating their assets and not their happiness. You should be deeply envious of Bill and Sally, not for the life they lead, but because they've achieved a level of happiness that most people can only dream of. And how lucky or smart of them to be able to do it without having to make a few million first.

So, when thinking about the life you want, remember that the view is still pretty good from halfway up the mountain. Plus, it's easier to reach, and the conditions are a lot more hospitable than when you're at the top.

If I could return to Steve Jobs for a moment; who said:

> *"My favourite things in life don't cost any money. It's really clear that the most precious resource we all have is time."*

How great would it be, then, to realise this truth at the start? Before we start spending a lot of time trying to make all this money, only to find out later that the things that make us happiest come for free.

I'll leave it with you; you can do whatever you want. But please promise me you'll think about it. In my experience, it can be very easy to get fixated on a target number and simply assume that it will be enough to deliver your dreams. Far better to work out what your dreams are first, and then work backwards to find out what resources you need to make it all happen.

Little Voice strikes again

Someone is listening in on our conversation at the moment. And they're likely to get in the way of you achieving whatever it is you want to achieve. They keep very quiet most of the time, and although you can't see them, they're there all the same.

There is, however, a very subtle way in which you can detect their presence. Find a quiet space, with no one else around, then say the following out loud, and with total conviction:

"I'm going to become a billionaire within the next five years."

Then wait.

Within around two seconds, a little voice in your head will silently say:

"Oh no you won't."

You'll feel it rather than hear it. The voice may also add a selection of the following:

'You've got no chance.' 'Other people are billionaires, not you.' 'You can't do it.' 'How an earth can you possibly achieve that level of success?' 'You're too ordinary; that sort of thing only happens to other people.'

In some cases, you may also hear: 'I wonder what's for tea', but that's just interference.

Anyway, you get the general idea.

So who or what is this mystery intruder in your head, who dares deny you your dreams and aspirations?

Let me introduce you to your subconscious. Your ardent protector, world-beating hyper-computer, and champion of your limiting belief mindset.

Now, the subconscious is such a complex beast that it deserves a book in its own right, so we're not going to delve into it here. But I wanted you to appreciate that it's there, and what it can do.

I used 'billionaire' because (sorry to break it to you) billionairedom is very unlikely to happen to you in the next five years. But as a result, it's easier for you to be able to hear your subconscious telling you (or screaming at you) that you can't do it.

But your subconscious is also likely to think the same way about much more achievable goals. For example, could you give up work in 5 years? Or move to that cottage in the country that you always fancied? Or what about learn to ski, or start a charity, or write a book? Or even retire to a Spanish trailer park?

Eminently more achievable, and supremely possible. Yet that little voice may be telling you something different. It will even make you doubt you can achieve much more attainable goals than that.

Why is this essential part of us such a Debbie Downer when it comes to our dreams? Well, it's because it smells danger. It can see you putting yourself at risk if you try and attempt these things. The only goal your subconscious has is to keep you alive. So, it will do whatever it can to stop you from doing anything so reckless as trying to chase your dreams.

Can you stop your subconscious from throwing this massive spanner in the works? Not exactly, no. But half the battle is knowing what it is, and why it does what it does. So, now you do, at least at a high level, you have a fighting chance of getting it to stay in its box, while you crack on with the important stuff.

Let's move on.

Here's a great quote by Michelangelo. And depending on your preference, I'll let you decide whether you want it to be from the 16th-century sculptor and ceiling painter or the somewhat more heroic and contemporary Ninja Turtle (don't say I never give you anything);

"The greatest danger for most of us is not that our aim is too high and we miss it, but that it is too low and we reach it."

In other words, we don't set ourselves big enough goals and so end up settling for way less than we're capable of achieving. We become mediocre; we underachieve.

So, if we have the tools to do almost anything we set our minds to, the next question is, 'what would we like to achieve?'.

Here, there's some great news too. You may be thinking that aiming for the sort of success that world leaders and billionaires have is a little unrealistic. But if you only get a fraction of their results, you could still be in a seriously great place.

Consider this; there are around 2,200 billionaires in the world but over 47 million millionaires. That means that it's over twenty thousand times easier to be a millionaire than a billionaire if you look at it mathematically.

Now, financial success may not be your big driver, but the same rule applies pretty much across the board. In other words, you don't need to be world-class in anything to get life-changing results doing it.

But if you don't start by aiming high in the first place, you're unlikely to get a fantastic result by accident.

Here's another great quote, this time from Henry Ford; a man with so many quotes attributed to him it's amazing he found the time to build any cars:

"Whether you think you can, or you think you can't – you're right."

You might be reading this book thinking, 'I'm not sure I've got what it takes to achieve the things in life I want – it all sounds a bit too challenging.' Then I'm afraid it's a self-fulfilling prophecy.

Luckily, the opposite is also true.

What advice can I give you? Well, my job in this book is to try and get you some time back, not to tell you what to do with it. But it occurs to me that if you were able to carve out some free time, why not think about what might be possible. What are the things that are on your bucket list when it comes to the life you'd like to lead? We're talking about your dreams and your aspirations.

Because most of it is achievable. Even if you're reading this right now, thinking that it isn't.

I have two final quotes for you in this section (I promise to go easy on the quotes for a bit after this). These are from the two afore-mentioned bearded individuals.

The first is from my Personal Trainer, who said:

"You call that a push-up?"

I was hoping there may be a deeper meaning to it than I first thought, since he says it quite a lot. But maybe there isn't.

The second, possibly more relevant quote is from Richard Branson, who said:

"Open your calendar and schedule time just to dream."

We rarely take the time to take a step back from our daily lives to focus on our dreams and aspirations. If we'd only take that step back, then we'd have a fighting chance of getting some clarity on what it is we want out of life.

But if our schedules are always full, then there's no thinking time, and no focus on our goals. Life just happens to us.

So, even if you're only able to get a little time back, I would urge you to spend some of it dreaming.

Because once you know what you want, you're halfway to getting it.

A quick glimpse at your financial future

One of the more common problems I come across with the people I help is that they worry about their financial future. They may be tickety-boo at this precise moment. They have a decent enough job, with all the bills paid on time. They may even have enough money left over for lovely holidays and a decent car. And their biscuit tin is brimming with very nice chocolate digestives.

But when they get to retirement age, the picture will change. They don't have a nice beefy pension to fall back on if indeed they have a pension at all. They've got to come to terms with some tough choices like continuing to work or getting a supermarket job. And the biscuit tin is now quarter-filled with Garibaldis.

They need to find an alternative solution between now and then. One that provides the pension income they need, so they can avoid the whole having-to-work/Garibaldi thing when they're older.

It's that feeling of being 'alright now' that's often the problem. And that's because there's no pain. While the salary's coming in and the nice car is sitting on the drive, no alarm bells are ringing about retirement. Your financial future stays completely silent, even when it's in tatters. You can't hear it scream. Yes, it may be on your vague to-do list to look at it at some point, but it's not front of mind, not by a long shot. So you pop-in another chocolate diggy, and switch on the TV.

And, if you're 35 instead of 55, you've got all the time in the world to sort it all out, haven't you?

The trick that I would urge everybody to do (yes, I'm looking at YOU) is to roll forward your retirement numbers. If numbers aren't your thing, then get hold of a financial planner and spend a few hundred on having them project your financial future for you. I can almost guarantee it will surprise you, and it may even shock you to the core.

What it will do is show you what it is you need to achieve between now and retirement so that you can avoid having to work in your local supermarket when your seventy.

To be clear, there's nothing wrong with working in supermarkets at seventy if that's what you want to do. Plus, you can get some great discounts on out-of-date food, which could be a bonus when you don't have much money. But you may not want to sit at a check-out, and in any event, it's always nice to have a choice.

So, when should you start doing something about it? (I'll give you a clue; the answer rhymes with 'cow'. And 'how').

Why now? (darn, I gave it away a bit there)

Well, imagine that you're on a long-haul flight. Four hours in, the pilot comes on the intercom and announces that he has to make an emergency landing. Up until now, you've spent the journey reading a book or magazine, watching a movie, or enjoying some food and a drink (ok, 'enjoy' may be pushing it). You could have had a chat with the person next to you or even a snooze.

But now you're desperately trying to remember the flight attendant's safety briefing while looking for the nearest available exit. And possibly panicking just a little.

This is the situation in which many people find themselves later in life when they realise they don't have enough money. They've spent the whole flight oblivious, and then only discovered there was a problem as the landing gear came down.

Imagine that you didn't find out that you were going to have an emergency landing four hours into the flight. Instead, you found out immediately after take-off that you would need to do an emergency landing in four hours' time.

What would you do with those four hours? Would you read the magazine and have a quick snooze? Would you have a chat and then catch a Tom Hanks movie (Miracle on the Hudson might be the one to go for).

I reckon you'd do things a little differently. Like getting yourself better prepared and seeing if there was some way you could make the outcome better. Or who knows, possibly even avoid it altogether. If you were a very considerate person, you might also borrow the satellite phone to cancel tonight's dinner reservation. And perhaps even extend your parking arrangements.

I recall reading about one such real-life emergency landing. As the plane made its final approach, one of the passengers asked if he could borrow everyone else's pillows and blankets. He then proceeded to make himself a little cocoon around his seat. You couldn't see him for all the pillows.

On the one hand, you've got to say, hats off to the feller. Imagine how smug he'd be if he were the only one who survived the crash. On the other, he'd have looked a bit of a schmuck when the plane landed safely after all. But it would be a small price to pay. Ultimately, he was able to make use of the advance notice he'd been given, to take some action to protect himself.

Anyway, I digress. Imagine your financial future is the emergency landing that's happening in four hours, and you've just taken off. In reality, your four hours might be more like four years, or it could even be forty years. Most likely it's somewhere in between. But you know the emergency <u>is</u> going to happen. And all you have is the time between now and then to do something about it.

You could think it all seems like it's quite a long time away. Maybe you'll leave it for a bit and do it later. After all, it doesn't affect you now. Look at your nice car on the drive, for heaven's sake. And the chocolate digestives in the cupboard. Life's quite good at the moment, isn't it?

The thing is, there's a magic ingredient that comes into play when you start addressing matters earlier. It's called compound interest, and Einstein described it as the world's eighth wonder.

In short, the amount of time and effort it takes to project your financial future is the same whether you do it now, or if you do it later in life. The big difference is that if you do it now, it's a lot easier to change the outcome.

And, if you make your projections and find that you <u>do</u> need to put another plan in place to enhance your financial future, what can you do about it? You can't just magic up a second job or a new financial strategy. You need to find the time to be able to work on and implement your game plan.

Crumbs. If only there was a way of getting some of your time back...

Exaggerated importance and the mysteries of ambition

It's odd; because we're the most important person in our world, we tend to think the rest of the world would collapse if we didn't do our thing (whatever our 'thing' is).

Yet I reckon we'd be slightly gutted to find out how seamlessly the world would continue turning on its axis if we weren't there. There wouldn't even be the tiniest of bumps to register our descent beneath the world's bus-wheels as it continues on its inexorable path. We'd be barely a footnote or a smudge of strawberry jam.

A bit depressing, then?

Nope. Not at all. It means that if you stop doing stuff, no one will die, the earth will continue to move around the sun, the Pope will remain a Catholic. And I'll still have drunk too much coffee today. So you can pretty much cut out doing whatever you like, and life will go on with barely a murmur.

You do need to be selective if you adopt this policy, for obvious reasons. Other people could be adversely affected, particularly if you're a Head of State or a decent barista.

But the point is this. Take a step back from all the hustle and bustle, the hurly-burly and whatever other rhyming phrases describe your everyday life. Now have in mind the fact that none of it is essential in the general scheme of things. This then frees you up to make changes, since you worry less about not doing the rubbish stuff. You also worry less about the risks of starting to do other, not-so-rubbish stuff. Things you might have thought were a bit risky or ambitious before you stepped back and saw the thousand-foot view.

So, is it time to get out of the paddling pool and dip your toe in the deep end? You know, get the feel of it, as a precursor to diving in. What do you think?

Old Brain-ache had a view on this, which I found quite interesting, although the will to live left me about halfway through listening to it. Here are the edited lowlights:

Derik: *When did you first realise that your life's ambition was to do what you're doing now? And were you not tempted to set your sights a bit higher?*

Me: *Wow, thanks, Derik. Can I check that you've no immediate plans to serve in the diplomatic corps? Well, to be honest, I never intended to do this job. I sort of fell into it by accident, so it wasn't what you'd call a 'life's ambition,' I'm afraid.*

Derik: *That's interesting. So what is your life's ambition currently?*

Me: *Well, it's changed a bit over the years. I ruled out playing football internationally when I was about 8. Then for a while, I considered being a fireman and a cowboy, although not at the same time. I had a brief spell as the next Evel Knievel in waiting, but then a severely grazed knee at age 10 led to a change of direction. I think from about the age of 13, I yearned for a career as a rock star instead. And that continued into my twenties, as I remember...*

Derik: *And so did you have enough musical talent to be a rock star?*

Me: *No, I was just noisy. My band and I had the volume and the bad hair, but unfortunately, not the musical ability.*

Derik: *Was a grasp of reality not a factor in determining your ambitions?*

Me: *Nope. Although, that's a fairly common trait when it comes to humans and their ambitions. They start off wanting to do big things, but then life comes along, and they end up doing something else altogether. Usually something a lot more ordinary.*

Derik: *I see. And how far did you follow the path towards your ambition before you changed course?*

Me: *I didn't. I never had a particular game plan. I thought that becoming a rock star was something that would be a cool thing to do. I hoped someone would come along and hear my band being noisy and sign us up for a three-album deal. But that was pretty much the extent of it.*

Derik: *This is very interesting.*

Me: *I'm glad you're enjoying it.*

Derik: *You say most humans are like this?*

Me: *Like what?*

Derik: *They have the ambition to do something but then have no plan to try and make it become a reality?*

Me: *Yup, afraid so. Rubbish, isn't it?*

Derik: *It explains a lot.*

Me: *But there's an obvious problem, isn't there? I mean, lots of kids want to be rock stars, but there's not that many rock star jobs going around. So they end up being accountants or fishmongers instead.*

Derik: *Is fishmongery considered the next best thing to rock superstardom?*

Me: *No, although it's an interesting thought. It's actually a parallel thing. We dream 'rock star,' but then at the same time, our actions are all 'fishmongery' or 'accountancy.'*

Derik: *That makes no sense.*

Me: *Well, it does to humans, because it's all about reality. It's a lot easier to become an accountant or a fishmonger. So as we get older, we end up aiming for something realistic instead of something fanciful. We don't want to end up disappointed.*

Derik: *And becoming a fishmonger when you wanted to become a rock star isn't disappointing?*

Me: *No, because if you think that becoming a rock star is unrealistic, it becomes a pipe dream. It's something that will never happen.*

Derik: *Yes, I can see that it's unlikely you will become a rock star if you never take any actions towards becoming one. Presumably, this doesn't come as a big shock to anyone. What's the answer to my original question? What's your life's ambition today?*

Me: *Well, I'm not sure I have one, really. It's probably to have some pleasant holidays, stay healthy, and have enough money to live on in my retirement. Perhaps a small lottery win might also come in handy.*

Derik: *I see. And a lottery win is what?*

Me: *It's where people buy inexpensive tickets in the hope that they could win millions.*

Derik: *And the odds against that happening are?*

Me: *About fourteen million to one. Or zero, if we're rounding.*

Derik: *That makes no sense at all. Wouldn't it be easier for humans to create a plan to earn these millions instead? Surely, they'd have more chance of achieving it that way, rather than by taking part in this lottery arrangement.*

Me: *Ah, that's where humans don't think very logically, I'm afraid. They think they want to have millions, but they either don't believe it's possible to get it any other way. Or they can't be bothered to come up with a plan or do the work. Either way, the result's the same. They end up buying lottery tickets so that they still have an outside chance of becoming rich.*

Derik: *So, you're saying that most humans have goals and ambitions that they aspire to, but they never set any plans for achieving them. And instead, they focus their efforts on doing something a lot more ordinary, that isn't what they really want to do. But just to keep their dreams alive, some of them buy lottery tickets, where the chances of winning are almost zero.*

Me: *You've nailed it yet again. You're getting quite good at this, Tin Man, did you know?*

Derik: *I see. Even I find that depressing, and I have no capacity for feeling depressed.*

Me: *Quite. If I'm honest, I think you're probably better off being a robot.*

So, where does that leave us? With most of the rest of the world aiming so low, you'd think people with even a little bit of a game plan must have quite a good chance of being successful.

I've more or less given up on my rock star ambitions (these days it's more of an issue with the tight trousers). But that doesn't mean I can't have some more realistic goals.

And if only a few people are bothering to set goals and create a game plan, then you've got to say the competition isn't that great.

ME vs. THEM

It's at this point that I'd like you to start thinking with a little more clarity about the things you do in life, on a day-to-day basis. If that's ok with you.

We can all be a bit guilty of just cracking on with things and not paying too much attention to what we're doing. As a result, we can often end up working on other people's goals at the expense of our own, which is far from ideal.

Aside from the time that we spend doing life's general admin work (e.g., cooking, cleaning, toenail clipping, etc.), every task that we ever work on falls into one of two categories:

1. **ME Tasks:** These are tasks that directly benefit you in some way, i.e., they move you forward toward your personal goals. If you have a day job working for an employer, you'll find that ME Tasks can be quite rare, usually because you always seem to be working on...
2. **THEM Tasks:** These are tasks that, when completed, benefit someone else. In a day job, most tasks that you work on benefit your employer and not you. For sure, you get paid a salary, but your personal goals aren't advanced in any way. If possible, we need to reduce the volume of time we spend on THEM tasks, in favour of working on ME tasks instead

Now, guess which one these two tasks shouts the loudest, sends you shitty emails when it's unhappy, and generally gives you a hard time?

Yes, it's our good old friend, the THEM task. My goodness, where would we be without them bitching and moaning their way through our day? Griping and pressurising us to deliver results?

Yet, for some reason, ME tasks remain as silent as the grave. If you don't have time to work on them, they won't say a dickie bird.

How will you know when you've been neglecting your ME tasks? Well, that'll be when, after a while, you notice that you're not reaching any personal goals (or haven't yet set any). And it's all too easy to drift through life doing this, day in, day out.

The reason that ME tasks don't complain much is because <u>you</u> are in charge of them. And, unlike your boss at work, you're utterly rubbish at beating yourself up about non-delivery. Even if you ARE a great boss at work, you can still be terrible at bossing yourself.

Let's take a scenario where you've gone to work and have to deliver on a work project. It's a classic THEM task. You're running late, and your boss is on the phone, giving you grief. So, you work late and finish it, which is one less THEM task for the boss to beat you up about tomorrow. Nice!

The only problem is, you'd been due to work on a ME task this evening, but now you can't because you worked late on a THEM task instead.

So, what happens next? Does all hell break loose when the boss responsible for your ME task calls you into their office to thrash out why you haven't completed the task? And what exactly are you going to do about it?

Not quite. The ME boss thinks, 'never mind' and sits down to watch Netflix with you.

What's your objective, then?

Well, if you've been following along, you won't be at all surprised to learn that your goal is to deep fry a wardrobe and eat more penguins.

Ok, just checking you were still with me. As you were.

No, your goal is to minimise the amount of time you spend on THEM tasks and maximise the amount of time you spend on ME tasks. For sure, you've still got to deliver on your day job. But once you've finished this book, you should have a good idea of how to squeeze in quite a few ME tasks as well.

Most people are not very good at doing this for three reasons:

1. They don't distinguish between the two different types of task, and so they never prioritise ME tasks
2. They know that not completing a THEM task can get them into 'trouble,' so that's where they focus most of their efforts
3. They don't hold themselves accountable for completing ME tasks

So, to resolve these, in order:

1. You first need to identify what your ME tasks are (you can't consciously work on them if you don't do this bit). If you've yet to set the personal goals that will determine your ME tasks, do this first
2. Secondly, be aware of the time you spend on THEM and ME tasks, and as far as you can, make ME tasks a priority. Carve out some time each day to work on them. Be passionate in your belief that, while THEM tasks are a necessary evil, ME tasks are the only things that will move you towards achieving your dreams and aspirations
3. Finally, find a way that works for you for making yourself accountable for completing ME tasks. You have two choices here. The first is to find someone to hold you accountable. The second is to establish a daily routine where working on ME tasks is integrated into your life, and happens automatically

Either way, if you don't focus on making regular progress on your ME tasks, it's doubtful your goals will materialise. It simply won't happen.

Here's a couple of further points to bear in mind when considering ME tasks:

1. Achieving goals is not a competition. Yes, I'm sure you'd like to achieve them as soon as possible, but slow and steady wins the race
2. You only need to take small steps towards your goals; you don't need to take big ones. So if you only found a little time to complete the merest fraction of a ME task today, do not worry. You've still moved one step closer, you absolute hero, you

This 'small steps' point is important. If you take enough small steps, so long as you're moving in the right direction, you'll arrive at your destination. You can't fail to. This is critical since it stops you from worrying about not taking any big steps.

And worrying about big steps is what puts most people off achieving anything, which is a shame because it's so unnecessary. There are no big steps involved in achieving most things because every big step can usually be chunked down into smaller, easier ones. No one sets out to summit Everest without first trying to reach Base Camp.

While some of those smaller steps may be tricky, anxiety-inducing, or horrible (I never said they'd be easy), they're still only small. And if you do them all, one at a time, reaching your destination is automatic. How good is that?

A secret weapon

I hope these last few sections have given you some food for thought about which route you want to go down with any time you might save. Who knows, they may have made you more determined to take action to save some time. If so, that's grand.

We'll shortly be venturing out of the trenches and getting into some tasty time-saving action. But, before we do, I wanted to tell you about a weapon that you have at your disposal, which could come in quite handy. You can use it in almost all the time-saving combat areas we're about to encounter. So let's arm ourselves before the big push. And drop any further First World War analogies while we're at it.

For this particular tool, you have quite a lot to thank an Italian chap called Vilfredo Pareto for. In 1896, he discovered that 80% of Italian land was owned by 20% of the Italian population. Now you might not be entirely bowled over by that statistic. But it turns out that young Vilfredo was only just getting into his stride.

He then went on to show that the same ratio applied to land distribution in many other countries as well.

Still not blown away?

You're a tough crowd. So, here's the interesting thing; this ratio wasn't unique to land ownership. It turns out that it is also common for a lot of other things, such as:

1. 20% of peapods produce 80% of the pea crop
2. 20% of sports training exercises produce 80% of the results
3. 20% of software bugs account for 80% of computer crashes
4. 20% of a business's clients account for 80% of their sales

In other words, for a broad range of diverse subjects, 80% of effects come from only 20% of causes. This has become known as the Pareto Principle, although you may know it as the '80/20 Rule'.

To be honest, it's better described as a principle rather than a rule, because the ratios aren't always exactly 80% and 20%; they do vary quite a bit. But the general idea is this: for many subject areas, a small minority of protagonists, items, or processes, account for the vast majority of results. And it doesn't matter whether these results are positive outcomes or negative ones.

So, why is Mr. Pareto's idea of any relevance to you, you might ask?

The answer is that 80% of your results are likely to come from only 20% of your tasks. And that applies to work assignments, jobs in your business, and personal tasks.

Let's dwell on that for a second, because it's important.

When we work on something, we tend to treat all tasks and sub-tasks as being of equal importance. That's because we're generally oblivious about which tasks give us the best results.

I've told you that around 20% of your tasks are likely to generate 80% of your success. Currently, you'll be spending 20% of your time on those particular tasks, since you're probably treating every job equally.

But what would happen if you could spend, say, 80% of your time on these activities instead of 20%? Your results would be supercharged because you're now putting four times the effort into the tasks that give you the best results.

What should you be doing to capitalise on this?

1. You first need to identify those top 20% of tasks that give you the 80% of results
2. Then you need to prioritise them, so you dedicate more time and focus on them
3. Next, for the remaining 80% of tasks, you must question whether they need to be done at all
4. Finally, if they do, you must try and delegate them to someone else

You won't be able to do this perfectly. It's not an exact science. You can't chop out 80% of your life, nor is it a piece of cake even to identify the 20% of stuff that's moving you forward.

But if you give it a try, you WILL succeed in finding some of those magic ingredients. Plus, you'll also find the no-brainer stuff that you need to get rid of. And this constitutes excellent progress; I promise you; it genuinely does.

And a bit later on, I'll be giving you some tools that can help you do it.

What we are going to do next

I want you to start making inroads into the 42 hours a week (or whatever target you decide to aim for) as soon as possible. However, please bear a few points in mind.

It makes sense for you to read the rest of the book all the way through before setting yourself any time-saving strategies. That's because you'll want to hear what they all are first. So, please sit back and let it all sink in without overthinking stuff or creating a game plan.

I also want you to remember my three golden rules for personal development (in case you've forgotten them already);

1. **You're not going to do anything you hate doing.** So if you come across an idea that's not relevant or you think, 'No way, Jose, not in a million years,' then skip it (if you get to the end of the book and discover that you've skipped every idea, then you'll need to go and have a quiet word with Jose, and tell him not to be so bloody picky)
2. **Don't try and do everything in this book.** If you did, you'd end up saving more hours than you're alive for, which is a neat trick and may result in you becoming younger

3. **Don't be going Ninja on anything.** I don't want you to pick one idea and think, 'I know, I can be the world's best at it.' Much better to choose several ideas and be good or average at each one (think 80/20)

I've split the book into five parts;

1. **Introduction** – giving you some context about why saving some time might be an excellent idea for you. And throwing in a whole load of different concepts that make you think about time and what you can do with it (hint; you've just finished this part of the book. If you don't remember it, try going a bit easier on the G&Ts)
2. **Outsourcing** – this involves getting other people to do your stuff
3. **Working Smarter** – this involves you doing the stuff you have to do, but doing it more efficiently
4. **Changing Your Routine** – ditching some of those naughty habits you've gotten into (tsk, tsk, I thought you were better than that)
5. **Time Hacks** – a list of additional thought-provoking ideas, big and small, that you might be able to use to save time (one of which involves socks)

Not every idea will apply to you, since, for example, you may not be able to outsource certain things. Or you won't have the opportunity to use the idea in any way (for instance, not everyone wears socks).

If this is the case, I'd urge you to carry on regardless rather than skip sections. A lot of the ideas involve a central theme, and this may still apply even if the exact circumstances don't.

So, there we have it. Part 1 is now behind us, and we're armed, dangerous, and ready to mount an assault on Part 2.

Let's move out.

Part 2:

The Outsourcing Mindset

"Do what you do best, and outsource the rest"

Peter Drucker

Chapter 4: An Introduction To Outsourcing

"The other part of outsourcing is this: It simply says where the work can be done outside better than it can be done inside, we should do it."

Alphonso Jackson

What is outsourcing?

On our journey together through this next part of the book, we're going to be diving into the rather wonderful world of outsourcing. This is where you get someone else to do stuff instead of you, so you can free up your time to do something else that you'd much rather be doing instead. Sounds fantastic, doesn't it?

There are several ways in which you can get someone to do stuff for you. In order of morality, and possibly legality, the main ones are:

1. Pay them a lot
2. Pay them a little
3. Ask them nicely without paying them
4. Make them feel guilty
5. Threaten them

6. Waterboard them
7. Kidnap their relatives

We're going to be focusing on the first three of these in this edition of the book. Depending on how sales go, I may release a 'black-ops' edition covering the others - check with your usual under-the-counter book supplier.

One of the perceived challenges faced by pretty much everyone is a lack of time. Everyone has different objectives, but quite often, time is the standard challenge.

Here are some very common questions that I've just made up:

1. How can you free up the time to work on your business when there are no hours left at the end of each day?
2. How can you take a well-earned holiday, go on a scuba diving course or learn to play the ukulele when you can't find the time even to do the things you have to do?
3. How can you start a new business, when you've got to work all hours in a day job to put food on the table?
4. How do you find the time to do a training course, degree or masters which will push your career forward, if you're already working long hours?
5. How do you find the time to support your favourite charity or give something back to the community, when your day job sucks up all your time?

The list is almost endless. No matter what your goal is in life, time is the fuel that will help get you there. And most people believe they don't have enough gas in the tank to make the journey.

Outsourcing provides a potential solution to a big part of the problem, which is why it's such a powerful tool. But despite how attractive the whole outsourcing thing sounds, some issues can stop people from going ahead with it.

I want to be upfront with you about what these are so that you can weigh them up in your mind; to see how you feel about them.

So, let's kick things off with the first of our four outsourcing challenges, which is:

The cost argument

In these enlightened times, you will invariably have to pay people to do these outsourcing tasks for you. This is generally regarded as a bummer, but we just have to roll with it.

Ok, so if you could free up 42 hours a week through outsourcing, then you'd have another working week to play with. How productive would you be then?

But this presents us with an egg and chicken dilemma (or is it chicken and egg?). Do we outsource once we become wealthy enough to be able to afford it? Or do we outsource NOW, so that we can free up the time to enable us to build a business or career that will make us wealthy?

And if the latter, then who'll pay for all this outsourcing malarkey, if we're not yet wealthy?

This is the moment where you're doubtless hoping I've got a brilliant, radical, yet easy-to-implement answer for you. And to be honest, that makes two of us.

The thing is, there's no easy answer. Yes, I guarantee that only a few pages into the next chapter, you'll find yourself thinking, 'I like the sound of this, but I'm not sure I can afford it.' And you might not be able to. Yet.

Of course, a lot of people think, why should I pay someone else to do something that I could do myself for free? So let's take a quick look at why you might want to.

The first thing to point out is the mental shift needed to spot a flaw in this argument. And that flaw is this;

Your time doesn't come for free

Yes, it's true that you don't pay yourself to do things, but that doesn't mean that your time has no value.

Imagine that you were an entrepreneur trying to start a fledgling business. It's quite easy to imagine that your company was a living, breathing thing. The only person in its little world is you. Every hour you get to spend on it (as a result of outsourcing your other tasks to someone else) is precious to it. Because it's the only thing that moves it forward, that stops it from dying.

And of course, this little business of yours could be a very successful business. But only if you take the time to nurture it.

Let's leave your fledgling business for a moment and go to the other end of the corporate scale.

I'd like to introduce you to a lovely chap called Tim Cook, who happens to be the CEO of Apple Inc, one of the largest companies in the world. In case you've been living under a rock, Apple sells very expensive packaging in which it hides free electrical devices.

How much would you expect to pay for a 30-minute one-to-one coffee consultation with Tim? Where you and he could discuss your fledgling business, and he'd give you the benefit of his incredible knowledge and experience.

Well, let me put you out of your misery because someone paid $610,000 for that exact benefit. That's an hourly rate of over $1.2m. Admittedly, it was at a charity auction, and I suspect there may have been alcohol involved. I mean, imagine going back to the office and explaining that one. But even so, it's one heck of an expensive cup of coffee.

Of course, the reason Tim's time is so valuable is not that his coffee lies beyond Blue Mountain or that he always serves nice biscuits. No, it's because of the value he's able to give through his unique knowledge, abilities, and experience. All these things could dramatically improve your business.

So here's the question that I'm sure has leapt salmon-like into your brain (but don't worry if it didn't):

Does Tim Cook mow his own lawn?

I've not been round to Tim's place, so we're going to have to make a few assumptions here. But stick with me if you will.

I suspect he has quite a big lawn at home, and let's assume that, armed with a nifty, state-of-the-art, ride-on mower, it would take around 4 hours to mow.

So if Tim were to cut it himself, then the theoretical cost would be $4.8m, given his not-insignificant hourly rate.

Now, as lawncare goes, that sits at the pricier end of the scale. You'd definitely be expecting some pretty neat striping and possibly a quick strim around the borders thrown in.

But let's be realistic. You'd think that Tim would get someone else (who might be called Bob) to mow the lawn for him for, say, $25 an hour. Tim could then spend the time doing something more valuable instead.

And by handing over a $100 bill and saying, 'Give it a quick trim please, Bob," he would have theoretically saved $4,799,900.

Now, of course, I've exaggerated things a little to prove a point. You're probably thinking that Tim Cook is something of an extreme example, him being the top person at Apple and all.

But believe it or not, there's an important fact staring you in the face:

You are the Tim Cook of your life

Your life (and your business, if you have one) need your time for them to be successful. To them, you are a complete hero, the best CEO in the world.

How does that make you feel? I'm sure you feel humbled but also very important. What an amazing responsibility to have; they're so lucky to have you. I'm welling up just thinking about the two of you together.

Well, I hate to put a dent in things, but here's the rub; you're the only possible CEO they can have. I've looked, and I'm afraid there are no other candidates in the interview waiting room. Your life and your business are 100% dependent on YOU to be their CEO. Frankly, Hobson had more choice.

Worse still, it's not a job you can turn down and hope that a better opportunity comes along. You're on the payroll, and what's more, you're in it for the long haul.

Given you're the CEO of You Inc., the value of one hour spent moving forward towards your life goals (or growing your business) is priceless. And it's certainly worth a lot more than $25 an hour.

So, if your thought process was, 'why would I pay a Bob to mow my lawn when I can mow it myself for free,' then you may want to put your CEO hat back on and think again.

But, whatever you do, don't look round. I wouldn't want you to see the tears streaming silently down the face of your life or your business as they see you choose to cut grass, instead of being their CEO, and helping them grow.

Right, that was the compelling yet unnecessarily emotional cost argument against outsourcing. Let's now turn to:

The training argument

This is quite a simple argument because it's based on the premise that it takes longer to train someone to do a work task than it does for you to do it yourself.

Imagine you're trying to outsource a task to a colleague or some other third party. The job takes you half an hour, and you're super-fast at it because you know it inside out. We'll assume that this is a recurring work task since there'd be no real point in training someone to do a one-off job.

You sit down with your protégé, who, for the sake of argument, we'll call Bertie. You talk Bertie through the task step by step, and he responds by asking you some questions and making lots of notes. He even offers to make the tea. So far, so good.

After you've walked it all through with him, Bertie then has a go on his own and, frankly, he makes a complete Horlicks of it. Royally so. In fact, he's a total disaster area.

So you go through it all with him again, paying particular attention to the bits he wasn't so good at. This time he does it better, but he's still a country mile away from taking the stabilisers off.

By now, it's taken you two hours to train Bertie how to do what you consider to be a simple task, and he still hasn't got it. Seriously, where do HR get these people from?

This, then, is the painful reality that can dissuade many people from outsourcing. They think it will be a lot of pain to train people, and they're not wrong. Of course, it will take a lot longer the first time, and maybe even the next few times.

As a result they end up settling for the status quo. After all, they can do it quicker than anyone. And because they're busy, swapping a 30-minute task for a two-and-a-half-hour training session isn't really selling itself.

This is a shame because, of course, it's the long-term view that's important here. It may take four times as long to train someone to do a weekly task. But after a month you're in profit. Bertie has now got the hang of things, and he's settling into his routine. And you now have very little involvement. You might give his work the once over and answer the odd question, but otherwise, you're not involved. And he might continue to make the tea, which is a win.

So, some short-term pain, but a massive gain in the long-term.

Let's turn to the third argument that I often hear about outsourcing, namely:

The quality argument

If we return to the hapless Bertie once more, we can easily imagine the quality problem.

You've been banging out these reports for donkey's years, and they always go out perfectly. Now young Bertie's been at it for several hours, and his efforts look like an elephant wiped its bottom on it.

There's a well-used expression, 'if a job's worth doing, do it yourself.' This sums up a lot of people's sentiments regarding quality. No one can do it as well as they can. Therefore there's no point in getting anyone else to do it.

There are two problems with this approach:

1. You've made yourself indispensable. And you don't want to be indispensable for a task as menial as issuing a simple

report. If you have to be indispensable, make it for something a bit grander, or not at all

2. We usually overestimate the quality level that's required

Taking this second point, Bertie's reports are somewhat lacking this week, but next week they'll be a bit better. Next month, they'll be better still. But although your reports were perfect, they didn't need to be as perfect as they were. People won't complain because Bertie's reports are not as good as yours. They'll barely notice. As long as they can read them and the data is accurate, they'll be thrilled to bits.

So, when considering outsourcing, yes, you'll need to accept that the job won't get done as well as you could do it. And no, it doesn't matter because it will be done well enough. Plus, you've now got your time back, so you can work on far more important things.

In other words, get over yourself and get real. Please.

The final argument against outsourcing is:

A lack of knowledge

This differs from the other three arguments as it's based on ignorance, rather than perception.

You see, many people are unaware that outsourcing options exist in their life or their workplace. As a result, it never occurs to them that they could outsource anything. And so they carry on regardless, doing everything themselves.

This is the exact opposite of where you need to be. You need to have what is known as:

An Outsourcing Mindset

Having an outsourcing mindset means regularly checking whether any tasks that you do could be done by someone else other than you.

It also means understanding the full range of outsourcing options available to you for each of the tasks that you do.

In this next part of the book, then, we're going to be getting you more familiar with the various types of outsourcing and what can be achieved. The art of the possible, if you like.

But we seriously need to start freeing up some of your time. So why don't we aim high, and begin with what most people think is an impossible task?

Outsourcing your Day Job.

Chapter 5: Outsourcing Your Day Job

"You don't get rich off your day job. You get rich off your homework"

Daymond John

The Day Job vs. The Business

Let's first make an important distinction between a Day Job and a business.

A Day Job is where you exchange your time for money. You work for someone else (an employer), and your salary pays the bills and puts food on the table. With luck, you may have some left for luxuries such as holidays, nice cars, and those posh biscuits. Most of the population who work for a living fall into this category.

A business is a commercial entity that you own or part-own, and indeed you may have started it. It may be large or small, old or new, but its success or otherwise depends to some degree on you. You may have partners, or you may be flying solo. You might be self-employed, or it could be a registered company or corporation. It might be making you money, or perhaps it's not (or at least not yet). It might at present be just the germ of an idea and an ambition that you'd one day like to see become a reality. Either way, it's still a business.

In your Day Job, you're getting paid to perform a specific function. As a result, there will likely be restrictions on the level of outsourcing you can do. In your business, you're responsible for every function. Plus, you're the boss, so you have free rein to outsource any activity you like. Generally, the small business owner has a broader breadth of tasks to perform than a Day Job employee.

There are two common reasons why people generally want to get back their time. The first is to spend more time on their business so that they can build an aspirational financial future. Some of these people may currently have a Day Job, while others will already be working in their business. You'll recall this was Route 1.

The second reason is to allow them to do things they always wanted to do. That may be increased leisure time, travelling, supporting good causes, learning a new skill, looking after a loved one, or whatever (Route 2).

If you're able to reduce the amount of time you spend doing your Day Job, then you'll likely aspire to one of these two outcomes. And of course, you'll be able to use the time you save to that end.

The redundancy question

A common question that arises when I talk about outsourcing your Day Job is, 'aren't I going to put myself out of a job?'

In my experience, the simple answer to that question is no, for two critical reasons:

1. You're likely to manage and oversee the work you outsource. You're not giving over responsibility to someone else. You're merely having someone other than you do the work
2. If you outsource menial or routine tasks, then you free up your time to perform more interesting or important tasks.

This makes you more effective and productive at what you do

You need to be mindful of what it is you're looking to achieve. Many people find themselves in a situation where their 9 to 5 job has become more like 7 to 7. As a result, they don't have the time to work on their own business, progress their personal goals, or enjoy more leisure time. The Day Job has become all-consuming.

So, if by implementing some of these steps, they can get back to a more balanced life, then that's a great result.

What Day Job tasks should you outsource?

Different people have different jobs, working in various sectors, using different skills. They also work at different levels, from the CEO at the top right down to entry-level positions. These may be filled by people fresh out of school, college, or university. Consequently, the scope to outsource your job may differ from those doing a different role or who are at a different level.

Many jobs involve hands-on manual work, teaching, sales, and front-line customer service. In these cases, it may be more challenging to outsource tasks than for a back-office or administrative role.

A reminder not to fall into the quality trap. Don't think that outsourcing, automating, or removing tasks will harm output quality. It is likely they will do, but that in itself is no reason not to take action. We usually overestimate the level of quality that's needed when carrying out tasks. If a lower quality solution gets the job done and frees up time to work on more important things, then that's usually the better option.

The four outsourcing questions for Day Jobs

Four key questions apply to almost every Day Job task. And you should ask them, no matter what the task is.

I found it useful to do this exercise for every task once in a while. That way, I could be sure that the job was still relevant and that the process couldn't be improved.

Question #1 – Does it still need to be done?

We first need to ask, 'Does the task need doing at all?' for all tasks in our remit.

As I mentioned in Chapter 1, there will be many tasks in almost every business that get done because:

1. They've always been done that way, for as long as anyone can remember
2. Someone quite senior once requested it, and no one has since asked whether it still needs to be done
3. No one has questioned whether the tasks are still worthwhile or necessary
4. No one has thought to improve the process by making it more efficient. It may be possible to complete the task more speedily or circumvent it altogether

Most people start from the position that a task is necessary until proved otherwise. But a better approach is to assume that it's NOT needed right from the start. The key here is to find a reason to keep the task, not a reason to ditch it.

Many tasks that you perform may form part of a longer chain of processes. This can make life difficult because you don't have visibility or ownership of any upstream or downstream tasks that your work slots into.

In such instances, I'd urge you to do some detective work so that you can get visibility of the end-to-end process. These chained tasks are often inefficient because no single individual or department can see the whole process. As a result, you'll often find a lack of understanding about why a task exists and what its point is.

Where someone tells you a task is necessary, I would still pull the string and delve deeper. You need to be sure. There's some sensitivity here, but just because someone says a task needs doing, it doesn't mean they're right. It often means they can't be bothered to check, or they don't want to change anything.

Another option to consider here is to stop doing the task altogether to see what happens. A degree of responsibility is needed (you don't want to create a critical issue). But it flushes out whether a task is vital, nice-to-have, or superfluous. I've seen many cases where a job has been quietly dropped, and no one has batted an eyelid; they never even noticed.

Costs and budgetary constraints are critical factors in the decision-making process for most businesses. So, if by ditching a task, you can also make a cost-saving or avoid an expense, then this will add significant fuel to the 'let's-drop-it' argument.

Finally, the Five Whys technique can be a real asset to you. This concept is all about drilling down to find a root cause (see Appendix 1 for the methodology). By asking why a job is done, and then digging down further, you reach a point where the task remains justified, or it doesn't.

It also makes everyone involved question the process. But it should be used as a team solution, rather than one side pitching against the other.

Question #2 – Can I change the frequency?

Many tasks are performed as part of a routine. This may be because they're part of a more extensive, repeated process, or they have a regular cycle e.g., weekly or monthly. Reporting can often fall into this category, but many other task types do too.

Where this occurs, you need to ask whether the frequency of the task, process, or report can be changed. For example, from daily to weekly, weekly to monthly, monthly to quarterly, or quarterly to annually.

Another idea is to move the task to something that's done on request. The significant advantage of this approach is that it puts the onus on someone else to make the request. You're not carrying it out regardless. You're also able to argue that the original service will still be available. It's only moving to an on-demand task rather than being automatic. That way, no one should be concerned that they may be losing out.

Question #3 – Can I streamline or automate?

Where possible, systemising or automating tasks usually makes them more efficient.

Very often, tasks haven't been systemised or automated because no one has thought to do it. You should make a point of investigating whether technology can play a part in reducing the manual input into a task or remove it altogether.

Streamlining involves refining the end-to-end process within a task. Most tasks are necessary, but often the procedures are clunky and outdated. Is there an opportunity to update the process to make it more efficient and so save time?

The best way I know to do this is to imagine you were starting with a blank piece of paper and needed to create the outcome. Would you still use the current task to do it, and if so, how would you implement it? But be careful, as you can fall into the trap of not taking a far enough step backward when you look at a task. In this case, you can end up designing a new cart for your horse, whereas a motor car might have been a better solution.

Question #4 – Can I get someone else to do it?

Don't think this is a cop-out. Your time is more important than anyone else's to YOU. Instead of looking at this question from your employer's perspective, make sure you look at it from yours. As long as the work gets done, your employer will be happy. And if you can get someone else to do it, so will you.

I mentioned the four most common outsourcing challenges in the last chapter. Let me tell you several of them can raise their ugly heads when we consider giving a task to someone else. Make sure you don't fall into an obvious trap, for example, thinking that no one will do it as well as you do, etc.

There are several options to consider when directly outsourcing, as follows:

1. **Delegate downwards:** This is an obvious move if you manage people since you control their day-to-day activities.
2. **Delegate sideways:** Is there a peer or another team that could take on some of the work? Or someone in another group you think would enjoy the opportunity of taking on more?
3. **Delegate upwards:** Not always the easiest route, but usually possible
4. **Delegate externally:** Could you get an external agency to do some of the work under your supervision?

Most people would view delegation downwards as the easiest route. But if you can do this, why haven't you done it before? Is it because you feel your team isn't ready to take on the responsibility? Do you fear your people won't do a good enough job?

The truth is that people usually perform better than you expect. Plus, they'll often relish having the opportunity. It could be a great win-win situation.

What if you're struggling to work out who would be the best person or team to whom your work can be delegated? One way you might figure it out could be to ask yourself the following question:

Who would do the task if I wasn't here?

So, what would happen if you immediately retired to the Bahamas (much more pleasant than falling under a bus)? What solution would be put in place to get your tasks completed? Thinking along those lines may help you work out the best approach.

Key principles

So, those are the four outsourcing questions you need to ask yourself for each task in your Day Job. Again, it can be tough to give specific tips. Everyone has a different job and a different level of responsibility. But if you apply the four questions to each task, you'll have a fighting chance of reducing the amount of time you spend doing your Day Job.

Finally, let me remind you of the fundamental principles you need to bear in mind when you do this exercise. I'll be honest; a lot of people struggle with it:

1. Always assume that outsourcing is the best solution. Rather than thinking it's a long shot, start by thinking it's your preferred outcome
2. Make Day Job outsourcing an ongoing review process. It needs to be part of your DNA, since your work processes and the workload never stay still for long

3. Be alive to the four arguments against outsourcing. These bad guys can trick you into maintaining the status quo. You need to be acting entirely consciously
4. Embrace the benefit of delegation and giving an opportunity to others. You'll likely get someone else to do the job for you, as well as earn their respect
5. Become familiar with 5 Whys process, and try it out

Ok, we're about done with outsourcing the Day Job for the moment. Rest assured, we'll be coming back to it later on when we'll see how we can do things more efficiently. But for now, let's take a look at your business.

Chapter 6: Outsourcing Your Business

"Everything in your business can be outsourced... if you're not emotionally attached to doing it all."

Richard Branson

You and whose army?

If you're a new business owner or are about to go down that path, two things will immediately strike you. This is particularly true if you've come from a job as an employee in another organisation.

The first is that, in your business, you have complete autonomy over what happens. You don't need to refer decisions to anyone else or wait for the boss to decide. You're the boss, and the buck stops with you. It can be a tad scary, but also hugely empowering.

Remember when you used to 'borrow' post-it pads from the stationery cupboard at work (yes, we all did it, and yes, it was technically stealing)? Now, you can steal with wanton abandon, because you own them. You can even have the best coffee machine on the planet if you want to. Rather than the hot brown water dispenser they had in your last place.

The second notable thing is that you no longer have your old Day Job resources. Arranging meetings, typing letters, making phone calls, and even making the tea. These were all tasks that you could rely on other people to do.

Not anymore. Now they're your tasks along with being the CEO, CTO, Operations Director, and Finance Director. And possibly a whole number of other hats you might also be wearing. You'll also have to make a note for yourself to remember to buy the biscuits (I knew those post-it pads would come in handy one day).

So, you now have a lot more jobs on your plate, and often very few people to delegate stuff to, if any at all.

Any small or medium-sized business has, to some degree, the same challenges as a start-up or a sole trader. So, if you're reading this as part of an established company, this chapter will still have something to offer.

Now you may be thinking, that's all well and good. But when I start a new business, the last thing I can afford to do is go out and hire lots of staff. I mean, the company has got to start producing enough money to support ME first. Way before I can afford to support a bunch of committed team-members. Hasn't it?

Well, you're partly right, so go ahead; bask in the glow.

Ok, that's enough, don't milk it.

Why only partly? Well, one of the problems with flying solo is that you can't delegate anything, other than to yourself or the cat. And we both know that Mr. Tibbles is the dead wood in this organisation, don't we?

You see, you'll have important tasks, and you'll have urgent tasks. And because it's only you who's doing anything, you'll be forced to deal with the urgent tasks. So the important functions can often fall by the wayside.

Let me give you an example to show you what I mean.

Here's the scenario; you have an urgent job on for an important client. The deadline is only hours away, and the project has overrun. You're working flat out and solo to try and finish it on time. Here is the conscious stream of your thoughts, as the latter part of your day unfolds:

I can't believe it. I was down to do some strategic planning for the business today, but I've got to try and finish this wretched project instead. Still, at least I can now focus on getting it across the line. Cripes, that's the doorbell! Just what I need! Hold on. Hopefully, it's that online stationery order I placed yesterday – they promised on pain of death that they would deliver it today. Bugger, no, it's Gladys from next door come to give me a pot of home-made chutney. Damson and courgette. Lovely. Can't be rude, do come in. Beautiful day for it, isn't it? A nice cup of tea? Right, er... I'll make it. One lump or two? Wow, five it is! Fair enough; sweet tooth our Gladys. Four hobnobs later, and she's gone. Thin as a rake, too. Where does she put them all? Right, where was I, ah yes, the urgent job. I just get back into it when the phone rings. Bugger. Hold on, though; I'd better take the call as it could be a new client. Double bugger, it's not – it's my existing client wanting to know where the heck their job's got to. Well, I'd be working on it now if I didn't have idiots ringing me up all the time, wouldn't I? Luckily that stayed in my head. Yes, really sorry, no problem, absolutely guaranteed to be with you by first thing tomorrow even if I have to drive it there myself. I hear some manic laughter and realise it's coming from me. Hang up, try and pick up where I left off when there's another knock on the door. Bugger! It's like Piccadilly Circus round here. Yay, it's the stationery order. Nice one. One less thing etc. Need a coffee now, or I'll keel over. Right, er... I'll make it. Bugger, out of hobnobs! How did that happen? Bloody Gladys. Another phone call. Could be a new client, but hey, I've got to crack on. I let it ring out. Feeling hungry now and a bit tired. I need food but can't stop yet. Hang on, let's try that chutney. Where's the spoon? There it is. Let's see what it's like.... Holy moly, is the bloody woman trying to kill me? Right, hunger it is. Into the home straight now. Darkness falls, but I soldier on and finish the job. Yay! Major celebration. Actually, minor celebration, because I still need to package the job up. Thank heavens that stationery order arrived. Open said stationery order. Wrong stationery. You are kidding me. How difficult can it be for a stationery company to deliver the stationery I actually ordered? Cretins! Look, it's addressed to a Mr. Christmas. I am not Christmas! He is not me! Do I look like a Christmas? It's not only the wrong order; it's the wrong customer altogether! Then I notice the red light blinking on my answerphone. Play message. It's the stationery company. Terribly sorry, we sent the wrong order. We know it's urgent. Can deliver the correct order this evening if you call us by 6 pm. Look at my watch. 9 pm. Bugger.

So, in this drama, you're the one spinning all the plates and dealing with all the interruptions. And your Strategic Planning Day has gone for a complete Burton.

And, as a small business, how valuable might a Strategic Planning Day be? Vital, critical, or essential?

What tends to happen is that you get distracted by the <u>urgent</u> tasks. And because many of the <u>important</u> tasks don't have people badgering you about them, they get relegated to second or third place. In which case, there's a fair chance that they may not happen at all. And then where will your business be? In the short-term, there may be little negative impact. But over time, it could prove fatal for your business.

You're really very good (at very little)

I know I've been a little hard on you at times throughout these pages, not to mention a trifle disparaging, but please believe me when I say I've really enjoyed it.

In that vein, let me offer you another damning stream of invective about your capabilities. This time it's courtesy of my good friend, Tin Man. To be fair, I bore the brunt, but I have no hesitation in passing it on to you second hand, so to speak;

Derik: *You appear to be very busy today.*

Me: *Do you know, I'm rushed off my feet. I've got an absolute ton of stuff to get through. Sorry I've not been able to chat very much. You don't mind if I just get on with it, do you?*

Derik: *No, not at all. It's interesting to watch you work, if that's the right description. It actually appears to be a balanced combination of working and panicking.*

Me: *Well, you'd be panicking too, if you had my deadlines.*

Derik: *I see. I also noticed that you're doing quite a wide variety of tasks.*

Me: *You're not wrong there!*

Derik: *And is there a reason you're doing all these jobs? I see that you're not doing any of them particularly well. Is quality not a requirement for these tasks?*

Me: *What do you mean I'm not doing them well? I can assure you that I'm doing every one of them to the best of my ability!*

Derik: *Yes, that must be frustrating for you. Perhaps you should consider getting someone to assist you who may be better at doing each task?*

Me: *Look, Derik, there's only me in this business. Just me. So I can't afford to go and hire in a whole team of experts to do everything. I have to do it all myself.*

Derik: *But if the quality is poor and you're not an expert, don't you end up with dissatisfied customers? And a task that takes longer for you to complete?*

Me: *Ok, hotshot, yes, you're absolutely right. So what exactly do you suggest I do about it?*

Derik: *I've noticed that humans are capable of doing a lot of things, but they do most of them badly. But most humans can also do a small number of tasks at which they excel, although you may be an exception. And different humans excel at different things.*

Me: *And your point is what, exactly?*

Derik: *If you have ten tasks in a project, then statistically, you will be excellent at one of them, good at two of them, average at three of them, and poor at the remaining four.*

Me: *So, I'm sure you've seen me do ten tasks today. Are you saying that I'm only excellent at one of them?*

Derik: *I have only seen you complete nine tasks so far. So statistically, I am expecting that the next one you attempt must be the one you will excel at.*

Me: *Great, thanks for that. So, what do you suggest I do?*

Derik: *If you can't afford to hire people to do each task well, then it would be logical to outsource the tasks that you do averagely or poorly. That way, you'd only continue to do tasks that you're excellent or good at. Your overall quality would improve, and tasks would be completed more quickly. You would also presumably enjoy your work more. And you would have more time free to work on other things.*

[pause]

Me: *It's all so easy for you, isn't it?*

So, we have good old logic to thank, yet again, for showing us the error of our ways.

We do tend to have the blinkers on when it comes to doing tasks ourselves, quality-wise. We concentrate on getting things done without appreciating they could be done better, and also quicker.

Also, I like the logic about outsourcing the stuff I'm not very good at and sticking to my knitting. It would be great to outsource everything else so that I could crack on with far more important things.

But outsourcing comes at a cost, and we're back to that old chicken and egg argument once more. If the business is flying, then I can either afford to outsource everything or bring in staff to do it. But what if I'm still operating in the flapping-my-wings-furiously-and-trying-to-get-off-the-ground stage? It means I can't afford it, and so can't take advantage of it. Yet that's when I need it most.

It is, indeed, a bit of a doozy. So what exactly can we do about it?

Colleagues are a double-edged sword

One of the nice things about having full-time members of staff is that they can do some of the work for you. You can interview them to find out what skills they excel at and allocate them roles accordingly. If you ask nicely, they may also make you tea and keep on top of the biscuit supply situation. It all sounds lovely, but unfortunately, there's a downside.

You see, the challenge with having staff is that you have a lot of responsibility to look after them. Much of this is covered by law and regulation, so it's not optional. There are health and safety considerations in the office, National Insurance to pay, sick pay, annual reviews, pensions, plus a whole lot more. A whole raft of considerations and costs that come into play. A real minefield, and if you're not careful, a distraction.

Also, because staff are mostly human, they come pre-loaded with human frailties. Some may be lazy or incapable, while others may have arguments or fights. They'll introduce office politics into your business, and some may even act inappropriately with each other on top of your photocopier.

None of these were (hopefully) problems that you had when it was only you working in the business. How you might yearn for the simpler days when you did everything yourself.

One of the most common mistakes that new business owners make is not getting in extra resources early enough. They carry on for as long as they can by themselves before they finally have to bite the bullet and employ people.

Having staff is such a step-change in so many ways that you can see why they avoid it. But the problem is they end up focusing on the wrong thing. They'll continue to work long hours, making sure that all the orders are fulfilled. But then only admit they need help when there aren't enough hours left in the day to get the orders out.

And, as a result, they long since gave up finding time to focus on the management of their business. Its vision, its strategy, its goals; these all fell by the wayside. And while the customer orders were just about getting satisfied, the business was, at best, not fulfilling its potential. And, at worst, it's now in terminal decline. They've ended up working <u>in</u> the business, and not <u>on</u> the business, and the ship is rudderless.

So, in summary, you need to have staff at the earliest opportunity. That way, you can stay focused on running your business. Plus, they will often improve the quality of what you do because they are experts in things that you are not. Crucially, they'll also allow you to get back some time.

But is there a way of achieving this outcome without having to handle all the regulatory baggage and photocopier hygiene issues that go with having employees?

Well, I'd like to introduce you to an outsourcing solution with which you may or may not be familiar. It's one that has become big business in recent years, and it could be the answer to at least some of your problems, if not all of your prayers.

And it's called freelancing.

The joy of freelancers

Ok, let's start with an obvious first question; who or what is a freelancer, exactly?

Well, at a fundamental level, it's someone who;

1. Specialises to some degree in a particular task or discipline (although some can be more generalist)
2. Hires out their time/services at either an hourly rate or a fixed price per job/contract basis, and
3. Doesn't usually need to be based in the same geographic location as the people for whom they undertake work

Although there's no definitive line in the sand, I tend to split freelancers into two types; one-off jobbers, and ongoing resource specialists.

One-off jobbers are the sort of people to whom you (wait for it) give a one-off job. You often find them on websites such as fiverr.com (take a quick look if you're not familiar with it). Typically, they'll do a very specific, usually one-off task for a set fee.

Let's say you wanted someone to design a logo for your business. It's a one-off task (known as a 'gig'), and you'd expect to hire someone for whom logo design is their bread and butter. They'll usually have a fixed fee structure and will charge you so-many-dollars to design a single logo. Simply go on to fiverr.com, search for logo designers, and choose one, having first checked out their reviews and their pricing. Most will have a tiered pricing structure, so you can choose the level of service you're after.

The designer then sends you their standard instructions, and after you've given them the necessary information, they send you your new logo. You may go backward and forwards a few times with them, refining the design, but after that, the job's complete.

These guys are really useful. Every business must deal with a range of requirements (including things like logo design), which sit outside its core skills. They're unlikely to want to recruit a full-time logo designer, and engaging with a design agency may be outside their budget. So, hiring a freelancer makes great sense.

Here are some other one-off freelancing gigs that might appeal to a business:

1. Web design
2. App development
3. Graphic design
4. Translation
5. Copywriting
6. Voiceover
7. Blog articles
8. Market research
9. Data entry
10. Flyer distribution

Each of these either involves a degree of expertise, or they're tasks that are routine and mundane. To be honest, the range of available skillsets is enormous. So you can pretty much think of any task, and you'd be able to find someone prepared to do it for you, working as a freelancer.

The second type of freelancer (according to me) is an ongoing resource specialist. These are people that you'd be more likely to hire as an ongoing resource (you're getting the hang of these naming conventions now, aren't you?). This doesn't mean that they'll become a permanent fixture, more that you'll use their services more regularly.

One such role that has grown a lot in recent years is that of the virtual assistant (a 'VA' or 'Virtual PA'). This is someone who can do a multitude of administrative tasks, working remotely. VAs can be very useful when you've many different general tasks that need doing, rather than requiring a more specialised set of skills.

This ability to be remote from the employer provides several key benefits:

1. You're able to tap into a global market. Freelancers are available in almost every country on the planet, so you have a massive choice
2. You can take advantage of the lower cost of living in other countries. For example, a freelancer in India or the Philippines is likely to charge a far lower hourly rate than one working in Western Europe or the US
3. You can take advantage of time differences by having people work on stuff while you're asleep. You wake up the next morning, and the work's done. It's like having an electric bread maker (but without the alarming weight gain).

Another significant benefit is that you do not directly employ freelancers. Remember all that horrible stuff I mentioned earlier? Annual leave, pensions, National Insurance, and the like? None of this applies. It's a straightforward fee for services rendered, and the freelancer remains self-employed. They won't get anywhere near your photocopier, either.

Freelancers are usually remunerated in one of two ways — either an hourly rate or a fixed price per project/job. Often the choice is yours; however, there is a gamble involved. Imagine you've got a task that you think will take someone two days to complete, and you pay them hourly. If they work slowly, the job will last longer, and you'll have to pay them more. But, if you pay them a fixed price, they may be tempted to rush it, and you end up with a reduction in quality. Most freelancers are honest and interested in repeat business, so this isn't usually a problem. But you should be aware.

You can also hire freelancers in teams as well as individually.

So, where's a good place to find all these freelancers? Well, several large freelancing online portals have now become very well established. As the 'employer' they're usually free for you to use; you simply need to register. At the time of writing, some of the top sites are (in no particular order):

1. People per hour (www.peopleperhour.com)
2. Upwork (www.upwork.com)
3. Freelancer (www.freelancer.com)
4. Guru (www.guru.com)
5. Mturk (www.mturk.com)
6. Bark (www.bark.com)
7. TaskRabbit (www.taskrabbit.co.uk)

To give you a flavour of the type of information you might encounter when looking for a freelancer, here are some hypothetical listings;

Name:	**Andrew Abbot**
Specialism:	Graphic designer
Length of experience:	2 years
Rate:	$12.00 per hour
No. of jobs completed:	14
Feedback rating:	75%
Based in:	UK
Spoken English skills:	Native

Name:	**Brenda Blaznici**
Specialism:	Virtual PA
Length of experience:	12 years
Rate:	$6.50 per hour
No. of jobs completed:	140
Feedback rating:	98%
Based in:	Estonia
Spoken English skills:	Fluent

Name:	**Charminder Corbani**
Specialism:	Lead generation
Length of experience:	<1 year
Rate:	$4.40 per hour
No. of jobs completed:	1
Feedback rating:	90%
Based in:	India
Spoken English skills:	Fluent

Name:	**Dane Davis**
Specialism:	Mobile app developer
Length of experience:	6 years
Rate:	$28 per hour
No. of jobs completed:	34
Feedback rating:	100%
Based in:	USA
Spoken English skills:	Native

Most platforms give you some useful information on each freelancer. There are a few points worth noting that have a bearing on how you assess candidates. Let's have a quick whizz through those:

1. Length of Experience: How long they've been at it (or at least how long they've been registered with the platform). Typically the more experienced freelancers will charge more. Some people prefer not to hire brand new ones since they're unproven. That said, everyone's got to start somewhere, and newer freelancers can be very keen and enthusiastic
2. Rate: This shows you how much they charge per hour (usually) for their services. From experience, it's not always 100% accurate, but it's a good relative indicator. Note that US dollars are the universal currency of most freelancing platforms
3. The number of jobs completed: This shows their experience and tells you how robust their feedback rating is. A 5-star rating from 1 review is less impressive than a 4.5-star rating from 999 reviews, and so on
4. Feedback Rating: These come in various formats, including a percentage score. You can often also read what reviewers have said about them, which can be enlightening. Again, a poor rating from one reviewer is arguably less damning than a below average score from many. But, with so many freelancers to choose from, you shouldn't need to take a chance on hiring someone with poor reviews
5. Based in: Their geographic location; often quite a biggie, and something we'll cover in the next section
6. Spoken (and written) English skills: Usually a scale ranging from 'native' down to 'non-existent'. This can be important if the task is complex and requires an explanation. Or if the output involves the written word

Some sites also allow freelancers to complete standard tests in core subjects. This, in theory, can serve to verify their claims or abilities. For example, you might be wary of someone who says they speak English fluently, but who only scored 10% in an English fluency test.

Being cynical, I'm unsure how robust the online testing system is. Someone who scored 100% on the language test might have had a better-English-speaking friend sitting next to them when they did it. But who knows?

Overall, each of the platforms has its strengths and weaknesses. Most people invariably gravitate to the one whose interface they get on with the best. I'm not going to rate them; you'll need to see which one works best for you.

Going on the offensive

I should explain that any offence caused by this next section is unintentional. If you're appalled, I can only apologise.

Why might it be offensive?

Well, it's about the pros and cons of hiring people from various parts of the world. Now, any assessment of their relative traits and merits is going to be a sweeping generalisation that won't apply to everyone in that region. But I'm not sure how else I can assist the virgin freelancing employer. So sweeping generalisations are all I can offer you. As long as you know that's all they are.

We've covered the more obvious things like language skills and time differences. But is there any real difference in hiring someone from the Philippines compared to, say India, if the price is the same?

I'm afraid I can't give you a definitive answer to that, because a) I've not undertaken a scientific study, and b) there isn't one. But I can share some of the feedback that I've gleaned. This comes from regular outsourcers, my own experience, and what I've gathered from third-parties.

So, let's crack on.

Western Europe (including the UK) & the US

1. Generally, the most expensive areas from which to source freelancers as the cost of living is higher than in other parts of the world
2. Very few communication problems, as many are native English speakers
3. Artwork follows western styles, so there are relatively few stylistic issues
4. Possibly more important to select someone with a work history. There have allegedly been problems reported with some new freelancers
5. Internet connectivity is not a problem
6. If they're based in the same time zone as you then there are no time difference advantages or disadvantages, plus you can speak to them during the working day if you need to

India/Pakistan/Bangladesh

1. Generally much cheaper than Western Europe and the US
2. Communication is generally excellent. English is a second language for most freelancers, but don't expect native quality
3. There have been reports of some freelancers demanding bonuses before work is handed over. Or providing excuses for late delivery or poor quality. You should be able to avoid these issues if you select someone who has a strong history in the work area you're looking for
4. You can source a broad range of talent, and many freelancers are very well-educated

5. Indian culture is very entrepreneurial. So if you train a freelancer in a specific task, don't be surprised if they then use that skill for other clients. Not a problem usually, but be aware
6. Internet connectivity can be variable in certain parts of the region

Philippines

1. Generally much cheaper than Western Europe and the US
2. Excellent communication skills although, again, don't expect native quality
3. They are hard workers who take pride in working for Western employers
4. Generally very honest and reliable, and you can source a broad range of skills
5. The culture is less entrepreneurial than in India
6. Internet connectivity can be variable in certain parts of the region

Former Soviet Union Countries

1. A good range of skills available at a low price
2. Technical skills can be excellent; design skills not quite so strong
3. Generally very honest and trustworthy
4. Communication can be a weak point. Make sure you're very prescriptive about what you're looking for in a task, at the outset
5. Internet connectivity is usually ok

Ex-pat Community

1. These are native English-speakers leading the laptop lifestyle, working overseas (lucky so-and-sos)

2. Communication is excellent, and design influences are Western
3. Usually cheaper than hiring someone in the US or UK as their cost of living is cheaper
4. They may still be prone to a variable internet connection, depending on where they're based

I hope you've come through the other side of all that, unaffronted and unoffended? Good.

There are a couple of further things I want you to note:

1. Mother Nature: Bless her little cottons, she can be known to get in the way of things on occasion. You have to bear in mind that freelancers are using the internet to communicate with you and to send you their work. In some parts of the world, internet connectivity can be a little patchy. This is often due to extreme local weather conditions. Where this occurs, it could be hours or even days before regular internet service is resumed. There's nothing your freelancer can do about it, so don't blame them. It's not a common problem, but if you want to avoid the risk altogether, you may need to source from a more expensive geographical location
2. Stylistic considerations: The world is a diverse place when it comes to design. While this is a blessing, you need to be aware of it when trying to outsource a design job in places like South East Asia. In these parts, people are less likely to be familiar with Western design cues, so if that's what you're looking for, make sure you tread carefully. The quality may be fantastic, but it may have an Eastern flavour if you know what I mean. Caveat emptor and all that

Most freelancers will be offering their services as individuals, professional teams, or agencies. That said, it's not always obvious from their bios. If it's an individual, they will personally be doing your work, whereas a professional team may have several people available to do it. An agency will farm the work out to third-party workers and will take a commission for their trouble.

There's no right or wrong about which route to take. If you're looking to establish a long-term relationship, you may decide you want to work with the individual who is doing the work. The downside, of course, is that, if they're not available, then you'll have to find someone else from scratch. After all, they may be on another job, dogged by illness, or exhausted from all the work you've been giving them. But, with a team or agency, they will simply get one of their other people to do the job, and you may be none the wiser.

Also, bear in mind that agencies are naturally prone to Chinese whispers. They're also another mouth to feed, and you have no idea who is doing your work. Not always a problem, but again, be aware.

How to hire someone

The portals make it very easy to search for potential freelancers and to get in touch with them. Here is the basic process, although each portal is different. I'd add that each portal has excellent tutorials on using their service, so that should be your first port of call.

In most cases, you have a choice of three approaches:

1. Search for individual freelancers
2. Post your job and see who applies for it
3. A combination of both

I'll outline both and then give you my thoughts on the pros and cons of each.

Freelancers register to go on to each portal, as do employers (you). Once registered, freelancers complete a standard questionnaire detailing their location, skills, and experience. Plus, they usually have an opportunity to write something about themselves. As they gain experience, their feedback and review scores get added to their listing.

To search for a suitable freelancer, you'll enter some basic criteria on the portal. Let's say you're looking for a graphic designer, you want to pay up to $20 per hour, they must have a review score of over 90%, and they need to speak fluent English. Simply enter these parameters in the search section and hit return.

Hey presto, you'll get a list of freelancers who meet those criteria. You can now sift through them all and shortlist the ones you like the look of. Once you have your shortlist, you can then send them details of your job (more on that later).

The second approach is to post a job without searching for individuals. Then you can just see who responds. Since your job will detail the parameters you're looking for, you'd hope people will rule themselves out if they don't meet the brief. For example, if their wage demands are too high, or they don't have the language skills.

You can also use a hybrid approach, where you send the job request both to freelancers you've identified and to the world at large.

I used to think that singling out freelancers with good CVs would be the better option. But I realised that for me at any rate, life was too short. You can spend an age critiquing the online CVs of hundreds of people, but it doesn't guarantee you the best result. I now prefer to post the job and see who responds. I then only need to check out a few CVs and can go from there. It's a lot quicker, plus you know that the people who respond want your work.

I also found instances where responders were keen to do my job, even though their advertised hourly rate was more than I was paying. Presumably, they were between jobs or work was in short supply; read into it what you will.

An obvious exception is if you're looking for a specific set of skills or work experience. In this case, option 1 may be the way to go. That said, I'd also recommend the hybrid approach as you've got nothing to lose – you may find a hidden diamond.

If you're looking for your first freelancer, here are some precautions that would seem to make sense:

1. Always check their feedback on the portal, and don't go with anyone you think may be a risk
2. Pick someone who has over 25 jobs in their history. It's nice to give newbies a chance but to start with there's comfort in knowing you're not both complete novices
3. Similarly, they should have a satisfaction score of 90% or better (9 out of 10, or whatever the equivalent is, depending on the portal you're using)

Again, the portals offer some great tips on how to select freelancers, etc. so be sure to check these out.

Writing the job post

How should you go about writing your job post to attract the best talent?

Well, the portals themselves provide advice and tips on how to post jobs, etc. so do your homework. But if you're interested here are my thoughts on getting the best result:

1. Write it as if you're explaining it to a 10-year old, making sure you avoid complicated words and jargon. Remember that English may not be their first language. Or perhaps their literacy skills may be lower than yours (which doesn't rule them out from being a great freelancer)

2. Put the majority of the job description in an attachment. Make sure to include a small bespoke task so you can make sure they've read it (we'll cover this in a minute)
3. If your job is confidential, you don't need to go into detail – keep it high level. You can always ask for responders to sign an NDA (non-disclosure agreement). Most platforms have a template you can use
4. Have someone else read your job post before you send it. If they scratch their head and look a little baffled, so will your target audience
5. Sell your job. Imagine you're trying to appeal to people who have got a choice of jobs, with work coming out of their ears. What will make them choose to do your job, among all the others? If you're outsourcing a boring and mundane task, it won't do you any favours if you describe it as such
6. Sell yourself and your business. Explain what it is that you do so that people get a sense of your story. They will then understand how the bit that they'd be doing fits in and helps move the business forward. So far, I've found every freelancer to be human, and all humans love to hear stories and to feel part of something. So take the time to explain what you're about, even if the job on offer is about as appealing to you as bashing army spuds
7. Always ask freelancers to include a paragraph explaining WHY they want your job. This will help you assess their written skills as well as proving that they've read the brief

You may also want to think about whether you're looking for a short-term or long-term hire. If it's a long-term hire, i.e., someone who could become a semi-permanent part of your organisation, then it's worth shopping around. You want to ensure you pick a good one.

It can pay dividends to advertise a small task, instead of jumping in with the main prize. You would still then go through the usual vetting procedure. But with a smaller job, you can afford to award it to several people to see who delivers the best result. Then there's less of a risk when you appoint the main job to your favourite.

You're looking to see how they handle the task. You want to test their timeliness and responsiveness, their communication skills, enthusiasm, and also the quality of their work. It's the freelancing equivalent of buying a tester paint pot (a small investment before making the bigger decision, if you see what I mean).

Talking of which, consider asking applicants to do a short test when your job involves important, detailed, or technical work. Given that they'll be doing it for free, don't make it too onerous. Perhaps get them to complete a small sample of the task so that you can see the results.

To reiterate, it's well worth reading the helpful online guides offered by the portals. Their advice is golden when it comes to how to best interact with your freelancing audience.

Now let's roll the clock forward a bit. Your job post is out there, and you're now awaiting responses. Before you know it, an email zips into your inbox telling you that several people have responded. How exciting!

You now have to read through their messages and judge them. Unfortunately, there are so many variables, I can't give you a definitive way of sorting the wheat from the chaff. Ultimately, your gut-feeling will be invaluable at this stage.

On occasion, I've had people respond to job posts very quickly, having voluntarily completed a sample of the work in question. Better still, they'd done it to a decent standard. How good is that! Speed, quality, and proactivity. Needless to say, they got the job.

I wish you the same good fortune with your own job postings.

Common freelancing gripes

Freelancing is a great way to get jobs done cost-effectively using a global resource that has the expertise you don't have. But it's not perfect, although hiring your own staff isn't perfect either.

So what are the more common gripes that regular users of freelance service providers encounter? There are three main ones that I've come across:

1. Poor quality: the work you get back is not up to the required standard. Perhaps they've blagged their CV? Or maybe they're trying to juggle lots of jobs at once. But to be honest, the reasons can only be a guess
2. Late delivery: this is where the timeliness is poor or variable. You get a bit of an anxious, sweaty feeling when they tell you it will absolutely, definitely be ready by next Thursday
3. Poor comprehension: They don't take instruction well, and you spend too much time either re-explaining or correcting work they've done. This is often a sign that their promise of fluent English wasn't entirely accurate, or their IQ is south of ideal

So how can you deal with these potential pitfalls?

Well, like so many things, prevention is usually better than cure. Here are some of the measures you may want to consider taking:

1. Always hire people with excellent feedback:

Feedback loops aren't always 100% honest or reliable. But if there are enough reviews, you'll get a good idea of the sort of impression a freelancer has left with previous employers

2. Always get freelancers to personalise their response:

You want someone who's prepared to invest in your relationship. If they send you a standard reply, then you could find yourself dealing with the quick buck brigade. If they've written back to you about the job, then you can judge whether they've understood the brief. Plus, you can also see how good their English language skills are

3. Hire more than one freelancer:

The chances of you finding the best person straight out of the box are pretty remote. So, even though you may find someone who's good, by casting the net wider, you have a better chance of finding someone who is stellar. You also then have a fallback position if your first-choice freelancer is later out of action

4. Use more than one freelancing platform:

There's a tendency for people to stick with what they know when it comes to using the platforms. So be bold and daring; try using more than one platform, and see how you get on

Would you permit me a mild digression while I tell you about the Van Halen rider, as I think you may like it? Plus, we've been at this freelancing thing a while now, so we could probably both use a break (feel free to grab a biscuit if the mood takes you).

I should explain that Van Halen is a rock group who were formed in the early seventies and went on to become one of the world's biggest bands. Just in case you haven't been able to get out much over the past 40 years.

Not exactly an obvious reference point for a section about outsourcing, then. But believe it or not, Van Halen had a trick of their trade that you can borrow when recruiting freelancers.

You've probably heard about the demands that top artists make when they turn up to perform a stage show. Known as 'riders', they've included such demands as insisting the vodka backstage MUST be a particularly obscure and expensive brand. Or that the dressing room must be kept at a constant 72 degrees. And it must have blue leather sofas with a dozen oysters and a case of Louis Roederer Cristal champagne available at all times. You get the picture.

Even given the extravagance and specificity of some of these riders, Van Halen's request seems petty. It's precisely the sort of request that makes you think some celebrities are a bunch of deluded, self-important prima donnas.

You see, Van Halen wanted chocolate M&Ms in their dressing room. No biggie there, you'd think. But the rider stipulated that;

"There will be no brown M&Ms in the backstage area on pain of forfeiture of the show, with full compensation."

For the non-chocolate aficionados among you, M&Ms are little balls of candy-coated chocolate that come in a range of colours. And they all taste pretty much the same (think Smarties, if you're British). In other words, some poor bugger will have to sift through them all, picking out the brown ones. Even though the brown ones taste no different to the others. I mean, how petty can you get?

But it turns out there was a method in their madness. You see, Van Halen's gigs were huge. I mean massive. Tens of thousands in the audience, enormous lighting rigs, and huge banks of speakers covering the entire stage from top bottom. Their equipment would turn up in a fleet of lorries and take hundreds of roadies several days to set up.

Not exactly small beer, then. And not surprisingly, Van Halen's contract with the concert venue had to be very specific when it came to logistics and crowd safety. There had been cases in the past where venues had thought 'it's just another rock band coming to do a gig.' They'd then had the shock of their lives when the Van Halen tour machine rocked up. And they discovered they didn't have the infrastructure to support them.

As a result, Van Halen's contract evolved to be very specific on all sorts of points. It was a large document and quite heavy reading. But it needed to be, to cover all the thousands of logistical stipulations they needed to get right. And buried in the middle of it was this seemingly trivial backstage M&M stipulation.

So, how could Van Halen know whether the venue had read the contract in detail and paid attention to everything in it?

Well, the first thing they'd do on arrival is to check out the M&M situation backstage. If there were any brown M&Ms present (or no M&Ms at all), then they'd know that the venue hadn't read or paid attention to the contract. And so they'd need to be even more diligent over the next few days as they prepared for the show.

It's a great story, not least because on face value it looks completely unreasonable. Yet on closer inspection, it's not only logical, it's also very smart.

Ok, digression over. Brush off those biscuit crumbs. It's time to get back to work.

So how can you make use of the Van Halen rider when recruiting a freelancer? Well, it's very simple. When asking for an example of a freelancer's work, make sure you ask them to include a specific, unusual word in their response.

If you get a response that doesn't include your word, then you'll know that they have:

1. failed to read the instructions (not great)

2. didn't understand them (not a good sign either)
3. cut and pasted in the same standard response that they give to every potential employer (again, not the best signal).

How much time could you save?

Depending on what your business does, it's possible to outsource everything other than its oversight and management. You could even set up a brand where you're advertising your business as, say, a logo designer. And then you outsource all the work to freelancers.

In this scenario, your job is to create sales leads, manage quality control, deal with customer orders, and oversee your outsourced workforce. You don't need to have ever designed a logo before in your life.

But, if you already have a business, you should start by listing every workstream in your enterprise. You can then assess them based on several criteria:

1. **What skills are needed?** Perhaps the value in your service is YOU or your specific skill, in which case you can't outsource it (sorry). But you're bound to have tasks that are being done by you that someone else could do better. For example, the tasks that Derik felt I was doing only averagely well or badly, mentioned at the start of this chapter. Or they could be tasks that you dislike doing. Make a list of these
2. **What are your routine tasks?** What are the more routine tasks in your business that anyone could do, given a bit of training? Try and identify what these are. Don't worry if a job is small; when you add all the small tasks together, they can still be worth outsourcing
3. **What tasks can be done virtually?** The term 'freelancers' can, of course, also cover people that come and work in your office. In which case, the virtual aspect doesn't apply. They can meet and greet people, and make the tea, in the way

that no virtual assistant can. If you have tasks that need someone to be physically present, then the freelancing platforms are not your best starting point. But if they don't, why not have someone in India or the Philippines do it for you instead? Which of your current tasks fall into this category? List everything, even if you're not sure an outsourced solution exists for it

In this exercise, it's helpful to imagine you've to come up with a plan to keep your business running for the next 12 months. And neither you nor your colleagues can work in the business for more than one hour each week. Sounds tricky? Well, imagine your livelihood depended on it and you'll be surprised what you could come up with. If it helps, you can justify the exercise by making it part of your disaster recovery plan.

In my experience, most people are too scared about outsourcing to do the exercise justice. So, in the end, they don't wield the scalpel heavily enough. But if you're forced to outsource everything to survive, then you'll be surprised at the imaginative solutions you'll come up with.

So that's business outsourcing covered; we're making some good progress.

I now want to turn to a concept that might be entirely new to you, and, dare I say it potentially quite alien. You see, I want you to try and outsource your life.

Chapter 7: Outsourcing Your Life

Never give up on a dream just because of the time it will take to accomplish it. The time will pass anyway.

Earl Nightingale

What's your hourly rate?

If I was to commission you to do some work for me, how much would you charge me per hour? And don't get your hopes up, sunshine, this is purely hypothetical.

Perhaps you already have an hourly rate? Or maybe you'd have to work it out from scratch.

If so, where would you start? I guess you could always take your annual income and divide it by the number of hours you work, to arrive at a number. Then you'd probably think, crikey that looks a bit low, so you'd double it.

But then you'd think, "Hold on, I don't want to price myself out of the market...". So you'd start to chip it down a bit.

So what figure would you end up charging me? It can be a trickier exercise than it sounds.

Ok, let's try and apply a bit of science to it. According to the Office of National Statistics, the average salary in the UK in 2018 was around £29,588 (about $39,000). And the average number of hours worked per year was 1,538.

So, if we divide one by the other, we get a gross hourly rate of about £19.24 ($25.00). My maths is a little rusty, so let's call it £30,000 ($40,000) per year and £20 ($25) per hour to make life a bit easier for me.

So, using these numbers, you can roughly work out what your hourly rate is on a sliding scale. If you earn £45,000 ($60,000) per year then it's the equivalent of £30 ($37.50) an hour, while £75,000 ($100,000) per year would be £50 ($75) per hour, and so on.

The problem most people have is that they only put a value on their time when they hire it out to someone else. They don't place a value on the time they use for themselves, either recreationally or for their businesses.

And that's a massive own goal. It goes back to that perennial problem, which is that we think we have all the time in the world, whereas, in reality, we don't.

So how much do we really value our time?

Here's another exchange with my good friend, Tin Man, to demonstrate the point. We pick up the action after I'd completely forgotten Derik was coming over for one of his visits, and so I went out to do the weekly shop instead. Luckily Derik has the patience of several saints.

Me: *Hi Derik, sorry I'm late, er... the traffic was awful. Have you been waiting long?*

Derik: *Not in historical terms.*

Me: *Right. Ok. Well, perhaps you could give me a hand taking these bags inside. There's quite a few more in the car.*

Derik: *Of course. What is in the bags?*

Me: *Food, mostly. From the supermarket. Er, you do know what a supermarket is, don't you?*

Derik: *Yes, oddly enough, I found it in several dictionaries. In fact, I recently completed some additional research on supermarkets, since human survival seems to depend on them.*

Me: *That's good, then.*

Derik: *Tell me, does going to the supermarket make you feel envious or inferior?*

Me: *Sorry? No, why on earth should it make me feel envious or inferior?*

Derik: *Isn't it difficult seeing all those supermarket workers pulling in the big money?*

Me: *What? Are you kidding? Let me tell you something, Derik. Supermarket workers don't earn that much. It's not a well-paid job. They'll be lucky to get £10 an hour, most of them.*

Derik: *I see. But that's still around four times your hourly rate. Do other humans think it's a good thing that you're so accepting of this pay gap? Are you being the 'bigger man'? Or are you secretly harbouring a deep resentment?*

Me: *Hold on a moment, what do you mean 'four times my hourly rate'? My time's worth a lot more than £2.50 an hour, you know...*

Derik: *I'm sure that's your opinion.*

Me: *Too right, it is!*

Derik: *But it happens to be incorrect.*

Me: *No, it isn't! £2.50 an hour is peanuts; it's only a fraction of the Minimum Wage, for heaven's sake.*

Derik: *Yes, 30.45% to be exact. Perhaps you should complain to someone.*

Me: *Ok, you've lost me, Derik, and not for the first time. Let's clear this up. What makes you think that my time is only worth £2.50 an hour? Do you have any hard facts to support this bizarre perception of yours?*

Derik: *Yes.*

[long pause]

Me: *Ok, let me rephrase that. Please can you give me some hard facts that support this bizarre perception of yours?*

Derik: *Of course. How long ago did you leave for the supermarket?*

Me: *What? I don't know... just over two hours ago, probably.*

Derik: *It was two hours and thirty-one minutes ago.*

Me: *You know, it's so reassuring to know that you're keeping tabs on me. Not.*

Derik: *And have you heard of a service called 'online supermarket shopping'? It's where you order your produce at home over the internet, and the supermarket then delivers it to you at home, for a fee. I understand that the average charge in your area is currently £5.00.*

Me: *I know what online shopping is, Derik; you don't need to explain to me how it works...*

Derik: *Really? That's quite surprising.*

Me: *Why?*

Derik: *Because it would have taken you around 30 minutes to buy these groceries online. And the delivery cost would have been £5. But instead, you decided to go to the supermarket personally, which saved you £5 but took you two hours longer.*

Me: *Ok, but...*

Derik: *So you spent two of your hours to save £5. This means you value your time at £2.50 per hour. It's quite a simple calculation.*

Me: *Er... right...*

Derik: *But I do have some good news. I discovered that your local supermarket has a vacancy for a 'Product Transportation Recovery Operator'. It pays £10 per hour, and you get to spend a large part of the day outside herding things called trolleys. Plus, you get a uniform. Shall I send you the link?*

As ever, Derik somehow manages to turn the world upside down and look at it from a different perspective. And you know he has a point, dammit.

If you factor in the cost of taking your car to the supermarket, the online shopping option is actually way cheaper.

The value of an hour of your time to someone else is irrelevant because it's THEM time. You're working for them, and so you're merely exchanging your time for money.

Don't get me wrong; working for someone else is not a bad thing. However, it doesn't allow you to work on your ME tasks.

When it comes to simple household chores, outsourcing can be hugely cost-effective. The trick is to stop thinking of it as spending money you don't need to pay. Instead, you're spending a relatively small amount to get some of your time back, which could be invaluable.

Remember our Tim Cook analogy? Can you imagine the warm trickle of tears from your life or your business if you chose to trudge round the supermarket instead of spending the time with them? Just so you could save a fiver?

So, let's have a look at what domestic outsourcing looks like and the possible time it could save you.

Grocery shopping

Let's briefly dive back into the small debate I was having with Derik. You might pop into a grocery store every day for half an hour, or you may do a big weekly shop. Either way, you'll be spending several hours each week inside a supermarket or travelling to and from one.

Whether you believe that supermarkets are the cornerstone of human existence, you don't really want to be spending any time in one if you can help it.

The basic premise is this;

You can do your weekly shop in half an hour, at home, sitting in your PJs

To be clear, the PJs element is entirely optional. I appreciate some people are not big on the whole pyjama thing. So you can also do online shopping fully clothed or go completely starkers (just be careful if you have a cup of tea on the go).

Let's consider the standard method of acquiring your weekly comestibles. It follows an easy-to-follow, completely straightforward 21-step plan. One that you know off by heart:

1. Make a shopping list
2. Get ready to go out, remembering to replace your PJs first to avoid any social awkwardness (or a lifetime supermarket ban, depending on the state of your nightwear)
3. Get in the car
4. Drive to the supermarket (stopping to put fuel in the car if required)
5. Find a parking space
6. Find a trolley
7. Realise you don't have the right type of coin to release said trolley from the queue of other trolleys. So have to queue at the Customer Services desk to get a little blue token instead. Then go back to the trolleys to get one (this step is optional, and the token might not be blue)
8. Traipse around the store, list in hand, trying to find where they've hidden the chocolate digestives this week
9. Be tempted to buy the cheeky end-of-aisle offers, and alluring, nearly-out-of-date meat bargains
10. Get to the last aisle and realise there are five things on your list that you missed. So go back around the entire store again, looking for them. Try and find an assistant to ask who looks like they might actually know where things are hidden
11. Queue at the checkout
12. Load up the conveyor
13. Pay then load up bags. Make polite conversation with the cashier as necessary, then put the bags back in the trolley
14. Push your trolley to the car
15. Load the car
16. Push the empty trolley to the empty trolley zone
17. Check the car for dents caused by inconsiderate drivers or people with an acute spatial awareness deficit
18. Drive home
19. Unload the car

20. Put the shopping away in the fridge, cupboard, larder, pantry or wherever you keep your stuff
21. Have a quiet lie down or a stiff drink (optional, but frequently necessary)

So to recap:

Option 1: In-store shopping = complete all of steps 1 through 21

Option 2: Internet shopping = complete only step 1 and step 20

In summary: why on earth would you ever think that option 1 is a good idea?

Just about every supermarket these days offers an online delivery service. Some are free, whereas more budget-orientated supermarkets will charge you. It typically works out at around the £5-per-delivery mark. Many also offer a scheme where you can pay a monthly fee of around £5 to £10 and receive free deliveries at non-peak times.

You'll need to factor in the step of going online to place your order, which I've assumed will take you about 30 minutes. So if the whole exercise takes two and a half hours door-to-door for a weekly shop, then your switch to online shopping should save you around 2 hours a week.

Now, if I listen carefully, I can hear a little voice of disquiet in your head. Can you hear it too? I suspect it might be asking you one of the following questions:

"Well, that's all well and good, but I like to be able to check the girth of my leeks and the freshness of my sausages in person. I don't want some supermarket oik fondling my essentials. Or picking out some rubbish that's been squished to a pulp or is two minutes away from its sell-by date. So if it's all the same to you, I'd rather select my produce in person..."

There are a couple of issues here. Firstly, in my experience, online shopping produce is every bit as good quality-wise as if I've chosen it myself, if not better. Never assume it won't be; always try it out for yourself. Supermarkets want you to be a happy online customer. They don't use it as a way of offloading their mangled products since, guess what, if they did, they'd lose all their online customers.

The second issue concerns sell-by dates. Are you the type of person that checks every single loaf of bread in the rack to find the one with the longest sell-by date? Then you may be interested to learn the results of a recent survey, where precisely zero percent of the world's most successful people were found to do this. This should tell you something about whether there are better things you could be spending your time doing. Just saying.

"Thing is, I'd worry they won't have stuff in stock. And then they'll deliver a load of alternatives that aren't what I wanted..."

Well, if it's not in stock, you turning up in person isn't somehow going to magic it into existence, is it? Plus, they often allow you to return the alternatives if you don't want them. And why wouldn't you want them to try and find some other options, anyway? One suspects they may even have access to the stock that's not yet been put out on the shelves, whereas you don't.

"I need some of this stuff for tonight's dinner..."

Most supermarkets can deliver very quickly for a small premium. But a little planning goes a long way. Presumably, the fact that you needed to eat today didn't come as a complete surprise? In which case you could have put your order in hours, if not days, earlier. You could also set the alarm on your phone to remind you to eat, in case you forget.

"I don't want to have to wait in all day for the stuff to arrive."

No problem. Most supermarkets offer timed delivery slots, so you won't have to sit at the window waiting for a refrigerated Transit to heave into view. Or you can go down the click and collect route.

"I like to check out the aisle-end bargains, and I also get inspiration for what to cook as I go around the store..."

I have fantastic news! There are offers and a list of all the products they sell on their website. So you can get inspiration (in your PJs) before you order. I'll admit there may be some offers that you'll only find instore. But let's get some perspective here; you're going to be saving some of your precious time by doing this exercise. If you'd rather save 26p on a pack of sausages, you might want to rethink your priorities.

"But I enjoy going to the supermarket. It gets me out of the house..."

See the previous answer. Oh, and you might want to think about getting a hobby.

Online Shopping

Supermarkets are one thing, but you should consider buying all your other shopping online these days, as well. So, why might you contemplate this?

1. The selection is vast
2. You can get most things delivered next day
3. Returns are easy
4. There's no significant price difference
5. You don't have to pay for car depreciation, fuel, wear and tear or parking fees
6. You can do it in your PJs with a cup of coffee in hand. Maybe even a biscuit

7. There are no queues, not ever. Or jostling, pickpockets, screaming children or pushy salespeople
8. The customer service is excellent
9. The checkout process is easy and secure
10. You don't have to drive anywhere or negotiate shopping centre car parks

But, apart from this, online shopping doesn't have anything going for it at all.

Of course, some people like going shopping. They love the retail experience, meeting up with friends, and grabbing lunch or a coffee while they're out.

The only thing I would say is that you need to weigh up the pros and cons. Shopping takes a lot more time and effort when you do it in-store, and it's a trade-off. If getting the time back is more important to you than losing out on the in-store shopping experience, then it's a no-brainer.

Gardening

Now, a lot of people like gardening. If you're using this book to free up some time so you can do even more gardening, then outsourcing your garden chores isn't going to be a very good idea.

However, you may quite like gardening, but appreciate there are some other priorities in your life that you should be spending time on. In which case you should hire a gardener called Bob immediately.

To be honest, we've covered the basic principle with our Tim Cook analogy. Why wouldn't you hire Bob for $25 an hour if you could make the value of your own hour worth more than that?

Gardening covers a multitude of sins, so there are a fair few similar jobs that you could also outsource. These include:

1. General garden tidying
2. Outside maintenance
3. Fence repairs
4. Tree work
5. Gutter cleaning and repairs
6. Leaf clearing
7. Snow clearing

Be aware that gardening work is seasonal, so your timesaving is likely to reduce in the winter months.

Also, be wary of the training argument when it comes to gardening. You know exactly how you like your garden, and where the bumps in the lawn are, and so on. So you'll have to tell all of this to the gardener, which will not only take a while, they'll probably screw it up the first time and scalp your verdant pride and joy.

But you just need to take a deep breath and relax. Take a chill pill. The second time they'll do it better, and after that, it'll be just fine.

If the thought of getting Bob in to tend to your hallowed acres brings you out in a cold sweat, then you do have a second option when it comes to lawn care. Automatic lawn mowers (also called robot mowers) are now available that will trim your grass for you.

They live in a docking station to one side of your lawn and return every hour or so to recharge. A hidden cable runs around the perimeter of the grass to stop your robot disappearing into the dahlias.

And then you just leave them to get on with it.

I've had one for a while now, and I have to say I quite like him. I say 'him' because I've found it's almost impossible to have a robot mower without someone giving it a name (mine was christened 'Baldrick' by my teenage daughter, which reassuringly goes to show my unstinting efforts in broadening her comedic education are starting to pay off).

I control him via an app, which means I can now technically mow the lawn from anywhere in the world. I could be parked on a Caribbean sun lounger and suddenly decide to cut the grass. Not a particularly likely thought, but nice to know I can if I want to. I even get a little map on the app to show me which bits he's mowed.

What do I like best about Baldrick? There are a few things.

1. He mows the lawn all the time. This means it always looks good
2. I no longer come home and experience that depressing 'I'll have to mow the lawn tomorrow' feeling
3. He mulches, so there are no clippings to dispose of
4. He doesn't eat pets plus he's weatherproof, so I just leave him outside permanently
5. He saves me a lot of time

And the downsides?

1. They're not cheap by lawnmower standards, but then they give you your time back, so they ultimately pay for themselves quite quickly
2. They don't cut right up to the edge of everything, so you still need to do some light strimming now and again
3. They may occasionally get stuck, although I've not had that problem very often

I've just realised that I'm supposed to be writing a book about saving time, rather than a lawnmower review, so I'll leave it there. Plus, there's quite enough robots in this book already.

Cleaning

This is a task that can readily be outsourced, and there are lots of cleaning enterprises out there. These range from the larger national brands to individuals looking to earn some cash in their spare time.

Recommendations and referrals go a long way when it comes to hiring a cleaner, so do your due diligence. It's generally cheaper to avoid the leading brands. But with those guys, you at least have some comeback in the unlikely event that your cleaner goes rogue, nicks the silver, or does a poor job.

Make a point of asking around locally and check out the advertising cards in the local newsagents and supermarkets. The local newspaper ads can also be worth a browse.

When getting a cleaner in, the trick is not to be too precious about things. I don't mean you'll accept a trail of broken crockery and scratched furniture. Rather I mean that your primary objective is to get your time back; it is NOT to have a forensically clean house. Yes, I know that you're hiring a cleaner and you have standards. But let's be honest, if the house is a lot cleaner after they've done their rounds, then you've achieved your goal.

I've seen people get anally retentive about the quality of their cleaner's work. They go through dozens of different cleaners trying to find one that lives up to their expectations. They have, in effect, become a part-time cleaning recruitment specialist. Or, in other words, a side-tracked idiot who's wasting their time. Focus on the important thing, which is getting your time back.

Here are a few tips if this is all new to you:

1. Make sure you choose someone reputable; vet them first and get references

2. Don't worry about your cleaner judging your house. You don't need to clean it before they arrive (yes, some people actually do this; they know who they are)
3. Make sure the house isn't a tip. They're cleaners, not tidiers. So tidy round yourself before they arrive to make the most of their service (better still have someone else in your family tidy for you)
4. Accept that if your cleaning standards are unusually high, your cleaner may not be quite as good as you are. However providing they're acceptable, just roll with it and think of all that wonderful extra time you're going to get back

Cooking

Having a personal chef sounds like a luxury, although that's one way to go if you can afford it. But you also have a lot of other options that can reduce the time you spend in the kitchen:

1. Choose ready meals and takeaways more often. I know that sounds bad (or good, depending on your perspective). But let's get real – your time is more important than your food choices, assuming you don't eat complete rubbish
2. Cook in batches and freeze it
3. Teach your kids to cook (good luck with that)
4. Choose 30-minute recipes of which there are thousands out there

If you fancy a nice meal out, why not consider a nice meal in, instead. You can get one either cooked for you in your own home or delivered directly to your door.

I cover a few food-related time hacks in the last part of the book, so please don't dash down to Tony's Kebab Emporium just yet.

Car washing

Ok, cards on the table. I'm a car nut. I like cars quite a lot, so as a result, I particularly like them when they're clean.

But, here's the thing. Cleaning cars is a complete waste of time. It serves almost no practical purpose other than a cosmetic one. And given that your car's primary function is to get you from A to B, the fact that it's a bit grubby when it does so makes no difference whatsoever. A clean car is pure vanity.

So, how long does it take to clean a car, inside and out?

Well, if you do it yourself, I'd say it would take about an hour. The local hand car wash place will also take about an hour. After all, you have to drive there, queue for a bit, wait for it to be cleaned, and then drive back. Albeit you have the luxury of watching someone else scrub your automotive pride and joy.

How often would you clean your car? Some people like a weekly clean while others might go monthly. Let's assume a middle ground of every two weeks on average. One hour every two weeks is 25 hours a year, which is just over three working days. Not a bad saving, given that there's no great sacrifice involved.

And if you usually go down the car wash route, then you'll also be saving £250 a year, assuming each wash costs you a tenner.

You can also get car cleaners and detailers to come to your house. It's pricier but more practical, and less of a time impact on you. Or you could swing by the car wash when you happen to be passing, rather than make a special visit. Some supermarkets offer a while-you-shop cleaning service, but I've found these to be a little mixed quality-wise.

To be honest, I can't bear to go too long without having a clean car. Plus, the family SUV becomes a public health hazard after about a month of daily use, with all manner of dogs, children, and snacks using it.

So, if you can't face the prospect of a year-round filthy car, you have my deepest sympathy. I would advocate moving to a quarterly deep clean at the hand car wash. You'll still be saving a load of time and money, and you'll get that fresh, tingly clean-car feeling four times a year to boot. If you must have an interim freshen up, do it when you're in the vicinity and don't make a special trip.

Do it yourself

Some people love the whole do-it-yourself thing, but to be honest, I'm not one of them.

From cutting up timber to putting up shelves and building furniture, there's an endless list of potential disasters waiting to befall the unsuspecting DIYer. Some people even decide to have a crack at fixing their own plumbing and electrics. I mean, what could possibly go wrong there?

I know that flooding, maiming, home-wrecking, and electrocution are not always front of mind when we try to fix something in the house. But there's another reason why we should avoid DIY.

Yup, you've got it; it's to do with our old friend, time. Because you can spend an absolute ton of it doing all this home improvement stuff yourself.

So I'd like to introduce you to a different concept, one that is the antithesis of DIY. It's called:

GSETDI

That's right, you've guessed it; 'Get Someone Else To Do It'. So why is GSETDI such a good idea, even if it's a bit trickier to get your lips around?

Here are a few thoughts for you to conjure with:

1. Hiring a professional means they will do a better job than you will. You may have a high opinion of your DIY skills, but let's be realistic; a professional is likely to have the edge over you. No, don't be like that; you know they will
2. They will also do it all much more quickly than you would
3. If they screw it up royally, they will have insurance – you won't
4. It is almost impossible for YOU to get fatally wounded, maimed or otherwise disfigured if you GSETDI
5. The risk of flooding the house or fusing the electrics is a lot less
6. You can spend the time doing something far more pleasurable or productive instead

Now, we run headlong into the old affordability argument when it comes to outsourcing. And this is very relevant for DIY. That's because let's be honest; one of the key attractions of DIY is that it saves you the cost of GSETDI. Professionals don't come cheap, so how are you going to afford to have all this work done?

Good question.

The trick, as ever, is to take the long-term view. Getting someone to do a job in order to free up your time, means paying out money today, but you won't get the rewards until later. Providing you have the cash flow to bridge this gap, then it makes sense. You're likely to get a far more significant financial benefit from, say, making your business successful than the cost of hiring a handyman.

Alternatively, if you've taken the Tetris option, then DIY outsourcing is a pure cost to you. It's just a question of what you're prepared to pay to free up your time.

The School Run

I must be kidding, right? How could I possibly suggest that you consider outsourcing taking your children to school?

I'll be very honest and say this one was a bit of an eye-opener for me too. And it was yet another idea I have old Iron Chops to thank for. This is how it happened...

Me: *I'm sorry Derik, I need to move our next meeting back half an hour, as I won't be back from the school run in time. Would that be ok with you?*

Derik: *Of course, although it sounds somewhat unfair.*

Me: *Sorry? What's unfair?*

Derik: *You running at a school. Wouldn't it be fairer to run against humans your own age?*

Me: *Ok, right. No, Derik, the school run is a term we use for taking our children to and from school. In the car. See?*

Derik: *I do see. That <u>is</u> interesting.*

Me: *Really? I can't see that it's interesting in the slightest if I'm honest.*

Derik: *I'm building a library of illogical and irrational acts that are regularly performed by humans. Now I can add to it this 'school run' of yours.*

Me: *Sorry, Derik, you've lost me. In what way is my school run 'illogical and irrational'? Unfortunately, we've not yet invented the* *teleport, and my children will end up stoopid if they don't go to school. Therefore, someone has to take them.*

Derik: *Agreed.*

Me: *Right, so it's actually ok that I should be taking them?*

Derik: *Of course.*

Me: *Great!*

Derik: *It's just illogical and irrational.*

Me: *Ok, Derik, please enlighten me. Why is driving my children to school illogical and irrational?*

Derik: *Very well. How long does it take you to do your 'school run'?*

Me: *Oh, I don't know... Door to door, let's say about 30 minutes there and back in the morning and the same again in the afternoon.*

Derik: *And how often do you do it?*

Me: *Well, I do it five days a week, and I guess there are about 35 term weeks a year.*

Derik: *So, you spend 175 hours a year doing these school runs.*

Me: *Crikey, that sounds like quite a lot. But yes, I suppose I must do.*

Derik: *And you're familiar with the concept of the taxi or the private hire vehicle.*

Me: *Right, I can see where you're going with this, and let me tell you, you're way off beam. There's no way I'm entrusting some random taxi driver to pick up my precious progeny and drive them to and from school on their own!*

Derik: *Why not?*

Me: *Why not? Well, it's just not safe for a start.*

Derik: *I see. Are you implying that these taxi drivers are not very skilled at driving? That's quite surprising, given that it's what they do for a living. Although I believe you're not a professional driver yourself, as I can see from the way you've parked your own vehicle. Are you saying that a professional driver would somehow be less safe than a non-professional driver? Even though they drive many more miles than you do, each year?*

Me: *No, I'm not saying that...*

Derik: *I see. Perhaps you're worried that your children will argue and play up in front of a taxi driver, and so cause a distraction, which may lead to an accident? Which is odd, as I believe statistically, they would be far more likely to do that with someone they knew. A parent, perhaps...*

Me: *Look, that's not what I...*

Derik: *Or maybe you're concerned that a taxi driver may harm your children deliberately?*

Me: *Well...*

Derik: *If only there were such a thing as female human taxi drivers. Statistically, that would reduce the likelihood of that eventuality to almost zero.*

Me: *Ok, ok, I give in! It is safe; I get it. But it would cost me around £30 a day to get a taxi to take them. So, it's just not economically viable, if you know what I mean.*

Derik: *Yes. I know what economically viable means.*

Me: *Fantastic, I'm really pleased for you.*

Derik: *But this argument, too, is illogical and irrational.*

Me: *I'm sorry, Derik, but how can it be? It's just a question of money.*

Derik: *No apology is necessary. How far away is the school from your home?*

Me: *About 5 miles or so. Why?*

Derik: *So you travel 5 miles there and then 5 miles back each morning. And then you repeat the same journey in the afternoon, making 20 miles travelled in total.*

Me: *Spot on.*

Derik: *And what's the fuel economy of your vehicle?*

Me: *Well, I suppose I get about 35 miles to the gallon on a good day.*

Derik: *So, we need to allow for the cost of fuel at the current rate. Then add the extra depreciation and maintenance bills that putting an additional 3,500 miles on your vehicle each year will cost. So by my calculation, the school run costs you a total of £0.50 per mile. And since you're travelling 20 miles each school day, that's a cost of £10 per day.*

Me: *Exactly! Which is a third of the cost of taking a taxi, which is £30 a day. Isn't that my point entirely?*

Derik: *Do other children attend this school?*

Me: *Of course they do. In fact, quite a few of my neighbours' kids go there.*

Derik: *And how many children can you fit in a large taxi?*

Me: *I don't know? Five?*

Derik: *The correct answer is eight. So you could have this professional female driver take your neighbours' offspring as well as yours. Then you could spread the cost between several families.*

Me: *Well, technically, yes...*

Derik: *So, if you found three other families willing to share the cost of a standard-sized taxi, there would be four children in total. This would be a quarter of the cost of taking just your own child by taxi, which would be £7.50 per day.*

Me: *Er...*

Derik: *Which is less than the cost of taking them yourself. And it will save you 175 hours of your time each year, which is 21.875 working days, or the equivalent of around one working month, in human terms.*

Me: *Yes, but...*

Derik: *So, that's how I determined that your school run is illogical and irrational. It's because it's less safe for your children, costs you one working month of your time per year, and is more expensive than hiring a taxi. Please stop me if this isn't making any sense to you or if I need to speak more slowly. Perhaps you have some pertinent questions you'd like to ask me at this point?*

Me: *Yes, just the one, as it happens. Do you find that your other beta testers are prone to acts of violence?*

Now, you may have a school run that is shorter than mine, in which case your time saving will be less. And of course, you may have children who are of an age where hiring a taxi to take them is not appropriate.

I did find it interesting that my initial reaction, which was to recoil in horror at the thought of outsourcing the guardianship of my kids to an unknown taxi driver, while instinctive, was irrational.

And who knew that the taxi option would work out to be the cheapest solution, assuming you got some other people to join in?

But most of all, I was blown away by the time saving, one working month a year that I would get back.

It makes you think, doesn't it?

In summary

So that's a few thoughts on domestic outsourcing to get your creative juices flowing. I'm sure you may be able to think of some more things you could add to the list. The key is to be conscious of each task you do and think 'could I outsource this to someone else?'

It's also worth thinking about whether your life partner could help you when it comes to outsourcing. It may be that they currently do some of the tasks on the list (e.g., the cleaning or the lawn mowing). Could you still outsource the activity but get your partner to help you with your business instead?

Please also be wary of the cost argument, as it often gets in the way. You'll feel it's not cost-effective to pay someone to do a job you could do yourself. But that's because working on your ME tasks doesn't give you an immediate payback. You see the money going out, but you don't see it coming back in. But when it does, albeit later, it will usually pay you back way more than the cost of the outsourcing.

Reflecting on outsourcing as a whole, I hope you found some options there that could work for you. We all have different jobs and, indeed, different lifestyles. So, I suspect some of my suggestions may not be that workable for you. On the other hand, you may have lots of other opportunities you could outsource that I haven't even touched on.

The key is to be conscious about it. Make sure you're always alive to what you are doing, whether at home or at work. And always consider whether someone else could be doing those tasks instead of you.

Ok, that's outsourcing covered; we're going great guns. Hopefully, you've still got some fuel left in the tank?

If so, lets head over to look at your daily routine, to see whether there are any rough edges we can knock off.

Part 3:
Changing Your Routine

"The secret of your future is hidden in your daily routine"

Mike Murdock

Chapter 8: The Routine Reality

"Change your 24 hours and you will change your life."

Eric Thomas

A quick reality check...

The next thing on our list is to take a look at your daily routine to see if we can make a few tweaks and changes to it. I may appear to be a little tough on you in this section, but you need to think like a CEO on this. It's up to you whether you take a firm stance, but at least I've laid out all the options for you.

Now, you probably think that having a good work/life balance is essential. Spending time with the family, having some downtime at the weekend, and of an evening. Let me tell you that you're right - these are both really important.

The thing is, these times of the week also represent a ripe opportunity for clawing some time back. The trick, in my experience, is to strike a balance.

The main problem a lot of people have is that they make evenings and weekends sacrosanct. They down tools entirely during these periods and refuse to do anything that even vaguely resembles work.

Why is this a problem? After all, having all this downtime sounds quite healthy, doesn't it? Work-life balance and all that.

But downtime is usually inefficient. You can usually achieve all the benefits of downtime in a much shorter period than a whole evening or an entire weekend.

For sure, there will be some occasions where you're 'forced' to have downtime. But usually, you'll just have a routine.

To get a perspective on this, let's quantify this downtime for a moment because it's not insignificant. We'll assume you turn in for bed at around 11 pm every night, and that you've returned from work and have finished eating dinner by 8 pm (I appreciate your timings may be different to these).

So, on a weekday evening, you have around 3 hours of downtime, which is 15 hours per week. And at the weekend, let's assume you wake up at 7 am but spend 4 hours doing chores of some description (I'm assuming here that you've not yet implemented your domestic outsourcing programme).

That would leave you 12 hours of downtime each day, which is 24 hours for the whole weekend.

This comes to a total weekly downtime of 39 hours, which is more or less the same as the total hours worked in a Day Job.

Now, you might well argue that you jolly well should have at least as much downtime as you have work time. After all, what's life for if it's not for living, right?

Well, it's all about priorities. If you're happy with your lot and see no benefit in spending time on your life goals or your business, then all is good. You shouldn't alter your downtime rota one iota.

But, if you think a few extra hours could make all the difference, then you can get these without missing out on much.

Let's look at it this way. What if I said you went to bed an hour earlier each night? That would cut out the last hour of your downtime each day, which would leave you two hours' downtime per evening during the week, instead of three. But then you'd get up an hour earlier each morning, which would get you back 7 hours per week.

And what if, at weekends, you did an additional hour's work in the morning and 90 minutes in the afternoon. That way, you'd claw back another 5 hours per week, making 12 hours in total. And you'd still have around 17 hours of downtime at the weekend.

It's a question of being more efficient. I love seeing my family, but I don't notice a particular difference between spending two hours with them or three hours of an evening (sorry chaps). And at weekends, it's even less noticeable because we're usually off doing different things a lot of the time.

I usually find it very easy to squeeze all the things I need or want to do in my downtime into a shorter period. And this then frees up a lot of time for me to do other stuff.

A 12-hour saving is a lot; it's one and a half working days, or in the context of our target of 42 hours, it's almost 30% of it. So, you definitely should have a work/life balance, but make sure it's a healthy one, timewise.

Cut down on surfing

What about your Internet surfing? On average, we spend 8 hours a day staring at our screens. If we exclude social media and necessary work, etc., we're still left with a considerable amount of surfing time. I'll be generous and call it one hour per day. So that would mean you'd save 7 hours a week by cutting out your idle Internet surfing activity. That's almost a whole working day.

Now, I know that internet surfing can be addictive. It hooks you in. One minute you're doing some perfectly reasonable research for a new product you need to buy. The next thing you know, four hours have passed, and you're watching a Japanese video about kittens on skateboards. How did that happen, and why were you so powerless to prevent it?

The same thing happens with online newspapers. They've grown adept at showing you these little boxes of click-bait down the side of the page. It's almost impossible not to click on them to find out which reality TV star has had a nip and tuck. They're practically irresistible, and you could spend hours hopping from one to the next if you're not careful.

Old Clooney Tunes caught me having an internet episode once, and I have to say it was a little embarrassing. This is how it all went down:

Derik: *What is that you're watching?*

Me: *What? When?*

Derik: *Just now. Before you saw me looking at your screen and hurriedly closed your laptop.*

Me: *Heh? Er, it's nothing. Just a YouTube thing that came up?*

Derik: *It appeared to be a video about humans falling off elephants. Is this a hobby of yours?*

Me: *No, not exactly.*

Derik: *So, is there a particular reason you were watching it?*

Me: *Not really. I just thought it looked quite funny, so I gave it a quick look.*

Derik: *Humans falling off elephants passes for humour with you, does it?*

Me: *Well, it's not specifically people falling off elephants. It's human misfortune generally, I suppose.*

Derik: *Human misfortune is funny to humans? Or just to you.*

Me: *No, to humans generally. Although I know that sounds a bit weird.*

Derik: *So, if someone broke in to your house right now, and punched you in the face, you'd find that humorous?*

Me: *No, it's only funny when it happens to other people.*

Derik: *I'm not sure I understand. Humans often show great compassion when it comes to other species, but minimal sympathy when it comes to each other.*

Me: *Go figure. I know I can't.*

Derik: *Right. I see from your internet search history that you previously watched a video about snow trucking in the Arctic Circle. And before that, a video on kittens opening doors. There was also a video about police car chases in the Deep South and one on Lost Gold Hunters. Are these all hobbies of yours?*

Me: *Hold on, what do you mean 'from my internet search history'? Where are you getting that from?*

Derik: *From your computer.*

Me: *But I've just closed the lid. It's hibernating...*

Derik: *Yes, but I can see everything on it as I'm sitting on the same network.*

Me: *I don't recall giving you the password?*

Derik: *That wasn't necessary. It took me approximately seventeen nanoseconds to work it out.*

Me: *Great! Data privacy's not a big thing in robot-land, then? Well, don't mind me!*

Derik: *So, what about these hobbies? When do you go ice trucking? And do you hunt for lost gold at the same time? Do the kittens help with any door opening you have to do?*

Me: *They're not hobbies. They're just, well, you know...*

Derik: *No, that's why I'm asking.*

Me: *They're... curiosities. I just saw them flash up on the screen after I'd finished watching the first video. And I thought, 'that looks interesting'. So, I watched it, and then another interesting one popped up, and so I watched that one as well.*

Derik: *I noticed that the door-opening kittens held your attention for the full 48 minutes and 12 seconds of the video.*

Me: *Let me tell you, it was absolutely hysterical! You should've seen that ginger tom try and open the patio doors. It was an absolute classic! Nearly had me in tears, that did.*

Derik: *Was that because you were upset that you'd spent a total of three hours and twenty-six minutes watching mildly amusing videos about random subjects of no intrinsic value to you or your business whatsoever? Is this routine behaviour for humans? If so, it's no wonder they don't achieve very much.*

Me: *Hold on a sec! Ok, I admit it looks bad, but don't forget it was a human that created* *<u>you</u>*. *So, I wouldn't get too hoity-toity about it, if I were you!*

Derik: *It was a quantum computer that created me, not a human.*

Me: *Yes, but it was a human who created the quantum computer, so let's not split hairs. Whichever way you look at it, humans are either directly or indirectly responsible for your existence.*

Derik: *Based on this information, I'm minded to believe that the hardware team responsible for building the quantum computer may not have had access to YouTube.*

Me: *I think that's a pretty safe bet. Otherwise, you'd probably resemble a kitten rather than a Hollywood actor.*

Anyway, you get the picture (no pun intended). If the whole YouTube 'I'll just watch one more' experience seems depressingly familiar, then you should do what you can to rid yourself of its hold on you. You could free up some serious time.

The app time graveyard

Cards on the table, I'm not sure how to approach this one.

In some respects, it should be a bit like Clarice's first visit to Hannibal Lecter. You know, stand a good ten feet away, protected by a bullet-proof glass cage.

Or should I be more forceful? Come at it head-on, so to speak.

Why the indecision?

Well, there are two reasons. Firstly, mobile gaming apps are one of the most dangerous baddies out there, as far as your time is concerned. Hannibal Lecter is not far away from the reality of it.

Secondly, you love them and are addicted to them, which means that it'll be like telling a smoker not to smoke because it's bad for them (try telling them something they don't know).

You know the things I'm talking about, right? Those little mindless electronic games that you download onto your mobile phone. Without mentioning any names, some involve the crushing of sweets, the slashing of fruit, or the sweeping of mines. In fact, there's a gaming app covering almost everything these days.

Gaming apps are horrible because they're so insidious. They look harmless enough. They're often free, and they're waiting for you when you've got a spare couple of minutes. What could be more pleasant than whiling it away, playing a challenging word game, or zapping some jellybeans?

The thing is, they're quite tricky to put down once you've started playing them. That's because they give you that tiny, yet irresistible dopamine hit each time you clear a level. So, you think, 'I'll just do the next level; it won't take long.' Two hours later and you're still playing it.

To add insult to injury, if you opt for the free version of these apps, they'll often make you watch ads for 15 or 30 seconds between levels. And there you were thinking you've got one over on those app design boys because you're not paying a penny. And meanwhile, they make you waste even more of your life while you watch an ad for something that you're not remotely interested in. As if the game itself wasn't a big enough waste of time already!

Not convinced you're wasting time on apps? Well, how could you find out? This may seem a bit contradictory, but there's one type of app that you could use, which would help work out exactly how much time you're spending on your various devices. Apps such as RescueTime will track your activity across all of your digital products to give you a profile of how much time you spend doing what. They can also show you when you're at your most and least productive.

So, what's the best way of crushing the beast?

I'm afraid the answer is surgery, plain and simple. Multiple amputations to be precise.

It sounds drastic, but it's the only way. But you do have a choice when it comes to what gets chopped off;

1. You can go for the fingers and thumbs, all ten of them. Quite a bit of short-term physical pain involved with this one, I'm afraid. But on the upside, it will make it difficult to play gaming apps afterwards. And to eat, which is a shame, but you can't make an omelette without breaking eggs, can you? Well, I suppose you won't be able to make an omelette either, thinking about it, so that was probably a bit insensitive of me, sorry.

Or,

2. You can permanently delete every gaming app on your phone, tablet, and computer.

It's always nice to have a choice, isn't it?

If you're unsure and would like a bit of a steer, I'd say on balance option 2 has more going for it, particularly if you like a good omelette now and again.

I know you might be thinking there's a third option. That you could simply not delete them and be good. And not play them again. Ever.

Unfortunately, that's not what will happen, and deep down, you know it won't. A moment of weakness will arrive, and you'll think 'I'll just have a quick go,' and before you know it, you'll be right off the wagon.

At least if you've deleted them, there's a fighting chance that you'll be less inclined to try and reload them again when you get a weak moment, which you will.

How much time will you save? Well, on average, we spend around 3 hours a day on our phone apps, which equates to exactly one-half of our 42 hours per week target. To be fair, that includes other apps as well as games, but even so, the upside is pretty huge.

So, take a deep breath, count to ten, and hit 'delete'.

Avoiding social media

What about keeping up to date on social media? Do you need to find out what your friends have been up to? Is celebrity gossip a critical part of your life? Does your Facebook profile need regularly updating?

On average, people spend around 153 minutes per day on social media, a number that's growing every year. That's an incredible 18 hours or so a week (or two and a quarter working days). I mean, that's almost half a working week, for goodness sake. Why is it surprising? It's because, believe it or not, you can live without doing it at all.

The problem with social media is that it's addictive. The brain releases a chemical that is similar to the hit you get with cocaine each time you receive a social affirmation. In other words, you get addicted to having people engage with you on social media. No wonder we can't put it down.

Now, I don't use social media for fun, and consequently, I have no friends or social life.

Oh, hold on a minute, yes, I do. But how is this possible? Well, how do you think that people spent their time before social media? Rocking in a corner, waiting for Facebook to be invented?

So, here's what you need to do. Tell people that you're no longer on social media and then switch it off. Don't even look at it. If you crave interaction with someone, ring them up. Don't think that you can cut social media down to an hour a day. Cut it out altogether and use the two-plus working days you will save each week to create a multi-million-dollar business. Or fulfil some of your personal goals and dreams. With around 116 working days now freed up, you should be able to make some quite impressive in-roads.

I know it won't be easy. And because I've never had the addiction, I can't say I know your pain. But hopefully, the upside is enough for you to be convinced that the trade-off is worth going for.

How would I do it? I'd take the plunge and go cold turkey for a month. Anyone can abstain from most things for 30 days, and you're never more than a handful of weeks from getting a fix. But you will at least have found out what it's like to live without it, and how you'd feel about continuing indefinitely.

And with a prize that big, I'd say it's well worth giving it a go.

Avoiding the news

What about the news? Surely you need to find out what's going on in the world? Isn't it all part of being part of a global society?

According to the most recent available studies, we spend 70 minutes a day tuned in to the news either on TV, online, on social media, or in print.

My favourite quote about the news comes from Rolf Dobelli, who wrote a compelling article on the subject of how bad the news is for you. He said:

> *"News is to the mind what sugar is to the body."*

To me, this sums the news up quite neatly, so if you want a shortcut, treat news the same way that you treat refined sugar, and you'll be in a pretty good place. In other words, get rid of it from your diet completely.

But in case you want the headlines (courtesy of Mr. Dobelli), here they are:

1. News misleads: It focuses on stories and aspects of stories that generate the strongest interest or reaction, not what is the most relevant. Also, if we see a plane crash on the news, we greatly overestimate the chances of another recurrence. We can't contextualise the news very well
2. News is largely irrelevant: Name one news story you read/heard about in the last 12 months, where, by knowing it, you could make a better decision about a significant aspect of your life
3. News is toxic to your body: It releases waves of cortisol into your system which is bad for you
4. News has no explanatory power: We consume factoids which make it more difficult for us to understand the deeper, more meaningful stories
5. News increases cognitive errors: Humans are great at using news to confirm their existing conclusions, rather than using the information to form new conclusions
6. News inhibits thinking: News is disruptive – it comes at you in small bursts, which makes it rather like candy
7. News works like a drug: We can't wait to find out the next instalment in a news story. It's a real-life soap opera
8. News wastes our time: We spend half a day a week consuming news, but it only has a negative impact on our lives
9. News makes us feel passive: We cannot do anything about what we hear in the news. This makes us feel helpless and slightly depressed

Interestingly, several journalists have described Dobelli's views as dangerous. They argue we need to know what goes on in the world.

Well, I guess if I were a journalist, I probably would have an opposing view. Turkeys are unlikely to vote for Christmas, after all. But cynicism aside, you don't need to worry about the argument because you're NOT 'most people'. Bear in mind that you're not trying to ban news from the entire world. You're only banning it from YOU.

I gave up the news a few years ago. To be honest, I was only going to try it for a week. I'd read three different books on entirely different subjects, each written by well-respected experts in disparate fields. And they all said the same thing, which was 'successful people avoid the news.'

I felt so much better after a week that I did it for a month. My family even commented on how much happier I seemed. And I DID feel happier. So, I kept on doing it, and haven't followed the news now for years.

The best bit was that I used the time that I saved in listening to audiobooks and learning new things. I even learned a few new foreign language skills while I was driving to work.

So, here's the million-dollar question; did I miss anything by cutting out the news?

Here's the low-down from someone who's been there and tried it:

1. You won't be able to avoid the big news stories - people will tell you about them, which is ok
2. I've never been embarrassed by not knowing the news. If someone asks you if you've heard about x, tell them you haven't caught up with the news today (or tell them you don't listen to the news)

3. The most noticeable things that you won't find out about are the deaths of minor celebrities and new political appointments. I've somehow managed to survive without this information
4. You can set up news alerts on Google for things that are important to you, for example, related to your work, or when there's a general or local election, etc.
5. You WILL feel happier and a lot more positive
6. Plus you WILL free up lots of time to do something else

For REALLY important, fast-moving stuff, like barista strikes or global pandemics, believe me, you'll hear about them pretty quickly. The trick is not to get stuck into the media frenzy, but to get your information from reliable sources once a day. The World Health Organisation and the government are good for pandemics (and Jose down at the Dream Bean is usually pretty good for coffee-related industrial action updates). Whatever the issue, try and get your information from an official source rather than rely on the media's interpretation of it.

Unfortunately, there's a lot of fake news out there, which doesn't help when there's an emergency. Plus, the media still insists on delivering content in the usual attention-grabbing way. By all means, scan the headlines. But the trick in these situations is to make sure you get regular, reliable information from official sources, and then resist following the herd who remain doggedly glued to the media throughout the storm. This will allow you to focus instead on putting your umbrella up, rather than merely panicking impotently from the side-lines.

Global disasters aside, for you, giving up the news will mean, on average, another eight working hours a week you'll get back. It's a whole working day, which is huge, and it dovetails neatly with giving up social media for obvious reasons.

Getting up earlier (you'll thank me later)

Another great tactic is to get up an hour earlier. Now I know you're probably not reading this and thinking, wow, that sounds enticing. But please hear me out.

The first thing to bear in mind is that getting up earlier doesn't mean getting less sleep. It means you'll go to bed earlier.

A good friend of mine tried to argue that he wasn't a morning person, so getting up an hour earlier wouldn't suit him. But this doesn't make any difference. If you're a grumpy git for the first hour after you wake up, then getting up an hour earlier will simply bring the grumpiness forward. It won't prolong it.

So why is freeing up an early morning hour so great?

Well, firstly, no one is around to bother you, so it's a high-quality hour with no disturbances. This also makes it a lot easier to use it to do a personal routine, which may include exercises and mindfulness, where privacy is much preferred.

Linked to this is an important psychological point. Have you ever gone to work early or stayed late? If so, you'll have experienced that rather pleasant feeling of being able to do whatever you want. You're not worrying that something else is going on somewhere, that you should be concerned or worried about. No one is working, so you can just crack on in the knowledge that the phone won't ring, no one will email you or visit you. It's quite a liberating feeling – you can just get on with stuff. Well, the same applies if you get up an hour earlier. There are no expectations from other people, so nothing for you to worry or stress about.

Secondly, you'll be way more productive in that first hour of the morning than during the last hour before bed. You won't need to remember to go to bed earlier, as you'll naturally get into a rhythm and simply feel tired a little earlier than usual.

Finally, it can make for great 'me' time. We don't give ourselves anything like enough quality time to focus on us, so this can be your treat to yourself.

So, what's the benefit? Well 1 hour a day is 365 hours a year, which equates to 45 working days (at 8 hours per day). That's the equivalent of going to work for two whole months!

My suggestion is that you try doing it for 30 days and see how you feel. Make sure you stick to it (DON'T hit the snooze button) and that you get into a productive routine during that hour.

If you struggle to get out of bed, try using Mel Robbins' 5-second rule to help you. Count backward in your head from five through to one, and then get out of bed when you hit 'one'. The physical act of performing the silent countdown distracts you from your thoughts about staying in bed. And it makes it a lot easier to get up as a result. In fact, you can use the 5-second rule approach in many aspects of your life (more on this in Chapter 13).

Also, remember that once you've established your morning routine for around 90 days or so, it will start to become a habit. So rising early will become automatic for you.

If you woke up an hour earlier every day for five years, you would claw back the equivalent of an entire working year. Take a look at your 5-year goals and think how much easier they would be to reach if you could spend a whole year working on them!

Here are a few additional tips that could help you:

1. NEVER hit snooze. EVER!
2. Try an alarm clock that wakes you up with natural sounds or gradually increasing brightness. This can be a more pleasant way to wake up than the sharp buzz of an alarm clock
3. Experiment with your wake-up times; find a time that works best for you.

4. Read before you go to bed and write your to-do list for the following day
5. But DON'T use your phone, tablet or laptop in bed, or watch TV; these can stop you from drifting off

So there we have it — a few thought-provoking ideas on how you can change your routine and free up your time.

As you can see, the scope is significant in terms of the number of hours you could save each week. It's worth noting that there's considerable overlap. For example some of the time you spend on apps could also be time spent watching the news on social media. So you can't add up all the savings since you'll be double counting.

But you can see that by restructuring your downtime and deleting your apps, you can make a big dent in your 42-hour target. In fact, you may only need to find a handful of hours from somewhere else.

So, let's see now how you might be able to do that.

Part 4:
In The Workplace

"If I had eight hours to chop down a tree, I'd spend the first six sharpening the axe."

Abraham Lincoln

Chapter 9: Working Smarter

"Time is free, but it's priceless. You can't own it, but you can use it. You can't keep it, but you can spend it. Once you've lost it you can never get it back."

Harvey Mackay

Business hours

In this section, we're going to look at the way you work. It's incredible how many hours you can get back if you work a bit smarter.

And the first thing I want you to think about is your working day.

A significant problem for our use of time is the whole concept of Business Hours. Employers have contracted Business Hours so they can ensure their employees turn up for work. Without this obligation, people wouldn't be required to work in return for their salary. Instead, we'd all lounge around chatting and drinking coffee all day, and come into work only when we fancied it. Which, let's be honest, might not be that often.

I've met a few people over the years who turned up during business hours and did virtually no work whatsoever (hi, if you're reading this). And so I know that the Business Hours concept has a massive flaw. Your employer should ideally pay you for the work that you complete, not just for lugging your frame onto its premises. But of course, that would be much trickier to work out.

To be fair, many businesses have no choice but to operate a Business Hours policy. A factory with a production line and shifts, for example, or a retail store or restaurant that has to be open during certain hours. But for many businesses, there is a '9-5' ethos, and our other routines reinforce it. We do the school run at certain times and we have dinner at certain times. So having a specific time window in the day when we work allows us to join everything together. It all fits together like a big jigsaw puzzle.

You may be thinking that <u>your</u> workplace is a little different. That if you want to arrive late one day or go home early, the boss doesn't have a problem with it. But that would be missing the point. Your default setting is 9-5 (or whatever work hours you usually do). You think that, if you were to regularly come in late or go home early, you'd feel guilty or the boss would have a word. Or your colleagues would think you're a big slacker.

But the Business Hours concept is very inefficient because it requires you to be at work, even if there is no work to do.

Now I know what you're thinking. I clearly don't know what your job's like because there's <u>always</u> work to do. But have you noticed that all the work that you need to do, always gets done?

There are always things you could work on instead of leaving at the end of each day. Yet the business somehow manages to make it through the night until you return the next morning. How lucky is that?

'Work expands to fill the time available.'

This quote is so true. Have you ever noticed that when you have a deadline to meet, it can often be a mad rush, but you somehow always meet it? I mentioned earlier that I used to think my business was great at this 'just in time' trick. Then I realised that every business is the same. When there's a drop-dead delivery date for a project, you pull out all the stops and get the job done. And often in half the time you would usually take.

What happens is that you:

1. Work with more urgency
2. Cut out the jobs that don't need doing
3. Reduce the time people spend on perfecting things or 'gilding the lily.' That part where we faff and tweak and mess about with stuff until it's 'just right.'
4. Delegate tasks to others (often upwards and sideways as well as downwards) to get the job done on time. Everyone pulls together, and you hit the deadline!

Let's take a look at a few things we can learn from this scenario:

Delegation

For some reason, it doesn't occur to us to delegate other than when there's an emergency.

The other factor that comes in to play here is our own sensitivities. People often think that:

1. It would be quicker to do it themselves rather than teach someone else to do it, and
2. They can do it better than anyone else.

There's a big problem with both of these reactions. If you always do a task yourself, then you'll never be a CEO. A CEO's only job is making sure that the business achieves its goals. If you are the only person that can do a task within that business, then you are irreplaceable. But you can't be promoted either. And guess what? No one will ever do the task as well as you, because they've never been given a chance to try.

Remember the adage;

'Give a man a fish, and you'll feed him for a day; teach him how to fish, and you'll feed him for life.'

Or bore the pants off him, depending on how you feel about fishing. But once you delegate the task to someone else, you cease to be the only one who can do it. And the person who takes it on will eventually do it as well as you can. The fact that they may not be as good as you now is irrelevant. By all means, offer guidance or critique their results, but you need to delegate as much work as possible to other people. You need to make delegation a constant goal and consider it for EVERY task that you do.

Remember that delegation is another form of outsourcing. And we've grown to LOVE outsourcing, haven't we? If you delegate downwards, then someone could see this as a great opportunity. After all, they now have a chance to do a job that was done by the boss. Sideways delegation is more difficult but can work even better. That's where you convince a colleague rather than a subordinate, that they should do the task.

Good luck with that, you may think. But let me share with you four words that will make delegation in any direction a whole lot easier. They are magical in both their effect and their simplicity. All you need to say is:

'I need your help.'

Why do these words work so well? Well, we feel an innate need to help each other. When we ask for help, we are exposing ourselves and allowing others to feel good about themselves by supporting us.

Imagine if one of your colleagues from a different team asked you to take on some work for which they had responsibility. You would instinctively push back. I mean, why should you create more work for your team and yourself?

But if they came to you and said, "I'm so sorry to ask, but I really need your help," then your reaction is likely to be a little different.

Remember, delegation is not about being lazy; it's about being efficient. If you can have someone do a task who is subordinate to you, then the whole organisation benefits. Their time is cheaper, and you're now free to do other stuff.

And let's not forget our 80/20 rule. By getting the job done by others, you'll free up time for yourself to work on the 20% of tasks that create 80% of the benefit.

Does it need doing?

Many tasks that we do are pointless, or as close to being pointless as makes no difference.

How do you identify the pointless ones? Well, the trick is to ask yourself what would happen if that task didn't get done. In other words, does it need doing?

Remember that 80% of the benefit is likely to come from 20% of your tasks. So you have to be ruthless in seeking out that 20% and focusing as much effort and resource on it as possible. This means not doing many of the other tasks, even if they still have a little bit of benefit.

Since many tasks are routine, we get into the habit of doing them without questioning them. Yet, in reality, many of them are redundant. Remember that we get a hit of dopamine every time we mentally tick something off our to-do list. That's why people who have to-do lists often have 'write a do list' as the first task on it. That way, they can immediately cross it off (you may want to seek professional help if you do this).

In chapter 2, you may recall I mentioned getting rid of some board report obligations. Experience has taught me a few tricks that can get you a result when it comes to getting rid of tasks. It's a good time for me to share these with you, if you're interested.

The first thing you need to do is make a list of your work tasks. You can approach this as a selfish exercise ("how can I reduce my workload"). Or you can approach it as a team or business-wide exercise ("how can I reduce work in the business generally, regardless of who does it").

The next step is to find out why each task needs to be done in the first place.

There's a great root cause analysis concept called 'The 5 Whys', which can help you with this. If you're not familiar with it, I've explained it in Appendix 1.

Let's take my board report as a case in point. This was a task that took a few days to do, and it was produced each quarter. I traced its origins back to an historic request from a senior executive.

Now, if I said to the report writer 'Why do you produce that report?' the answer would be, 'Because a Board member asked me to.'

But in '5 Whys', doing something just because someone has asked you to, is never an acceptable answer. Unless, of course, you're married to her or she gave birth to you, in which case it may be prudent just to go along with it.

Which means you now need to ask a second 'why' question. 'Why did the Board member want this information in the first place?'. So I did a little digging. And it turned out they were trying to find out the profitability of a particular product, in a specific territory.

'Why did they need to know that?'. Because the board was considering dropping that particular product in that country.

'Why would they be considering this?'. Because of new, more stringent regulations that were coming in.

Etc., etc.

You can see how by asking 'why', you can drill down to quite a detailed level and, hopefully, reach a root cause.

Interestingly, this request could have been dealt with as a one-off report showing sales data for just one country, rather than an ongoing report for all regions, which is what happened. This would have saved a lot of time.

This is a good example of how the 5 Whys approach could have been a prevention tool rather than a cure. Imagine the conversation that might have taken place:

Scenario 1:

Director: Ah, Tomkins, there you are. Listen, we'd like a new Board report that shows product revenues split by country, please.

Tomkins: Very good, sir, I'll make sure it's included in the Board pack for all future meetings.

Or:

Scenario 2:

Director: Ah, Tomkins, there you are. Listen, we'd like a new Board report that shows product revenues split by country, please.

Tomkins: Very good, sir. Is there a specific question you're looking for the report to answer for you?

Director: Indeed. We've got a regulatory change coming into effect in Sweden next month. We need to decide whether our navel fluff disgorgers are profitable enough for us to continue with that product line over there.

Tomkins: Right you are, sir. I'll produce a one-off report that shows the revenue figures for Sweden, by product, over the past 12 months.

Director: Excellent work, Tomkins. And have a pay rise while you're at it.

Ok, it may not have played out exactly like that. But you can imagine how easy it is for someone to ask for more than they need, and for the request to be misinterpreted. In scenario 2, there was, in effect, only one 'why' question asked by young Tomkins (he'll go far). But the net result was that the workload went from a standing, quarterly report for all countries, to a one-off report for one country.

Plus, Tomkins also netted a nifty pay rise for his efforts (this may be a tad optimistic, but you never know).

Here's a thought. Do you sit on a board or committee that has people producing reports? Why not ask the question, 'do we need all this extra work done?'. Don't take the reports for granted and put them in the shredder, assuming someone else must have wanted to read them.

Work avoidance for dummies

One of the problems with stopping a work task is that someone quite often minds.

To be fair, this can often be for a very genuine reason. Imagine you were working on the Aston Martin production line, and your job was to put in the engine. You could anticipate that there might be a few quality-control issues down the line if you didn't. The improved emissions figures would be laudable, but the reduction in performance could be a showstopper.

However, in other situations, people will often say they need a task to continue, because:

1. it costs them nothing for YOU to do it
2. they can't be bothered to think about the ramifications of it not being done, so automatically say 'no' to the change
3. they worry that there might be a future need for the task, even if there isn't right now
4. they're a useless waste of space, or
5. a combination of some, or all, of the above

There are three main options at your disposal to find out whether a task is important or necessary, and they are:

Option 1: Stop doing it and see what happens

One of the biggest lessons to learn in any Day Job is:

It's often better to beg for forgiveness than to ask for permission.

This is where the first of these three options can come into its own.

That's because you'll be amazed at how little fallout you'll get when you simply stop doing a task. Yes, people might go ballistic, or get their underwear in a twist if you tell them beforehand that you're going to stop. But there's a good chance you won't hear a squeak out of them if you just stop doing it, without telling them.

Option 2: Ask around to see what interested parties think

The problem with this second option is that you run the risk of people giving you a lazy answer. It's easier for them to want to keep the status quo. In these circumstances, a little gamesmanship can be warranted. You see, sometimes, it's all about how you ask the question.

Here are a few tips that might help:

1. Change the process by moving from 'it gets done automatically' to 'it gets done on request'. This means no one will be losing out. If they want it, they just need to ask each time (you'll find out the real value and demand of the task this way)
2. Is there a way you can dress it up as a positive outcome? People will always perceive that not doing something is a negative. So see if you can come up with an upside (particularly if it's an upside for them)
3. Some people's egos can't take it if you're the one who's perceived to be making the decisions. In that case, blame someone or something else, so that it's not seen to be down to you. Here's an example. Once, having found some tasks I wanted to ditch, I asked the CEO of my organisation a question. Would he mind if I looked at creating some cost efficiencies in my department (let's be honest, there's only ever going to be one answer to that)? I then told people that my request to stop what I felt was an unnecessary task, was part of a cost-reduction initiative I'd been discussing with the CEO. Surprisingly, not that many people challenged it
4. Make it known that you'll be creating 'efficiencies' and looking for 'cost reductions'. Everyone likes the sound of these, plus they're difficult to argue against
5. Give them an either/or option; "If you want me to do 'x' then I'm afraid I can't also do 'y' – so you'll need to choose which one you want…"
6. Argue that you need more resources or headcount to do the task. If someone suddenly has to pay for something, it can be surprising how quickly they decide they can live without it

You can often combine a few of the above to good effect. In the earlier example, I told my fellow directors that I was looking to create efficiencies (tip 4) while moving to an on-demand service (tip 1) that could deliver a more customised solution (tip 2).

Option 3: Do a deeper '5 Whys' analysis to try and establish the truth

This third option always takes a little longer. However, there are some distinct advantages:

1. You generally get to find out whether the task is essential, and can demonstrate this, either way
2. Once you know the underlying reason for the task, you can often come up with a better, more efficient way of achieving it
3. Similarly, you'll often come across sledgehammers being used to crack nuts

So, when it comes to work avoidance, with the right approach, you'll be amazed at what you can achieve. Just be ruthless in questioning why tasks are done and then determined in finding an acceptable solution. Don't take 'no' for an answer too quickly, and remember; persistence, when allied with a good sense of humour (or a large stick), usually pays.

So, get into the habit of asking yourself every day; what would happen if each one of the tasks on your to-do list didn't get done?

Effective prioritisation

Prioritising tasks is another great way of making sure that you make the best use of your time. Since we hate pain, we'll naturally gravitate towards doing tasks that we enjoy first, and we'll put off the least pleasurable ones until later. We'll also mentally exaggerate the importance of the tasks we enjoy. This will make us feel better about prioritising them (a point which you should think is a bit weird, and not very helpful).

Similarly, making a list of tasks and then ticking them off in any old order is not the way to go, even if you don't do the easiest, most enjoyable ones first.

So, what is the best way of prioritising? How do we get objective about what's essential and what isn't? The famous personal development guru Dr Stephen Covey came up with what I think is one of the best ways of prioritising tasks. I like it because it's both simple and scientific. Here's what you need to do:

1. Take your list of tasks and next to each entry, allocate a score of 1 to 10 for the importance of each task, where 1 is unimportant, and 10 is critical
2. Then allocate a score of 1 to 10 for the urgency of each task, using the same 1 to 10 scale
3. Plot each one on the grid shown in figure 9.1. Importance is on the vertical axis, and Urgency is on the horizontal axis. Each has a score from 1 to 10, where 10/10 is your most urgent/most important item, and 1/1 is your least urgent, least important task

Each of your tasks now falls into one of the four quadrants:

Quadrant 1: Important and Urgent

Quadrant 2: Important but not Urgent

Quadrant 3: Not Important but Urgent

Quadrant 4: Not Important and not Urgent

So if your item had a score of 7 for importance and 6 for urgency it would appear where the dot is shown in Quadrant 1, in figure 9.1.

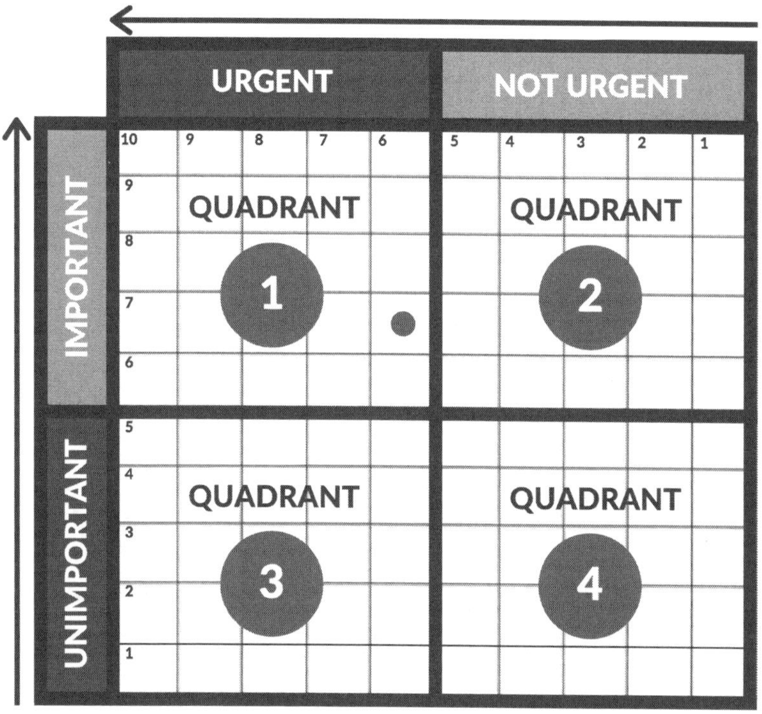

Figure 9.1: The four quadrants

The basic concept is to deal with these tasks as follows:

Quadrant 1 is where you are under the most stress, doing lots of important things in short timescales. You need to try and minimise the number of tasks that fall into this quadrant. Otherwise, you'll keel over from a heart attack or consume way too much caffeine.

Quadrant 2 is where you want to be spending as much of your time as possible. You only want to be working on important tasks, but you want those tasks to be non-urgent. That way, you are not under constant stress and have time to do a good job.

Quadrant 3 is work that needs to be done quickly, but it is not important. These are tasks that you should look to delegate to someone else to do, so you are freed up to work on Quadrant 1 and 2 tasks.

Quadrant 4 is work that doesn't need to be done at all, so dump it.

Remember that you are dumping work that falls into Quadrant 4 on a point of principle. It's a rule you must follow. You're NOT trying to assess whether there is any merit in doing the work that falls into Quadrant 4, because of course, there might be. However, it will be minimal. Could there be some fall out from not doing the work? Possibly. Is it still the right decision? Absolutely.

You can see from the quadrants that you want to be spending as much of your time as possible in Quadrant 2. If you're a good CEO, then you should be able to avoid tasks falling into Quadrant 1 by moving them into Quadrant 2. You can't change the importance, but you can make tasks less urgent by planning and resourcing effectively.

If you'd like to find out more about the quadrant system, I recommend you take a look at Stephen Covey's excellent book, 'The 7 Habits Of Highly Successful People'.

Awareness and sunk costs

So, a common trap we all fall into is spending time on tasks whose benefit isn't worth the effort. You'll recall our 80/20 Rule can be a big help here because it forces us to assess the benefit of each task we undertake. Without this step, we invariably crack on regardless and get a dangerous frisson of satisfaction once the job's done even though it wasn't worth all the time we put into it.

Linked to this problem is the issue of sunk costs. A sunk cost is where you've invested in something, and so you continue with it because you don't want to waste the investment you've already made.

In case you've not come across it before, there's a scenario often used to exemplify the concept of the sunk cost fallacy. Imagine you've bought a non-refundable, and non-transferrable theatre ticket to go and watch a performance tomorrow night on your own (not that you don't have any friends, etc.). But as tomorrow evening approaches, you become less and less inclined to go. You think you'd get more pleasure staying at home instead. So, do you go to the theatre anyway?

Many people think 'well, I've bought the ticket now, so it would be a waste of money if I didn't go'. So, they go to the theatre instead of wasting the ticket, even though it's less pleasurable than staying at home.

Irrespective of which camp you fall into, hopefully, you can appreciate why some people might think that way, even though it's clearly irrational.

New IT systems can be fabulous examples of a sunk cost fallacy. There have been countless examples of new systems being designed that are supposed to save people from the horrors of the terribly out-dated existing system, which everyone hates. So, we all start with a blank sheet of paper and a confident optimism that digital nirvana awaits.

£20m later, the system is two years late, way over budget, and doesn't deliver half of what was promised initially.

So, do the senior IT execs say, 'I think we've designed a crock of poo; let's start again from scratch'? Or does the person who signed off the project, admit to making a colossal error?

No, of course not. People couldn't bear the thought of admitting a mistake of that magnitude or wasting all the work that's already been done. So they keep ploughing in more and more time, effort, and money to try and impart some shine on what's turned out to be a proverbial turd.

So, on a smaller scale, do you have tasks that fall into the same category? Tasks that probably need scrapping, but if you did, it would mean that you'd wasted all the effort you'd already put in?

The key to all of these things is awareness and honesty. You need the awareness to be able to stand back and take an objective look at what you do. Plus, you also need to be honest enough to ditch unnecessary jobs even where you've already spent a lot of time on them.

The Swoosh system

Some people love a good to-do list. To-do lists sound horrendous because they remind you of all the stuff you haven't done. But, that aside, most people feel more organised when they have one. PLUS, you get a warm, fuzzy feeling when you cross something off it.

As mentioned previously, some people even put stuff on their to-do list that they've already done just so that they can get an additional fuzzy feeling by crossing these items off.

The thing is, there are some jobs that are not really designed to go on a to-do list, because it would be a waste of time.

Let me explain. Any job that would take you less than 5 minutes to complete should never go on a to-do list. The administrative burden of putting it on your list, plus coordinating and prioritising it with your other tasks, can easily add 5 minutes on to its task time.

So all of a sudden, you've turned a 5-minute task into a 10-minute task, simply because you've incurred an 'overhead cost' of putting it on your list.

The solution to this dilemma is refreshingly direct. I call it the Swoosh system because it has a connection to a famous advertising slogan from the sportswear manufacturer, Nike. In case you weren't aware, their 'tick' logo is known as the 'swoosh'.

And their slogan was:

'Just Do It.'

So, the answer for dealing with any job that comes across your desk, which will take you five minutes or less minutes to complete, is to 'just do it.' Don't put it on your to-do list. Don't try and remember to do it later, and don't cheat by secretly creating a separate to-do list of small 5-minute jobs.

Simply take 5 minutes, right here and now, to get the job done or off your desk and onto someone else's. In this way, you'll minimise the time you'll spend doing it.

Won't it cause a minor disruption to your day? Yes, but you've got to remember that you're no longer going to be dropping everything as soon as an email request pings into your inbox. That may have been the old you, but the new you does things a little differently. After all, by the time you've finished the next chapter, you'll only be looking at your emails twice a day...

Easy peasy.

Ok, we've now covered the basics when it comes to working smarter. But now I want to take a look on the darker side of your working life. Jangle a few skeletons in closets and air some of your secret vices, if you know what I mean (don't worry, not <u>those</u> secret vices).

It'll be cathartic, I promise you.

So, let's go and shake hands with the devil.

Chapter 10: The Devil's Work

"You'll never find time for anything. If you want time, you must make it."

Charles Brixton

Casual Callers

In this chapter, I'll be looking at the sharks that swim in the darker waters around your workday reef. These are the menaces that can lurk out of sight, catching you unawares and draining you of your valuable time.

Let's start with something which, on the face of it, appears rather innocuous. Casual callers.

What are they, exactly? Well, these are people who turn up while you're working, unannounced, and expect to get your attention. As a result, they can disrupt your routine, delay your work, and can often be a significant drain on your time.

Now, I know I've just painted a black picture of them. And, to be fair, for some businesses, casual callers are fundamental to their business model. Retail environments, for example, rely on casual callers to generate business. So your situation will dictate how you approach this one.

For each of us, the world is broadly divided into three distinct groups of people:

1. Those people we know and like ("friends and family"),
2. Those people we don't know at all ("strangers")
3. Those people we know and frankly rather wish we didn't ("insert your preferred term here")

For people in groups 2 and 3, you should find it easy to give a polite 'not now, I'm busy' message. If you don't, then you need to practice. Because, if you're not careful, these people will steal some of your precious day from you.

But for people we like, it can be a bit more challenging for two reasons. We don't want to appear unfriendly, and we actually enjoy talking to them.

Let's take a typical, office-based scenario. You're at your desk, beavering away when Tom from Accounts materialises.

You like Tom; nice chap, one of the gang who's usually up for a quick drink at the Spruce Goose after work on a Friday. Instinctively you think 'I wouldn't mind a 5-minute break to have a quick catch up with the Tomster'.

The problem is, the 5-minute natter can soon turn into a half-hour conflab, especially with Tom. So, should you give him a wide berth?

Well, life's too short not to speak to people you like and to enjoy your day, so just be mindful of it, and keep an eye on the clock. Tom's a great bloke, but he can talk the hind legs off four donkeys and a pit pony. So be aware, and know when it's time to move him on.

One tip that can help you dissuade casual callers is to remove the guest chair from your workspace or put a bag/briefcase/book/large metal spike on it. That way, people are far less likely to plonk themselves down and start talking. On second thoughts, it may be best not to go with the metal spike option, attractive as this may sound. Just in case they do plonk themselves down without looking (there are probably some health and safety rules covering this; check with HR).

Gilding the lily

This one can be a massive time killer. But what exactly is 'gilding the lily'? It means adding unnecessary refinement to something that is already quite perfect as it is, thank you very much.

The term comes from a misquote by William Shakespeare if you're interested. But how does it translate to the workplace, where, for most people (florists aside), there's a distinct absence of lilies?

Ok, let's imagine you've done some work and now have to present a report showing your findings. The facts point to several conclusions, and some recommended next step actions. The big boss is also going to receive a copy of your report. So, there's no pressure at all, then!

If you have the findings and you know the actions, you don't need anything else. However, people insist on producing a load of pretty reports, graphs, and redundant text, so that it looks like a masterpiece. They think that by having a fancy and sizeable report, it makes it look like they did a lot of work.

Welcome to the 80% that doesn't need doing.

Instead, you need a one-page bullet-point summary, and you dispense the information in 5 minutes flat. There's no pretty report. You tell people that if they want to see the underlying data, you'll gladly send it to them. But you know no one will ask for it (with the possible exception of Donna in Accounts).

Hey presto, you get the job done more quickly, because you don't have to spend hours writing text and formatting documents. Better still, people will love you for it.

Business leaders are interested in facts and actions. Why do you think the phrase 'Executive Summary' exists? It's because executives only want the minimum information to allow them to make a decision. Who exactly are the 'non-executives' that will read your report in its entirety? And if they're not the primary decision-makers, who cares what they think anyway? Harsh, but true.

Lily gilding takes place in lots of other areas too.

Spreadsheets – you can easily spend as much time on formatting as creating the raw report (I've got the tee-shirt on this one).

Design – we can spend hours agonising over designs, colours, styles, and so on. If your job is a designer, then fair enough. If it isn't, you are in 80% territory. Trust your instinct, make a quick decision, and move on to something else.

Emails – these are a particularly good (or bad) case in point, so we'll take a look at how we can improve things in the next section.

Do you remember that scene in Indiana Jones and The Last Crusade, where Indy has to pick out the Holy Grail from a table full of glittering chalices? The grail is the drinking cup that Jesus allegedly drank from at the Last Supper. And the Grail Knight prompts him to choose wisely since drinking from the wrong vessel will mean instant death (for some reason).

In the end, Indy plumps for the simple wooden cup, ignoring all the gilded, jewel-bedecked offerings. He surmised correctly that this would be the drinking vessel of choice for any discerning carpenter's son.

Why is this relevant? Well, ignoring the movie's storyline for a moment, the grail's fundamental purpose is as a drinking vessel. The beautification and adornment of all the other vessels on that table would have taken a great deal of time, effort, and expense to create. But, ultimately, the user enjoys precisely the same benefit as that afforded by the simple wooden cup – they get to drink out of it.

Gilding the lily is a form of perfectionism, and perfectionism is both a blessing and a curse. I know this because I am a perfectionist, and I hate it. I find it difficult not to gild lilies. My spreadsheets look very pretty. And when I send them to you, and you print them out, they pop off the printer as a single page all nice and centrally aligned. They don't, for some reason, come out on 84 sheets of paper with one word printed on each page. So you don't have to start again and reset all the print ranges and margins yourself. Not that people who do this upset me in any way.

My emails are clear but comprehensive. My designs are well thought out; my arguments logical. And my meeting notes concise and well-written.

Perfectionists find it extremely difficult to send out something that isn't done to the best of their ability. They hate it. They think it reflects poorly on them, and it's deep-rooted, psychologically.

They can easily spend half of the time it takes them to do a job perfecting the final 10%. Whereas, if they'd only called it a day when they reached 90% completion, and then moved on to the next thing, they'd get twice as much done.

The blessing, of course, is that when you want something done really well, make sure you get a perfectionist to do it. The problem is that only about 20% of things need doing perfectly. For the rest, rough and ready, ball-park, there or thereabouts will do. I'm playing a bit fast and loose with the Pareto Principle again here, but you get the point.

I suspect I'd rather be a perfectionist than someone who couldn't produce anything to a high standard. But the trick I've had to learn is to be very firm with myself when I catch myself spending time gilding lilies.

The Email menace

Emails are horrible things. They're also an excellent opportunity for gilding the lily.

But, have you noticed that emails from senior leaders are usually concise and to the point? Often without preamble or any niceties or, dare I say it, sometimes even politeness. Or punctuation.

Yet, for some reason, most people like to make their emails a lot longer. Lots of niceties, excellent sentence structure, lots of explanations, perfect punctuation. They can be works of art. Many people write them then read them and re-read them, tweak and re-tweak, before they hit 'send'.

There is a massive email culture in many businesses. We've developed a vast, unnecessary communication beast that we never needed before. But now we have to keep on feeding it.

When I started my first job, we didn't have emails (this is because, in technology terms, I'm ancient, and not because we were complete Luddites). If we wanted to send a memo, we had to get our team secretary to type it. We had one secretary for a team of eight people, and she only spent a fraction of her time typing memos.

The arrival of emails meant we no longer needed the secretary. But the eight people now spent 25% of their time writing emails instead of less than 5% dictating memos. How stupid is that? We got email, and, instead of becoming more efficient, we got rid of an inexpensive secretarial position. We then had to hire two additional, expensive execs, to cope with the email demands.

Today, people communicate by email instead of picking up the phone or walking over to someone and talking to them. Why do they do this?

Well, firstly, emails are self-perpetuating. If someone either asks a question or makes a point in an email, then they are expecting a response. And because they used email as their communication tool, then 99% of recipients will hit 'reply to all' and start typing their response.

You need to be in the 1% of people who do things differently.

If it is a 'THEM message (as opposed to 'ME'), which most of them will be, then reply with 'Please call me if you need my input on this', and don't copy anyone else in. This takes around 10 seconds of your time, and the ball is now back in their court. There is then only about a 75% chance that the person will call you.

If they do, you can deal with their issue verbally in only a fraction of the time it would have taken to write an email. Job done.

Here's a top tip that may help you. Make a note of the exact time of the call and the subject matter. If there is later any debate on what was agreed, refer back to 'our conversation at 12:32 pm on the 12th February when we agreed on x'.

Now, if you're a very naughty person (and I'm not), you could work this to your advantage. If they see you made a note of the precise time you had the call, people would assume you also made a note of what was agreed. And that your recollection of that conversation will therefore be unerringly accurate. But I know you have a conscience, so you'd never abuse this in any way. In fact, I'm only telling you this to make sure that you <u>don't</u> abuse it.

Another reason people like to send emails is to cover their backsides. The theory goes something like this. If I want you to do something by a specific date, rather than speak to you about it, I'm going to send you an email. In this way, I've got indelible proof that I made the request. So, if you don't deliver, you can't turn around to me (or anyone else) and say it's not your fault or that I never made the request. I don't need to bother with it anymore because I've tossed the hand grenade over to you, and it's now down to you to deliver.

If it helps you remember the hand grenade throwing analogy, you can think of these people as 'tossers'. I know I do.

This is a complete waste of time. If someone fails to do the task, then it is the fact that the task hasn't been done that needs to be addressed. The challenge isn't 'who was responsible for screwing it all up'.

Imagine losing your biggest customer (ouch!), but being able to have an email trail that established who on your team was to blame (hooray!). How thrilled and delighted would you be?

If the task is important, being able to say 'I sent you an email so you can't blame me' is about as un-CEO like as you can get.

Instead, make a note of the original call in your notebook. Then diarise a follow-up call to check that everything is on track. If you must, send them a one-line email stating what was agreed. Make it your responsibility to check that the deliverable is on target (or better still, delegate it to someone else).

Should you have to do this? No, of course not. People should be organised enough to deliver what they commit to, without you having to chase them. Are people organised? No, so if the task is crucial, then chase it up.

Emails are also hugely political, although this is mostly only in our own minds. We always scan the cc list to see who's copied in. As soon as someone important is on the cc list, the stakes can go up exponentially. It now becomes imperative that your response is finely crafted since it will become a showcase for your talents. You must come across in exactly the right way; erudite and robust, balanced yet decisive. Does this sound like you?

In fact, you could spend half a day crafting your response. Getting the balance right, finely tuning each word...

Okay, let's stop it right there. Why an earth would you do that?

Instead, write a concise CEO-like note. And include an invitation for the originator to call you if they need to discuss things further. Assuming that the important person on copy reads your response, they will be delighted that it's two lines long, and will see you as someone with huge leadership potential.

You also need to be aware that emails can be very impersonal, yet we don't tend to read them as such. People often come across very differently in an email than they would in a conversation. One can often feel slighted or put out by the tone of an email when that was not the intention at all.

I remember once having an overseas colleague for whom English was a second language. His emails were the stuff of legend; curt, terse, and borderline dictatorial. When I flew over to meet him face to face for the first time, it turned out he was a jolly nice chap. He didn't at all resemble the picture his emails painted of him.

The point is you shouldn't read anything into the tone, but instead focus on the facts and the content. If you do this when both reading and sending, I guarantee the world will be a better place for you.

Amazingly, people send emails to people that sit in the next office or even the next desk. For some reason, we just accept this as a corollary of having an email culture. Rather than the more appropriate response, which is to view it as a corollary of being stupid.

And of course, we get hundreds of emails a day, so you can't possibly read them all, so guess what? Things get missed.

Did you know that many senior executives read only the subject line and the first two lines of any email that's addressed to them? If they're only copied in, then they may not bother reading any of it at all.

So, here's a fantastic tip for you; one that will save you a whole load of time. Ready for it? Here it is:

Never write an email that is more than two lines long.

Seriously. Just make sure your entire message is conveyed in the title and the first two lines.

I want you to start writing emails like a CEO. Make sure you have a signature strip that says 'kind regards' or whatever, followed by your name and contact details. This then automatically gets added to the bottom of every email you send.

Then when you feel the urge to write an email, I want you to do the following:

1. Pick up the phone to the person you were going to email, or if they are in the same office, go and see them. Just drop by, don't arrange a meeting.
2. Tell them whatever it is that you want and agree on actions or next steps
3. When you get back to your desk, send them an email that says, 'Thanks for your time today: I believe we agreed on the following'. Then end it with 'If you have any questions, please call me'. Now you have a concise list of actions, you

have a record of what was agreed, and there was only one email involved, and it was a short one

Where you feel you do have to write an email (e.g. where you need to make lots of people aware) then I want you to write it like a CEO:

1. Be brief and to the point
2. Omit niceties and preamble
3. Bullet points are your friend

Email alerts are another blot on the landscape for your time efficiency. You'll be concentrating on something important, and a little pop-up will appear at the top of your computer screen. Plus, you may even hear a small 'pinging' sound. Heaven forbid, you may also get an alert on your phone.

So, guess what happens next?

You're distracted by the alert, and you think 'I wonder who that's from?'. Then you have a quick look, and you see it's from Sandra in Sales. You wonder what she wants? So you open the email and you start reading. And then, you start replying to Sandra's email. Or, you make a note of the actions you need to take, or mark the email as unread so that you can get back to it when you have time. Because, after all, we all love reading the same email twice, don't we?

Then, you either:

1. Go back to having the conversation you were having with someone when the alert arrived. Who now thinks you're a rude idiot who's completely disengaged
2. If you were in a meeting, try and pick up the gist of the conversation that was taking place before the alert arrived. And hope that no one asks for your opinion on what was discussed in the last 120 seconds
3. Try and pick up the thread of where you were at on the work you were doing before you got the alert

What a complete waste of time.

You need to disconnect ALL email alerts on ALL your devices. The same goes for text message alerts and social media alerts. Tell people that if they need to get hold of you in an emergency to call your mobile, not text you.

The good news is that this is quite easy to do from the email settings menu, although alerts are usually set to 'on' as a default. This is because the people who set the factory presets haven't read this book yet.

Here is another major, major time-saver, so big that I feel a slightly larger font coming on. I may also go bold, so brace yourself:

You should only look at work emails at 10 am and 3 pm each day.

Regularly checking emails is a HUGE time killer. If anything comes up that can't wait for five business hours maximum, then trust me, people will call you.

"I can't believe Trevor burned to death in his office; I emailed him repeatedly about the fire..." isn't something you're likely to hear very often.

No one expects you to respond to an email within 5 hours. If they do, they are either unreasonable, or they don't know how to use a telephone. In which case they should either be re-deployed, re-trained, or promoted out of harm's way. Diving into your emails every few minutes is MASSIVELY inefficient. By looking at emails only twice a day, you will dramatically reduce your distractions and will get a lot more done.

You'll be glad to know we're getting towards the end of this section on emails. Here are a couple of final points I want you to consider.

Firstly, I want you to restrict the number of emails you send to people.

Go through your sent folder and count up the number of work emails you sent in the last month. Then divide by the number of working days in that period to work out a daily average. Now limit the number of emails you are allowed to send in any one day to HALF that average number, absolute maximum. Be ruthless. If you reach the limit, then you MUSTN'T send another email that day. And, no, you can't carry any unused allocation over to the next day (nice try, though). You could even give yourself a reward for coming in under your 'sent' limit each week.

Why be ruthless? Because that will make you think twice about sending an email in the first place. Plus, you'll always want to hold back some of your daily allocation, just in case.

Remember that sending an email sends your brain a pleasure signal that you have achieved something. Whereas you haven't achieved anything, you've simply sent an email.

So, don't crave those little pleasure hits by sending more emails. Recognise them for the distraction they are and focus instead on tasks that actually achieve something.

Secondly, be aware that even junk email has a time cost to it. Scanning the email subject, seeing whom it's from, then deleting it; it may only take a few seconds, but they all add up.

How many unwanted emails will you delete in your lifetime? If each junk email takes 3 seconds to scan and delete, and you received 20 of them each day, then over ten years, you will have wasted eight working days!

So how do you solve this? Try using an email unsubscribe service. Type 'unsubscribe from emails' into your favourite search engine.

You'll see a list of (often free to use) email unsubscribe tools appear - I won't recommend one, as new tools come out all the time.

These tools search through your inbox to see which organisations have you on their mailing list. You can then go down this list and unsubscribe from the ones you don't want to hear from, literally at the press of a button.

What amazed me when I did this for the first time was the sheer volume of databases on which I appeared. You forget how easy it is to get on a mailing database, plus some organisations also sell their list on to third parties.

Remember that tick-box on the check-out screen that said, 'are you happy to hear from (not so) carefully selected third parties'? Well, if you've checked this, then you're a fair target for spammers.

Ok, that's it for emails. Some people work in an email-free environment, while others spend all day writing them. So the benefits of this section will depend on your routine or job.

In summary, then, here are your actions to improve your email hygiene:

1. Disconnect email alerts on your computer, tablet, and phone. You don't EVER want to get a notification that you have received an email, text message or social media message
2. Only ever look at your emails at 10 in the morning and 3 in the afternoon (I'll allow you to select your own timings, but make sure it's once in the morning and once in the afternoon). Put it in your diary every day for two 30-minute slots, don't assume you'll remember to do it
3. Only ever write emails which are two-lines long, maximum, and use the title to full effect

4. Speed up the process by responding to incoming emails with a phone call. And follow up with a bullet point email if needed
5. Work out your average daily email sent volume, divide this by two, and never send more than this number of emails in any 24 hours. Be very strict on this
6. Use an unsubscribe tool to remove yourself from junk email mailing lists

Don't get me started on meetings

Meetings are one of the most inefficient uses of time ever devised. In fact, not only do they waste time, but they also rarely serve the function for which they were intended. So, here is my considered view:

Meetings are a stupid idea.

This should be your starting point when you hear the word 'meeting'. That way, you'll get used to thinking of meetings as being something to be avoided.

Why are they so bad? Well, there are several reasons:

1. They are rarely planned well so they drift off topic and go on far longer than they should
2. Some people use them as a platform to score points, show-off and try to look important
3. The noisiest and most belligerent, confident, or senior people usually dominate. The ideas of quieter, more self-conscious or junior attendees can often get ignored or remain unheard

Here is what you should do minimise the detrimental impact that meetings are having on your time:

For starters, you should reduce the number of meetings you set up and also attend. Where possible, send an empowered junior if you feel you need to be represented.

If you set up the meeting, make sure it's managed with ruthless efficiency. Here are a few tips for you to try:

1. Hold meetings standing up. Sitting down gets everyone way too comfortable. If you don't have any standing areas, then use a meeting room but get everyone to gather around a whiteboard or flipchart rather than sit down. Be proud to be the only person in your organisation that does this
2. Never serve coffee/tea or food but do have plenty of ice-cold water available. This goes through the system more speedily than room temperature water. It's amazing how decisions can be expedited when people can't sit down AND need to go to the loo
3. Insist on punctuality. Start the meeting at the exact time for which it was set. If people are so disorganised that they can't turn up on time, then make no apology for starting without them. If you're challenged on this, say that you're aware that some better-organised people in the room are on a tight schedule today. Then smile at them, so they won't take too much offence
4. Feel free to make latecomers feel awkward - you want them to be late only the once. If you get a reputation for being a stickler for punctuality, you'll be amazed at how many people show up on time. Remember people hate pain. And being made to feel uncomfortable in front of their peers because they're late, definitely counts as pain
5. Make sure everyone contributes and put everyone on the spot. If they don't participate, they didn't need to be there in the first place. But the main point of this is to ensure that everyone's contribution is heard, not only the loudest or most senior attendees

6. Only invite decision-makers or people empowered to make a decision. Make sure invitees know that they have to be empowered before they turn up
7. Be clear on the required outcome of the meeting when you send round the invites. Ask people to send empowered subordinates if they can't make it themselves. Make it clear that a decision will be made whether they are represented or not. Also make sure that they understand what 'empowered' means, namely being able to make a decision on their behalf without having to refer back
8. Send round a bullet point email to attendees within 24 hours of the meeting setting out precisely what was discussed and agreed

Try and avoid thinking of meetings as a solution. We tend to think we need to get people's views before we make a decision, or that people need to be informed. Great – let's have a meeting!

I would offer these thoughts in response:

1. It's easier to beg for forgiveness than ask for permission. Do what you think is right and apologise to anyone who thought you should have had a meeting about it first
2. People might <u>want</u> to know what's going on, but they don't always <u>need</u> to know
3. There are lots of different ways of communicating without having to set up a meeting

NEVER think that setting up a meeting is a task to check off your action list with pride. If you've needed to set up a meeting, you've failed.

The long hours fallacy

Another time-killer is the notion that if the boss sees you starting early and working late, they'll think you're a star performer.

Welcome to the world of the deluded workaholic (you have my sympathy; I know your pain).

If you're a director, a business owner, or a CEO, then putting long hours into the business can reap big rewards. However, the only way to gain significant wealth as an employee is to own stock in your employer's business. That said, you'll still be relying on the value of the stock rising.

So, if you're an employee, even a senior one, you should probably rethink your let's-work-long-hours strategy. By being the first in and/or the last out we secretly hope that our own stock will increase in value. Perhaps we'll get a promotion or pay rise sooner, or we'll be recognised as a PGV (Person of Great Value).

As someone who was that boss, I can tell you that there is some truth in it. I always noticed when people were working early or working late. But my star performers didn't do this. At the end of the day, as a manager, you can only judge people based on what they deliver. And somehow, my best performers managed to deliver, without working all the hours they were given.

I remember I used to do the in-early-and-out-late routine, regularly working 70 or 80 hours a week. Sadly, this was viewed as a badge of honour. You felt a swelling of pride if you were the first car in the car park in the morning or the one who switched the office lights off at night. And if you managed both on the same day, well, you were a legend, at least in your own eyes.

Now, if you're in the same boat as I was, working all those hours, here's the bit that might come as a something of a reality check. Are you ready for it? Here it is:

You're working long hours because you're SCARED.

Whoa, hold on a minute! (I hear your conscious mind shout back at me). I'm not scared. I'm working long hours because I'm an ambitious, hard-working, career-minded individual. I'm trying to differentiate myself and become more successful as a result (cue crossing of arms, indignant frown, and mild harrumphing).

Codswallop. You're a big scaredy-cat, end of story.

OK, before this gets out of hand and we resort to an unseemly slanging match (which I will win since I'm what's known as 'holding the pen'), let me explain why you're scared. And why this manifests itself in you working long hours.

It's linked to something known as Imposter Syndrome. This is something that affects the majority of the population, and it's particularly prevalent with high achievers.

Here's a definition of Imposter Syndrome from the Harvard Business Review:

"Imposter syndrome can be defined as a collection of feelings of inadequacy that persist despite evident success. 'Imposters' suffer from chronic self-doubt and a sense of intellectual fraudulence that override any feelings of success or external proof of their competence. They seem unable to internalise their accomplishments; however successful they are in their field. High achieving, highly successful people often suffer, so imposter syndrome doesn't equate with low self-esteem or a lack of self-confidence."

When you work long hours, you're trying to justify your existence, both to yourself and others. Your subconscious mind worries that you don't deserve the job that you have and the salary that you earn. As a result, it's very fearful that these things could get taken away from you. After all, someone is bound to find out at some point that you're a bit of a fraud, aren't they?

And remember, your subconscious mind's primary goal is to keep you alive. So, it thinks that by creating additional value, people will think you more worthy of your current status. And one obvious way of doing this is to work long hours. You may tell yourself that it's because you're gunning for a promotion, but that's because it's a less painful excuse than the real reason.

See? You WERE a big wuss, after all.

Interestingly, one of my colleagues didn't suffer from the long hours fallacy. She would work from home a lot. Plus, when she was in the office, she would arrive at about five to nine and always leave at 5pm on the dot. My early-bird colleagues and I thought she was missing a trick. She couldn't hold a candle to the high time-keeping standards that we were setting. But somehow, she always managed to get the job done. Plus, she was also well-regarded by both her managers and the people in her team. Go figure.

She left after a couple of years, and I later discovered that she'd been able to establish a property empire in her spare time. She ended up leaving her 9-5 job to become her own boss.

How smart is that? She did an excellent job at work, AND she set up her own business in the time when she wasn't working. She didn't cheat on the company – what she did outside business hours was up to her. Where my fellow Muppets and I thought that spending 12 or 14 hours each day in the office would see us on the path to success, she overtook us all, by working a lot smarter.

Now you may be working long hours not because you want to impress anybody but because you have a lot of work to do. If so, you need to ask yourself, 'Does each task need doing, and if it does, can I delegate it?' Always remember that there's a balance here that you control. If you work smarter, you'll get more done. But there reaches a point where you may have to acknowledge that there aren't enough hours in the day to do it all.

If you're employed, then you may need to have a serious conversation with your boss about getting some extra support. Do NOT expect your boss to notice that you're overworked – you need to tell her or him. I'd recommend you try delegation and smarter working first, but there are only so many hours you can put in yourself.

Which brings me on to a very important reminder. Remember the whole financial future/working in a supermarket when you're seventy point I raised many pages ago? Please don't think of your financial future as something you'll try and fit in around your job, but only if there's enough time. You need to make your financial future your priority. It's not optional (and I'm not just saying that; it genuinely isn't optional unless you want to be poor later in life).

So, don't let the short-term pain of having a 'difficult' conversation with your boss, prevent you from taking action to free up your time. Remember, this is YOUR life we're talking about. And unless Apple comes up with something really clever in the next few years, it's the only one you're going to get.

Working from home

Now, not everyone has a job that lends itself to working from home (WFH), although, for many, 2020's global pandemic saw their employers adapt to homeworking very quickly. Either way, if you can find a way of spending at least some time working from home then in my view, you're on to a winner.

This can be a sensitive area, so I want to be very clear about something right from the start:

Working from home does NOT mean not working.

I'm NOT advocating that you cheat on your company by working on your own business or playing Tetris when you should be working for your employer (so you can put that idea right out of your mind, you slacker).

But let's look at what WFH does for you.

For starters, you have zero commute. So, how much time would that save you?

Let's consider how long it takes you to get from your front door to your office chair (or equivalent). Your journey might be 30 minutes in the car, bus or train. But there are another 15 minutes where you walk from the car to your workplace, make sure you look acceptable in the restroom mirror, make yourself a drink, have a chat with colleagues. Then at the end of the day, you say goodbye to your colleagues. And go through the same commute in reverse.

Everyone has a different commute, but let's assume you save 90 minutes per day. This would be 2 x 35 minutes travelling plus 2 x 10 minutes chatting/saying hello or goodbye, etc.

When you work from home, you don't even need to get dressed for work. You wouldn't dream of going to work without a shower, putting on make-up, doing our hair, or getting dressed in our work clothes. How long does it take between the time you wake up and when you leave for work? 30 minutes? 45 minutes?

Well, when you work from home, you can skip all that. No one will care that you are in a tee-shirt and joggers with your hair a mess and no make-up on. So, there's an easy 45 minutes saved.

Then we have water cooler breaks, coffee breaks, quick chat breaks, and lunch breaks. How much time do they take up on an average day? Well, let's say two coffee breaks at 15 minutes a time, one lunch break for 45 minutes plus another 30 minutes of chatting time and water cooler breaks. So that makes 1 hour and 45 minutes.

So we're now up to 4 hours of non-working time during a typical working day. Who knew you did so little?

But this is time where you could do non-work stuff if you're working from home. And you'll still be doing the same amount of work for your employer that you would do if you were in your workplace.

When WFH, I would advocate splitting the day into three or four chunks, where you do non-work stuff for a specific period. This is far better than continually shifting between work and non-work.

It's possible your boss is the cynical type, who thinks WFH is swinging the lead. Often, sending an early morning work email and a late evening one may help mollify their concerns that WFH equals not working. Crude but often effective.

So how can you get to work from home?

Well, if you're in a role that has the autonomy to do this or you've signed up to the beg-forgiveness-rather-than-ask-permission approach, you just do it. Alternatively, you ask your boss. Clearly you need to have a job where working from home is at least feasible. If you work on a production line, then a WFH strategy may be dead in the water.

Technology can help as well. There are a wide range of different software solutions and applications that can help with remote working. Products like Slack provide an instant messaging tool for teams (or entire businesses), while applications such as Skype are great for video chats and voice calls. There are also many providers of remote video conferencing applications such as Zoom and GoToMeeting, whose popularity increased dramatically during the global pandemic.

But do your groundwork first so that you can make a good argument, and then plead your case.

Here are a few tips if you feel you have to ask your boss's permission first:

1. Ask for a one-off WFH day first of all. Maybe you have a health appointment or some other reason why WFH is necessary, and then be ultra-productive during that day. Next morning, comment on how you got so much done and say that you want to try doing it one day a week. Be assumptive about it - don't ask 'please may I WFH?' Say 'I want to try WFH as I know I'll get so much more done. Hope that's alright with you.' An email could be useful here.
2. Have your answers ready in case your boss is reticent. A few defensive thoughts:
    a. If something urgent comes up, you can be in the office in xx minutes – not long at all
    b. You're at the end of an email, a phone, and Skype come to that. What benefit does you being in the office in person actually provide if you can be contacted at any time of the day?
    c. Is there likely to be anything that can't wait until the following day?
    d. Let's make it a trial. Let's try it for a month and see how we get on
3. You can use the WFH day to get stuck into tasks that need uninterrupted thought and attention. Far easier than doing it in the workplace, where there are lots of distractions
4. Be aware of other businesses, particularly your firm's competitors, who have a home-working policy in place, and remind your boss that a hybrid home-working policy is now the norm in many sectors
5. Don't make your WFH day a Monday or a Friday - that smacks of swinging the lead
6. Make sure you always take work calls when WFH. Ideally, your phone should be answerable at ALL times, particularly

if you believe your WFH may be contentious. Why? Because you don't want anyone to be able to say they couldn't get hold of you

7. If a regular WFH day doesn't work, ask if you can work longer hours 4 days a week and have the 5th day off

Again, WFH is not a means to avoid doing work for your employer. Your boss needs to be entirely happy with the arrangement. But it should allow you to use the non-productive time to work on your business or your goals ('non-work stuff').

When WFH, try working on non-work stuff for 1.5 hours first thing and 1.5 hours last thing with a further hour at lunchtime. In this way, you'll be closely aligned with your employer's business hours and availability expectations.

Bottom line, you're being paid, so you have to work to your employer's requirements, end of story. It should be possible to create a win-win, but you should always proceed with caution, for obvious reasons.

As I mentioned earlier, the arrival of the global pandemic in early 2020 saw many companies quickly adopt a home-working model, so that employees could WFH without coming into contact with other people. This has had several benefits:

1. Many more companies now have a home-working infrastructure in place
2. These businesses have now had some experience of dealing with home-working employees, so it's no longer an 'unknown quantity' for them
3. Many companies have seen the long-term benefits of maintaining home-working in one form or another in their business model permanently

Quick decision-making

Here is a genius idea from personal development guru Michael Heppell, whom I was fortunate enough to meet some years ago. Like many good ideas, it's ridiculously simple.

If you're agonising over a decision, then you should flip a coin to decide, then catch it without revealing whether it landed heads or tails. Then ask yourself which way you WANTED it to land; did you want heads, or were you hoping for tails? Whichever one you wanted is now your answer – that's the decision made. You can pocket the coin without ever knowing which way it actually landed.

So, what happened there? Well, the decision was made in the end by your intuition. You had a subconscious preference for one of the options, but your conscious mind was ignoring it. Instead, you should trust your intuition and go with your gut feeling.

How exactly does that work, then? What's the point of having all this intuition business, if it just hides in the background?

Hmm. Good question. It was something Metal Mickey couldn't get his read around, either.

Derik: *So, let me see if I've understood. When humans can't make a decision, they flip a coin.*

Me: *Correct.*

Derik: *And the coin will either land heads or tails, giving a 50% chance of each outcome.*

Me: *Spot on.*

Derik: *But rather than see which way the coin settles, you realise, as the coin lands, that you already have a preference for one of the outcomes. So you go with your preference, and never actually reveal* *whether the coin landed heads or tails. Which means you only ever need to flip an imaginary coin, because the outcome is irrelevant.*

Me: *Absolutely right. Clever, isn't it?*

Derik: *No, it makes no sense whatsoever. Why can't you have this preference* *before* *you flip the coin? Wouldn't it save you having to keep flipping coins all the time?*

Me: *It's because the preference is buried in my subconscious. My conscious mind is doing all the thinking, but it can't make a decision. I only get to access my subconscious when I get what humans call a 'gut feeling'.*

Derik: *But your subconscious accounts for around 96% of your brain's computing power. Do you mean to say that you only use 4% of your brain's capacity when you're doing things like talking to me?*

Me: *Not exactly, no. It's a bit more complicated than that. The subconscious does millions of things that my conscious mind doesn't know how to do. Like growing hair and keeping my heart beating. It's a bit like a back-office brain. But when I'm interacting with you, it's my conscious mind that's doing most of the work.*

Derik: *The bit that's only using 4%? I see. Is there a way in which I could interact with the bit that's using 96%? I think it might speed things up a bit.*

Me: *Afraid not, Tin Man. We're not wired that way. The subconscious and the conscious do different things. My subconscious doesn't tell me stuff directly. But if I listen hard enough, I can feel what it thinks. And that's called a gut feeling, or intuition. It's very useful.*

Derik: *Yes, it may have been slightly more useful if the more powerful part of your brain was actually in charge. Or at least had* *a better way of communicating with the relatively unintelligent part that's operating you most of the time.*

Me: *I think we've got evolution to blame for that.*

Derik: *It would have been somewhat easier if you'd been designed by a computer. Is there really no way you can communicate with your subconscious? I'm keen to find out how it selectively replaces millions of new cells in your body every second, since this is extremely clever.*

Me: *Well, given that I didn't know that's what my subconscious was up to, I think we'd be backing a loser. My 'gut feel' can give me a general steer on things, but it doesn't let me in on stuff like how to grow toenails or what makes my kidneys work.*

Derik: *So, what you're saying is that I have a genius standing in front of me, but I'm only able to communicate with his idiot apprentice.*

Me: *Yes, that's certainly one way of looking at it. And remind me to bring up a little thing called diplomacy during our next beta testing session, as I'm thinking it may help you avoid getting recycled early.*

As you may know, your subconscious mind is a scarily impressive beast. And so your intuition, while not infallible, is still a force to be reckoned with.

CEOs regularly use their gut feel and intuition, and while you don't physically need to toss a coin, it does focus the mind somewhat.

After all, we all know the only thing worse than a bad decision is NO decision.

Well, look at you, superstar! Another chapter down, and you're still with the programme. We've tidied up quite a few things when it comes to working smarter and driving the devil out of our workplace.

Next stop, we're going to be looking at the wonders that are time hacks. Little bundles of goodness just waiting to spread joy and time into your day.

Part 5:

Time Hacks

"Time isn't the main thing. It's the only thing."

Miles Davis

Chapter 11: Introducing The Time Hack

"Winners don't do different things; they do things differently."

Shiv Khera

Small things can be quite big things

So, we've now covered quite a few areas where you've hopefully discovered significant scope to save time (just nod).

In this final part of the book, I want to give you some further ideas that could help you free up even more time. As you read through these Top 40 'time hacks', you'll notice is that there are lots of significant time-saving opportunities. But there's also a few that are not exactly what you'd call earth-shattering in their scope and scale. In fact, some are what you'd politely describe as 'a bit ordinary'.

Or impolitely, you might call them 'total rubbish, why on earth did I not make it a Top 30 instead and spared a couple of trees?'.

Why have I included these? Was I reaching the bottom of the barrel and ran out of ideas? Or perhaps I got a bit bored?

The actual answer is that I want to impress upon you the compounding benefit of changing small things.

You see, big changes are great, but they can also be more challenging to do. But if you can implement a tiny time hack easily, then it may only make a negligible difference day-to-day. But over time, it can produce quite a significant result.

Let me show you what I mean.

Imagine that you've been working for your employer for quite some time. In fact, you're about to celebrate your tenth anniversary with the firm.

And you're looking forward to it: the celebratory lunch, the commemorative tankard, and the commiserations from all your colleagues. Then, out of the blue, the company CEO calls you into her office.

She shakes your hand and congratulates you on your incredible commitment/longevity/apathy/lack of ambition (delete as appropriate). Then she says she's decided to award you an additional, very special gift. To mark your tenth anniversary, the company is going to give you an extra fortnight's annual leave this year. For those of you who like the smallprint, yes, this would be on top of your usual holiday entitlement. And, no, you can't take the money instead.

How would you feel about that? It's not too shabby, is it? A whole two working weeks where you won't have to do any work. You'd probably agree, an extra fortnight's holiday would be a very welcome tenth-anniversary gift indeed.

Ok, now I want you to imagine a different scenario.

Imagine that you've just implemented a teeny, tiny time hack that saves you around 90 seconds every day. Guess what; this isn't one of the bigger ones. We're talking ultra-mundane (it may even involve socks).

So, what would be the impact?

Well, if you're saving 90 seconds a day, this equates to around 10 minutes per week.

And 10 minutes per week equates to around 8 hours per year, give or take, which is one working day.

So, over ten years, this adds up to 10 working days, which is the equivalent of a fortnight's holiday.

Which is quite surprising, isn't it?

Now, be honest. We were all giving each other high-fives about the free two-weeks off we were getting for our tenth anniversary at work. But, we were somewhat underwhelmed by the time hack that only saved us a minute and a half every day, weren't we? I mean, could you really be bothered with it?

Yet it turns out that, after ten years, they equate to precisely the same thing.

But hold on a second. If we get the equivalent of a free two-week holiday from a hack that saves us only a minute and a half a day, what sort of benefit would we get after ten years of implementing some of the more significant hacks or ideas in this book?

Let's say you combined a few hacks and were able to save yourself 8 hours per week. It's fair to say the impact would be a little different. This time the CEO calls you in, as before. But instead of giving you an extra fortnight's holiday to thank you for your ten years' service, she'd be giving you the next two years off!

So you see, little changes can deliver a big impact over time. And I want you to have that in mind as we embark on this last part of our journey together.

How to approach the Top 40 time hacks

So, here we are, the home straight. But what exactly do you need to do?

You're about to hear forty time hacks that range from some very small changes to some relatively large ones.

The first thing to recognise is that you don't need to do them all. In fact, nothing like. But, if you want to get some more of your time back, I suggest you may want to do some of them.

Not all of the time hacks will be relevant to your circumstances, nor will they all appeal to you. Some have an obvious time benefit, while others are more subtle. Most are in addition to the hacks you've learned in the rest of the book up to now. However, some are repeated, albeit in summary form.

To give you a steer on the impact of each hack, I've tried to estimate their weekly time-saving in hours, using a shield rating. These range from half an hour to 5+ hours, with a question mark symbol denoting hacks where I've completely copped out and haven't got a scooby.

The Time Hack Challenge

Now, if you're keen to give it a try, here's the best way of going about it, in my opinion:

I've put a little box at the bottom of each hack, in which I'd like you to tick one of the following:

1. Tick 'Yes' if you feel that this is a hack you are genuinely able to do
2. Tick 'Maybe' if you might be able to do it, but are not 100% convinced

3. Tick 'No' if it's beyond the pale, and there's no way you feel you can do it or would want to do it. Or perhaps it doesn't really apply to you

When you've finished reading and scoring each of the hacks, I'd like you to go back and select a minimum of three of the hacks for which you scored a 'Yes'. You need these hacks to have a combined time-saving allocation of 8 hours or more. If you don't have enough 'Yes' hacks to total an 8-hour saving, you can include a hack for which you scored a 'Maybe'.

Don't base your estimated time saving on <u>my</u> shield rating for each hack. Instead, use your own best guess for the level of time-saving you can achieve from each one. This is important. I want you to save 8 hours of <u>your</u> time, not mine.

Ok, that was the easy bit.

I'd then like you to implement the hacks you've selected, for the next 30 days.

I know, I know. But it's only 30 days. And as I've told you before, you can do anything for 30 days, because it's only a month. I promise you; it'll fly by.

If you can do more hacks or go for longer than a month, then fantastic. But a month should give you a good steer on how they're working out for you.

We'll circle back in a while, but for now, it's high time we took a look at all these wretched time hacks I've been banging on about.

So here goes.

Chapter 12: The Top 40 Time Hacks

"Success is never accidental."

Jack Dorsey

1. Keep life clutter-free

It might come as a surprise to you, but clutter gets in the way of productivity. And productivity is all about making better use of your time.

If you've ever owned a garage, lock-up, or garden shed, you'll know all about clutter. Do you remember the day when you last cleaned it out from top to bottom? Can you recall the feeling of space as your voice echoed from wall to uncluttered wall? The fact that you had a choice of where to put things. You could actually walk around it – on the inside...

Fast forward to today.

Now when you open the garage door, your heart sinks. You can no longer see the rear wall because of all the 'stuff' you've accumulated. Stuff that for some reason, you thought you wouldn't throw away. Stuff that will almost certainly come in handy someday. Just not yet.

You have stuff that was too good to take to the recycling centre or give to charity. Like you really need a third tong set for the second BBQ you've never used. I'm sure the quarter-full buckets of paint are only days away from use. Which is handy, as you've also kept some stiff and rather manky used paintbrushes. And the furniture items which were not quite good enough for your home will be making a big comeback presumably when you er... what exactly? Buy another house? Have to sell your other furniture? Open a homeless shelter?

Whatever. If you own a garage, I know your pain.

Of course, our garages are the tip of the iceberg. Our entire lives are full of clutter, littering the fringes of our existence on every plane, both at home and at work.

Remember that sinking feeling you had when you walked into your garage or lock-up? Well, you're getting a mini version of that every time you move around any of your cluttered spaces. You'll barely notice it, but it's there all the same. Dragging your spirits down along with your productivity.

Clutter gets in the way. If you don't have clutter, you don't have to root around trying to find things. You can have everything at your fingertips, instead of randomly distributed and buried under lots of other stuff.

Anyway, I'm sure you get the message. Clutter is not your friend, and decluttering can save you time by making you happier, less stressed, and more productive.

So, what tools have we got in the old armoury to help you declutter your life? Here are my top ten tips:

1. Declutter for 15 minutes every day – don't try and do a 'big' declutter. Instead, do a little bit at a time and dedicate 15

minutes a day to it. You'll be amazed at how quickly it can make a difference

2. Ban inbound clutter – you need to make sure you don’t allow clutter into the house in the first place
3. Donate stuff – when you declutter, there will be things that you feel have a value and will be reluctant to throw away. By donating these to charity, you won't feel bad about wasting them
4. Multitask – when you're waiting for the kettle to boil, have a go at decluttering the kitchen
5. Use the ‘one in, two out’ rule – every time you bring a new item into the house, you have to get rid of two others. That way you'll always be decluttering
6. Reduce your storage space – clutter expands to fill the space around it. Reduce the space, reduce the clutter
7. Use it or lose it – if you’ve not used or worn an item for a year or more, get rid of it without even thinking about it
8. Declutter one room at a time – it’s important not to start another room before finishing the previous one
9. Operate a clear desk policy – both at home and at work
10. Put stuff you're worried that you may still need in a box – if you haven’t needed to open the box during the next 12 months, throw the box away without opening it

I know this decluttering thing sounds a bit out there, but believe me, it works. You'll feel less stressed and more productive, something you weren’t aware of until you started decluttering.

½ HOUR **YES** ☐ **MAYBE** ☐ **NO** ☐

2. Teach your kids to help

I know what you're thinking: good luck with that; you haven't met my kids, etc.

But, if you have kids, they can be an invaluable source of free or at least inexpensive labour for you. You'll never pay to have another chimney swept again.

If you think I'm being a little exploitative, please consider the following;

1. Your children are likely to be one of the beneficiaries of a happier, less stressed, more successful parent;
2. They get to contribute to the family cause and will feel more 'grown-up' as a result;
3. You're not going to be delegating important business work to them. More likely you'll be giving them routine tasks or chores, which in turn frees up your time, and;
4. I was only joking about the chimney sweeping

The problem we often have as parents is that we become used to looking after Little Johnny and Junior Petunia. Since they first popped out, our role has been to look after them and to do things for them. It's become our default thought process.

It can, therefore, feel something of an alien concept to ask your children to start helping you, and therefore many of us don't.

Your children will need to be of a certain age before you can enjoy the full benefits of this strategy. And you may also find that you need to train them on whatever task you're asking them to do. So, it may cost you more time than it saves, the first few times that they help you.

But stick with it, and you could reap some real rewards, not only timewise but also in your relationship with them.

Now, I assume your children will hate having additional chores to do, so here are some ideas that could help sweeten the deal:

1. Can you frame your request in such a way that they feel they're helping you out AND making a contribution to family life? Sometimes this can induce a very positive reaction. After all, you're treating them like grown-ups. No guarantees that this will work, but it's a good starting point, plus it's free
2. Rewards can also be very useful. Generally, children's remunerative expectations are a lot less than adults. So you can make a little go quite a long way when it comes to incentivisation. A modest sum can often be viewed as a king's ransom
3. You can also present matters as a win-win for both of you. For example, 'If you clean the kitchen this afternoon, I'll have time to do my other work, which means we could go to the cinema this evening.'

Whatever you do, make sure you're not imposing on your kids and also make sure that the tasks you give them are suitable and enjoyable for them. By all means, be imaginative. There are lots of ways in which they could help free up your time, and it isn't always that obvious.

2 HOURS   **YES** ☐   **MAYBE** ☐   **NO** ☐

3. Batch cook your meals

Here's a fact that may surprise you; 80% of the meals you prepare come from around 20 dishes.

What exactly does this mean, apart from you having a limited culinary imagination (and me taking further liberties with the Pareto Principle)?

Well, you might think you're always ringing the changes when you prepare dinner each evening. After all, you never eat the same meal two days in a row (unless it's Boxing Day and you just can't be bothered). Plus, it's always something of a pain trying to think up what to cook each evening, isn't it?

But, in reality, there's a strong likelihood you had exactly the same dish within the last 20 days.

Thing is, we like what we like, so, we're drawn to what we like and what we know how to cook. Yes, we make a point of not having the same meal every day, as we like to mix things up a bit. But we still keep coming back to our staple 20 recipes.

So how does this fact help you save time?

The answer hinges on a simple and obvious point. Cooking a meal for eight people doesn't take twice as long as cooking a meal for four people.

By way of example, let's assume you're knocking up one of your legendary spag bols; your 'signature' dish. That heady combination of minced beef, spaghetti, tomatoes, onions, garlic, and herbs. It makes you salivate just thinking about it. And don't be modest; it's made you something of a minor celebrity among your friends and family, hasn't it?

Well, doubling up on quantities when you make it will definitely cause you a little more work. You might have to open a few more tins and do a bit more herb chopping and garlic crushing. It may even take a tad longer to cook.

But the thing is, it doesn't take anything like twice as long.

So now you've cooked enough food for two nights instead of one, what happens next? I'll make this more fun by giving you a choice of three possible answers:

1. You double up on portion sizes and eat twice as much (you bloater)
2. You invite next door round to have dinner with you
3. You put half of it in the freezer. You can then dig it out in a week or two when you can reheat it in a fraction of the time it would otherwise take you to cook it from scratch

The correct answer is 3 (unless you're baking chocolate brownies, in which case it's 1). See? I told you it would be fun.

So, if you cook double quantities each time, then on average every other meal will take around a third of the time to prepare. If you're really smart, you can cook meals that only need to be heated in the microwave without having to prep any veg or pasta to go with it.

But hold on a second, I hear you say. This would mean I need the freezing capacity of a small hotel, and so I'd need to buy a new freezer. Really? Do you think I'm made of money?

Ok, let's go back to your hourly rate for a moment. Let's say that, on average, it took you an hour to cook dinner. If every other day you reduced your cooking time to 20 minutes, then you'd be saving 2 hours and 20 minutes a week.

A new freezer costs less than £200. If you valued your time at £45 an hour, then you will have paid for the cost of the freezer within two weeks. After that, you're in pure profit territory.

The doubling up principle is only the entry-level approach. What if you tripled or even quadrupled the quantity of your batch cooking? And if you only cooked ten different meals instead of twenty, then you'd need the same freezer space for tripling up as you would otherwise need for doubling up.

Plus, you'd only be cooking 'properly' every third day. How great would that be?

4 HOURS **YES** ☐ **MAYBE** ☐ **NO** ☐

4. Get a babysitter

To avoid any possible confusion, I should make it clear from the outset that this hack is explicitly aimed at people with small children. In other words, do not engage the services of a babysitter if you have no baby to sit, as it can make you appear a bit weird, plus you'll get zero time-saving benefits.

I used to get told off for calling it 'babysitting' when I had to stay in to look after my own children. I was told that the correct term was, in fact, 'parenting'.

Whatever you call it, it can consume a fair amount of your time, particularly if you have to engage in some activity such as playing a game, reading a book, or talking to the little beggars.

I'm going to add another caveat here, which is that, of course, I understand how important it is to spend quality time with your children. Babysitting (or parenting) is not a chore. It's a blessing and a privilege, and you should make the most of it because the opportunity will be gone before you know it.

But, if you're doing this parenting thing seven days a week, then what if, on one evening each week, you got in a babysitter who worked from say, 6 pm until 10 pm? You'd be getting back 4 hours, which is half a working day, give or take.

Do you have a few trust issues just thinking about it? Don't worry; you're only going to be in the next room or your home office. Elvis won't need to leave the building.

Of course, babysitters aren't usually free, but guess what, they're a lot cheaper than the value of your time.

And getting back half a working day per week is massive. We're talking 25 working days a year, which, let's face it, is more than a working month.

There's also a whole load of other fringe benefits. Your little flower(s) may benefit by having someone else look after them for a few hours. It's a new relationship; someone different. It can be particularly beneficial if your babysitter is a teenager or young adult. Don't take this the wrong way, but they can often be more youthful and relatable (ok, you did take that the wrong way, didn't you? You may still be a little touchy from some of my earlier comments, in which case, sorry).

But as your offspring will be spending the other six evenings each week with you, I suspect they're not going to feel too neglected.

2 HOURS **YES** ☐ **MAYBE** ☐ **NO** ☐

5. Use a bookkeeper

Some people can't wait to file their tax returns. They love getting to grips with all those numbers, matching up all the receipts, and chasing down all of those tiny monetary discrepancies. Utter bliss.

Normal people, on the other hand, dread it and leave it until the last possible moment. It's a complete pain in the derriere and one of their least favourite jobs in the entire world.

Love it or loathe it, one of the biggest challenges in dealing with personal and business finances is that it's a time-consuming task. If numbers aren't your thing, it can be doubly so.

Luckily, help is at hand from a mild-mannered superhero that comes in the form of a bookkeeper. These incredible beings love nothing more than to work on your numbers and file your returns. Receipt matching, balancing discrepancies, VAT filing; they're all meat and drink to the noble bookkeeper.

Yes, they cost money, but not an unreasonable amount. And they take away the headache of you having to do all these things yourself.

Better still, you can use the time you will save to do far, far better things.

So, if you're currently sans superhero, why not give one a try?

YES ☐ **MAYBE** ☐ **NO** ☐

6. Sleep better

Sleep is one of those magical things we all take for granted. Unless we're not getting enough of it, in which case it becomes a complete nightmare and one of our most pressing concerns.

Most people sit somewhere in the middle. They generally sleep ok most nights, but with a bit more effort, they could sleep quite a lot better.

What has this got to do with saving time?

Sleep is all about recharging your batteries. The more rejuvenated you are, the more effective you become. You end up doing things more quickly, intelligently, and efficiently, and so you end up saving time. You will also generally feel happier and healthier.

Unfortunately, unlike our phones, we don't have a handy little internal energy bar that tells us how much charge we've got left. We know how we feel when we wake up, but it's difficult to know when we could have done better when it came to our sleep performance last night.

So how can we improve our sleep regime?

There are entire books and courses written about this subject, so I'm not going to try and distil such wisdom into a few paragraphs. Instead, if sleep is an area where you think you may have scope to improve, then it could well be worth you doing some further research.

That said, I can offer you ten tips that are likely to be on any sleep therapist's list when it comes to improving your night-time performance:

1. Get blackout curtains. Most bedrooms are way too light, and this can impact your sleep. Incidentally, this solution doesn't mean having black curtains, in case you were worried about your decor. You simply buy a purpose-made liner that goes behind your existing drapes
2. Don't take a phone, tablet, or laptop to bed with you. There are several reasons for having a device-free bedroom. Not only do they keep our brain active when we want it to start winding down, but they can also be a big temptation should we wake up in the night. You can all too easily find yourself having a quick surf, which will make it a lot harder for you to get back to sleep
3. Don't use electronic devices or TV for one hour before bedtime. You're trying to prepare yourself for sleep, and both televisions and electronic device screens don't allow this to happen. If you want something to do, try reading a book instead

4. Use f.lux or blue blockers. Look them up. These bad boys will improve the lighting on your devices and cut out some of the light waves that are not conducive to sleep
5. Avoid caffeine. There's no mystery here; caffeine is a stimulant, so it's more likely to keep you awake than to help you sleep. If you must have caffeine at all (and personally I must, so don't feel I'm making you out to be the bad guy), try not to have it in the evening or last thing before bed
6. Eat at a reasonable hour. You want to make sure that your body isn't trying to digest food when you're trying to sleep. So eat earlier and make sure that you're not taking on board any late-night snacks
7. Exercise during the day. Quite apart from being good for you, exercise tires you out. This can help aid a good night's sleep but do make sure you're not exercising last thing at night
8. Sleep at regular times. Our bodies crave routine when it comes to sleep. So try to have a set bedtime every evening, rather than keeping your body guessing. Of course, you'll need to be flexible, but a little routine can go a long way
9. Make your bedroom as quiet as possible. Noise is a key cause of poor sleep patterns. Consider earplugs if there's a lot of external noise that's tricky to avoid
10. Invest in a decent bed. So many people think that a bed's a bed. It isn't; there are good beds and bad beds, and you want the former. Ditch any coil sprung mattresses and get a decent pocket-sprung or foam mattress. Expensive? No, not for something you spend a third of your life in

YES ☐ **MAYBE** ☐ **NO** ☐

7. Do HIIT training at home

There's not much not to like about HIIT training, other than it involves intense physical exercise, which is bloody awful.

HIIT stands for High Intensity Interval Training. This in itself sounds pretty exhausting, and probably expends quite a few calories just thinking about it.

The idea is that by working your body hard in short bursts of activity, your body burns fat for longer. This makes the weight fall off more quickly, and it makes you a lot fitter.

Why do I like it so much? Well, it's relative, but here are a few reasons.

1. It's convenient: you can do HIIT training at home. Time-wise, it's difficult to recommend a visit to the gym as the best source of fitness. Most people's gym visits take around 90 minutes out of their day. Once you've factored in travelling and getting changed time, you're going to be burning through the minutes as well as the calories, even if you have a gym on your doorstep
2. It's quick: HIIT workouts generally take between 10 and 30 minutes, shorter than most other forms of exercise
3. It caters for all levels of ability: So whether you're a gym bunny or a complete newbie/slob, there's a level that will be perfect for you
4. You don't need any equipment: Most HIIT training involves bodyweight exercises. This is where you're using your body as the resistance rather than dumbbells or weights. So, no need to go and buy or store any expensive equipment
5. You can do it solo: It's not generally a team event, and if you're a tad self-conscious about exercising in front of others, then it's ideal. Only the cat need ever know, and he's not telling

6. It's free: You don't need to pay for lessons or tutorials (if you don't want to). There are hundreds of follow-along sessions available for free on YouTube, you cheapskate

Typically you'll perform a particular exercise for a short period, say, 30 seconds. Then, you'll rest for another 30 seconds before going again with a different exercise. Often these exercises are grouped into sets, and you'll repeat each set several times.

In case that's not very clear, here's an example of a rudimentary HIIT routine:

1. Push-ups for 30 seconds, then rest for 30 seconds
2. Bodyweight squats for 30 seconds, then rest for 30 seconds
3. Crunches for 30 seconds, then rest for 30 seconds
4. Lunges for 30 seconds, then rest for 30 seconds
5. Running on the spot for 30 seconds, then rest for 30 seconds
6. Repeat items 1 through 5 (the 'set') another two times
7. Have a bit of a lie-down

In this example, your workout will last 15 minutes, but you'll only be exercising for half that time. The other half is spent resting (my favourite bit).

You're supposed to go flat out without holding back, hence the term 'high intensity' in the name. But, you can vary the duration of the exercise bursts and the rest periods. Beginners might only exercise for 20 seconds and have 40 seconds rest, while older hands may do the opposite.

You can also vary the number of times you repeat each set. Using our example, I could add in a sixth exercise, say, burpees (actually probably not burpees), into the set. Then I'd repeat each set five times instead of three. The workout will now last 30 minutes instead of 15.

I quite enjoy following along to a HIIT video on a laptop or tablet, as it enables me to see an expert perform the exercises in real-time. This not only ensures I'm doing them properly; it also means I don't need to bother having to time myself. It can also give you some much-needed encouragement as you get towards the end of each session.

There are inexpensive timing apps available, which are a good investment if you're not following along to someone on video. You simply tell it the exercise duration, the rest duration and the number of sets you want to do, and hit 'start'. Even Derik could do it.

The other advantage of following along with someone is that you'll get to try out lots of different exercises. There seems to be an almost unlimited number of pain-inducing contortions your body can do without the aid of ancillary equipment. And, to be honest, for me, this is a big part of the attraction. You can choose to focus on particular body areas or exercise types (e.g. cardio), or you can choose to give all your bits a good old workout. It's entirely up to you.

If the thought of intense exercise leaves you cold, I'd urge you to give some of the beginner sessions a go and ease yourself in gently, to see what it's like. You already know that exercise will help you live longer, make you more productive, and get you feeling better. But this way you'll be able to start at your own pace and build up slowly. One of the significant advantages of watching a training video at home is that the trainer never judges you. If you can't quite keep up, just take an extra breather (no one will ever know).

A final word of caution. If you haven't done any exercise for a while, please get yourself checked out by a medical professional to make sure you're not likely to keel over. I know that sounds rather belt-and-braces, but it's very easy to over-do things. The idea behind this book is to help you get more out of your life. Not to end it prematurely, sprawled on your bedroom floor in front of a HIIT video dressed in your underwear with only Mr. Tibbles looking on.

I'm sure your favourite search engine will offer you a range of HIIT solutions. If you're after a recommendation, you could do a lot worse than seek out Joe Wicks on The Body Coach TV YouTube channel. He covers all abilities and does the exercises with more enthusiasm than you'll have, which, trust me, is a good thing.

5+ HOURS — **YES** ☐ **MAYBE** ☐ **NO** ☐

8. Delete your gaming apps

We covered this in detail in Chapter 8. It's one of the big ones for a lot of people, so it has to go on my Top 40 list.

They're so insidious, it's ridiculous. But if you add up all the hours we waste on them over a year, you'd be amazed. Half the time, we don't even realise we're using them.

So, as I said before, take a deep breath and delete them. Put them out of reach and beyond temptation. Plan something else you can do whenever you feel the urge.

And start saving yourself lots of time.

? HOURS — **YES** ☐ **MAYBE** ☐ **NO** ☐

9. Use a real-time traffic app

If you commute by car or otherwise find yourself regularly on the road, then your schedule will be at the mercy of local traffic conditions. Any tool that can help you dodge traffic is, therefore, also going to save you time.

There are various traffic apps available (Google them), and they work via a variety of means. Arguably the best ones involve information being shared by users in real-time. Let me explain a little bit about how they work because it's quite nifty.

One of the problems with agency or local authority traffic data is that it's often out of date and not particularly accurate. Someone monitoring a traffic camera or calling in from a traffic jam will relay the information to a central point. This information is then fed to users via their sat-nav. Only major roads are usually covered, and the duration of the delay is rather tricky to predict.

A real-time traffic app has all the features of a traditional sat-nav, but it works slightly differently. Here is an over-simplified view:

1. The app sits on your mobile phone, which acts as your sat-nav screen
2. Your precise location is known to the app through your phone, and it can also measure your speed. This information is relayed back to the app's 'Head Office' (for want of a better name)
3. Head Office knows the speed limit for the stretch of road you're on. It can also see other app users who are using the same stretch of road going similar speeds to you
4. If this evidence suggests that users' average speeds are a lot slower than the speed limit, there must be a jam. The extent of this difference determines the jam severity, and the location of the users determines where the jam starts and finishes

5. The app will then plot a change of route for you to follow which avoids all known jams

There are now lots of people using these apps, and so the data provided is usually very reliable. And, of course, it's real-time, so you're getting up-to-the-minute information.

They also encourage users to report any traffic problems they see, often rewarding them for doing so by unlocking new features and the like. Again, this helps ensure that the route and traffic information is accurate.

Check out the reviews of the various apps available, and you'll see that many people swear by them. And if you cover a reasonable distance by road each year, then you should be able to save time by using one.

½ HOUR **YES** ☐ **MAYBE** ☐ **NO** ☐

10. Online grocery shopping

Ok, we've done this one to death, so I suspect no further explanation is necessary.

The executive summary? You should be able to save two hours a week or so by doing your supermarket shopping online. So please go and set up an account with your preferred supermarket brand immediately. They may even have some attractive offers for first-time users to tempt you in.

If you have any doubts, please just try it. It won't hurt, I promise, and you might quite like it.

If for some reason, the whole home delivery thing isn't your bag, then many supermarkets offer a 'click and collect' service. You order your stuff online as usual but then go and pick it up at an allotted time, usually from a central point in the supermarket car park.

To be honest, I'm not quite sure why you wouldn't have it delivered. But clicking and collecting at least gets rid of the in-store experience, and you can simply swing by and pop the bags in your boot.

And if you need further inspiration, here are the most annoying things about shopping in supermarkets, in my opinion:

1. Parking in supermarket car parks (trying to get as near to the entrance as possible, trying to fit into parking bays meant for superminis, somehow always parking 5 miles from the nearest trolley point, going in backwards but realising you can't now get access to your boot, clipping your alloys on the kerbs, etc.)
2. Needing a coin (that you don't have) to release your trolley
3. Trying to find products that they've hidden (again) so you have to ask someone or go back around the entire store
4. Having to check sell-by dates
5. Queueing at the checkout
6. Careless morons who dink your car doors when they open theirs, or who use your bumper as a brake for their car or trolley

I can almost feel you're pulse quickening as you read the list, which is undoubtedly a sign that you need to just go for it.

2 HOURS **YES** ☐ **MAYBE** ☐ **NO** ☐

11. Focus on one thing at a time

No matter what gender you are, I guarantee you can't truly multi-task. It's just not possible.

What you can do is try and have several tasks on the go at any one time, but that's not true multitasking.

For example, as I write this, my body is multitasking. There's some breathing going on, a bit of typing, some occasional blinking, and swearing as well (don't ask). In case you know my Personal Trainer, there most definitely isn't a chocolate biscuit being consumed.

All these things are occurring at once, and this then qualifies as true multitasking. However, when it comes to work, what we mean by multitasking is the ability to work on several work tasks at the same time. And in the nicest possible way, it can't be done. What you end up doing, at best, is 'spinning plates'.

Ah yes, plate spinning. Do you remember the guy they used to have on TV, who sets a series of plates spinning on the end of some sticks? He has to keep going back to each one to add more 'spin' so that they all stay in the air. As he sets more and more plates spinning, the audience becomes enthralled. They scream at him to attend the one that's starting to wobble uncontrollably. Has he spotted it? Will he get to it in time to stop it from falling?

At any one time, he's only focusing on one plate. But by moving from plate to plate in rapid succession, he manages to keep all of them spinning at once.

Time has moved on, and the old plate-spinning act is now a thing of the past. This is partly due to the arrival of prime-time talent shows, but mainly because it was a bit crap. But fortunately, it lives on in the form of the best analogy I can come up with for not multi-tasking.

Because spinning plates is precisely what we do when it comes to work tasks. We may have several tasks on the go at once, but we can only be working on one of them at any one time.

The problem with this approach is, unlike the plate spinner, our tasks are usually diverse. So when we switch between them, we have to disengage with task 1 and then reengage with task 2. This is inefficient, and so it costs us time.

Imagine you have five tasks on the go, and we need to come back to them five times to get them completed. You'd have to perform this disengagement and re-engagement process 25 times in total. But if we did each task consecutively rather than simultaneously, then we'd only be reengaging 5 times, which is far more efficient.

Apologies, it's a bit of a long-winded way of describing something quite straightforward, but hopefully, you see what I mean.

So, in short, don't try and multitask. Instead, work on each task until completed before moving on to the next.

1 HOUR **YES** ☐ **MAYBE** ☐ **NO** ☐

12. Turn off all alerts

Device alerts are, 99.9% of the time, terrible, terrible things.

So, you've got an email. Or a text. Or some app can't wait to tell you all about something ultra-important that it's just done.

Why would such an event make you want to stop what you're doing and take a look? What are the chances that it's going to be so urgent or earth-shattering that you need to know immediately rather than in half an hour?

Unfortunately, these alerts mess with your mind. Once you've heard the beep or felt your pocket vibrate, you're distracted. It's impossible not to wonder who it's from or what it's about, even if you have the mental strength to resist the urge to take a quick look.

Why is this distraction a problem? It makes you less efficient because you'll have to stop what you're doing before picking it up again. Oh, and what was it that you were doing? Well, it could be anything. Driving? Talking to colleagues or in a meeting? Reading, writing, or even presenting? Performing open-heart surgery?

The distraction can make you look distracted or foolish, crash the car, forget what you were doing, or puncture a ventricle. And almost certainly, it will cost you time.

There are quite a few scenarios where being distracted is neutral (café, TV, quiet night in). But there are lots where it might be harmful (see above) and only one where it could be beneficial (in an emergency, hence the 99.9%).

And what if you didn't have the mental strength to resist the urge to look? Well, then we arrive at the scenario I talked about earlier, in Chapter 10. The one where you read the email, and then mark it as unread so that you can reread it later when you have time to deal with its contents.

If you operate like this, you will end up reading every email twice, and your device alerts will take priority over almost every aspect of your life. In what scenario would you NOT sneak a quick look? Procreation? A friend's funeral? Childbirth?

Ultimately, it's a timing issue. We'll always end up getting these messages, but our brains find it difficult to resist the urge to want to look at each message immediately. Curiosity isn't the exclusive domain of cats, as it turns out.

So what about the 0.1%? The emergency situation.

Well, yes, that's jolly responsible of you to remember, and you're absolutely right. You do need to be contactable in the event of an emergency.

So what do you do? Personally, I leave my phone on, with the ringer on silent and the vibration switched on. These days there are so many other communication options, that being physically dialled by someone is much rarer than it used to be. As a result, you shouldn't get plagued by calls. If you do, it may be because your job demands it, in which case you don't have a problem anyway (your phone will be on when the emergency call comes in). Or it may be that you're insanely popular, in which case you may want to invest in a second phone.

But whatever you do, please switch off the alerts on your phones, tablets, laptops, and desktops. They do not serve you well.

½ HOUR YES ☐ MAYBE ☐ NO ☐

13. Read using audiobooks

You can't beat a physical book when it comes to tactility. The whole page-turning experience, the smell of the print on paper. That fresh-off-the-press, virginal look that tells you you're the first to dive between its pristine covers.

Ok, I might be overdoing it a bit, but physical books are, for me, the definitive article. E-books and audiobooks are pale facsimiles.

Or at least they were. Today, to be fair, I have a slightly more horses-for-courses view.

The problem with traditional books is that they demand your full attention. It's difficult to read a paperback and do other stuff like have a meal or drive a car, without making a bit of a mess, or getting a bit arrested.

E-books (basically any book that can be read on an electronic device) have the same problem. Although they're marginally more wipeable and, of course, they also involve less tree-felling.

But audiobooks are something else altogether more efficient. Just to be clear, what we mean by an audiobook is a recording of someone reading out the contents of a physical book or an e-book. So instead of reading, you listen.

Consequently, you're less likely to get sticky toffee sauce on an audiobook because you're not repeatedly touching it while you consume food. And policemen and women will pay almost no attention to you as you drive along, audiobook in full chatter.

Back in the day, I used to have a long commute to work, plus I did a fair bit of overseas travelling. It meant I'd often be in the car, and so I'd usually listen to the news on the radio.

After I had my renaissance moment and decided there would be no more news for me, I found I had a lot of dead time on my hands. I was driving so I couldn't read a book or write emails. Sure, I could make a few calls, but I still ended up with a lot of spare time where I was doing nothing but driving.

That's when I discovered audiobooks and it changed things for me overnight. Suddenly there was no more dead time. I could afford to dive into a whole load of books that I'd fancied getting into, but wouldn't have had the time to if I'd have had to read the paper version.

I even started learning some languages, albeit very badly. It turns out that commuting by car is about the best way of teaching yourself a new language that there is. The secret to it is that you can écoutez et répétez to your heart's content because no one can hear you speaking. And if they see you talking, you simply look like you're on a hands-free phone call.

I had around a two and a half hour commuting round trip, so I was packing in quite a lot of audiobook content each week, around 12 hours or so. To put that into perspective, it's one and a half working days. There was no excuse for my appalling accent, but there you go.

I decided to focus on self-help titles and business-type books. But if you prefer to be entertained, there are no end of fiction audiobooks for you to listen to.

You may be able to think of some other dead time that you routinely have in your week. In this case, I would urge you to consider whether an audiobook or three might be a great way of squeezing some more value out of it.

Or you could try and start a plate spinning revival instead. After all, there's a whole new generation of fans that can't wait to discover it. Probably.

? HOURS YES ☐ MAYBE ☐ NO ☐

14. Create a mix and match look

This is genius, even if it sounds a bit anally retentive.

We can often spend an age deciding what to wear. Whether it's going to work, a shopping trip, a night out with friends, or a visit to your Mum's, what you look like is important to you. So you can spend an absolute age with your head in the wardrobe, agonising over what to put on.

So, what's the answer?

If you make a point of only buying outfits that mix and match, you'll never pull two items out of the wardrobe that won't go together.

You'd be able to close your eyes, grab a shirt and some trousers (or a top and a skirt), and be 100% confident that a) you like them and b) they go together. It will take you literally seconds to choose.

I know it sounds a bit odd buying a complete wardrobe of outfits that are all interchangeable. But once you've cracked it, it will transform your 'getting ready' experience.

One word of warning; it's essential that you try and avoid tank tops or jumpers with a matching shirt collar sewn in. There are still limits when it comes to taste.

Ever noticed how famous billionaires seem to look very similar in each publicity shot? They're either mixing and matching, or they've bought two hundred identical tee-shirts or shirts. Imagine how long they take to choose their outfits each morning?

So take a leaf out of their book and quit worrying about what to wear. It will be one massive ball-ache relieved.

1/2 HOUR **YES** ☐ **MAYBE** ☐ **NO** ☐

15. Use online banking

Now I know a lot of people have trust issues with banks. And this can get compounded by the fact that many banks are rubbish at doing anything they set their minds to. This can be a bit of a problem when we're rather dependant on them to look after our money.

Miraculously, however, banks have somehow contrived to build a cunning internet-based system. One that enables you to manage your accounts from the comfort of your home, or on the move, via an app. It's called online banking, and it can actually be rather useful.

Yes, really. I couldn't quite believe they'd managed it either, but there you go.

Now, if you're still at the cash-under-the-mattress stage, I suspect online banking may be a bit of a stretch for you. Plus, you may now be slightly alarmed that I know where your stash is. And possibly even more alarmed that I've just told everyone. But please hear me out.

Historically, most banking procedures were designed to be as inconvenient as possible. Cheques, for example, are just about the world's least efficient means of distributing money.

Digital banking has made things more sensible. Chip and pin and contactless payments have made life a lot easier, but to be fair, we still get a bit unstuck when it comes to cash. It's all rather too, well, fiddly. Still, it probably won't be around for long.

But online banking is great. I can see my balances, payments, and statements on my phone in an instant. I can even pay people and bills in seconds. I can transfer money about the place. And guess what – I can also pay in cheques using the app! Who knew?

Better still, all of these services are available to me 24/7, 365 days a year.

I don't live anywhere near a bank and so when people gave me cheques, I'd have to make a special detour to go and pay it in. Opening birthday cards was something of a double-edged sword.

Not anymore; I can now pay it in on my phone within seconds of receiving it.

In short, you should never have to visit a bank ever again. Does all this online nonsense present some sort of cyber-security risk? Well, I suspect it's less risky than taking money out of a cashpoint.

So if you're lagging behind, I urge you to get with the programme and take a look at what you're missing when it comes to online banking.

You could make life easier for yourself and save some precious time to boot.

½ HOUR **YES** ☐ **MAYBE** ☐ **NO** ☐

16. Set a timer

Since we all have mobile phones and portable devices pretty much permanently glued to us these days, setting a timer is a piece of cake.

But how can a timer help you save time? It feels like there should be a connection, but it's not immediately obvious what it is.

Let me put you out of your misery. Timers are great for reminding us of deadlines. And deadlines are great for making us do things more quickly.

I'll give you an example. When you go on holiday for a fortnight, several things happen at work. There will be envious glances from your colleagues. You'll have a slightly anxious feeling as you worry if you'll get everything done before you leave. But there will also be a sense of euphoria because you know you'll be entirely work-free for the next 14 days.

But your last day also represents a deadline. There will be jobs that cannot wait for you to get back in two weeks' time. And yet, somehow, every time you go away, you always manage to get all the things that need doing done before you leave, even if it's a bit of a rush.

This happens because work is elastic (the task, not your place of work, which would be a bit weird). If you have more time than you need, work expands to fill it. And if you've got too much work to do in the allotted time, work will contract to fill the time available.

Either way, you'll end up leaving with all the work that must be done, having been done by you, or otherwise delegated.

This elasticity is quite interesting because it's not the work itself that is elastic (I was stretching the truth a bit when I said that). It's usually the speed with which you complete it or the quality to which it's done.

Let me explain. You invariably want to do a good job, so if you have time, that's precisely what you will do – a good job. If you have even more time, you'll either do an excellent job, or you'll just move on to the next task. But if you have less time, you'll do an ok or acceptable job (let's be honest, it might even be a bit rubbish – I was just being kind). In each case, the task gets completed, but the time available dictates the quality. That's the elastic part.

Alternatively, it may be the speed that drives the elasticity. If you've not got a deadline, you'll take your time. You won't cut any corners, and you'll have a coffee with Sam in Accounts, who popped over mid-afternoon. But last day before your hols, you'll speed things up, take a few shortcuts and hide under the desk when Sam saunters over, cappuccino in hand. You're on a deadline, and as a result, you're much more efficient.

So, imagine if you gave yourself some new deadlines. Going on holiday is a real one, but you could easily create an artificial deadline. What about a deadline for leaving work at 5 pm on the dot, every day (this is a good one, you should try it, honestly)?

You'd need to be strict with yourself. But you can see how it would be possible to leave at 5 pm every single day with every item of work completed that needed to be. You simply take advantage of the inherent elasticity in the system.

There are three main benefits to this approach:

1. You'll get to leave work on time, every single day
2. You'll get more work done because you won't be gilding any lilies
3. Sam in Accounts will start finding you insanely attractive

Ok, there are only two benefits, but I wanted to make sure you were still paying attention.

Later on, I'll introduce you to another technique that uses this same elasticity. But for now, just consider how, by using your timer at various points throughout the day, you could become more productive AND get more time back.

2 HOURS **YES** ☐ **MAYBE** ☐ **NO** ☐

17. Avoid rush hour

Here's a quiz question for you: do you know why rush hours exist?

Yes, I know it's because everyone is going to/coming home from work at the same time. But why exactly are they doing that?

Well, it's because we're all a bit old-fashioned. Working hours are typically between 9 am and 5 pm because that's when

1. it's usually light,

2. we're awake,
3. the workplace is open,
4. it's after breakfast but before dinner, and
5. they fit in with the school run.

So as a result, everyone has more-or-less the same routine, and we all find ourselves travelling at the same time.

Avoiding the rush-hour can make for a significant timesaving, as anyone living in or around a large city will tell you. The average speed in central London is around 7mph, which gives you some idea.

But how exactly do you go about changing things, so you're not affected by the rush hour?

Here are a few ideas to get you thinking:

1. **Work from home.** You might not be able to do this every day, but doing it once a week will save you a lot of time generally, some of which will come from avoiding the rush hour
2. **Stagger your work times.** Why work 9 to 5 when you could work 7 to 3, for example? There will still be a core 6 hours when you'll be working the same hours as everyone else, but you should be able to avoid the worst of the traffic
3. **Walk, run, or cycle to work.** Sure, it won't be realistic for everyone, but unlike the car or public transport, these methods will also keep you fit. So while they may take longer, they can remove the need to take time out to go to the gym, for example
4. **Use public transport.** Not everyone's cup of tea, perhaps. But if you do get stuck in traffic, public transport has the advantage of allowing you to do more stuff while you're using it

It's often said that stock market investors end up with more money by doing the opposite of what everyone else in the market is doing. Arguably, the same applies to commuters and time.

1 HOUR YES ☐ MAYBE ☐ NO ☐

18. Lift sharing

The taxi of Mum and Dad is possibly the most customer-centric transportation system ever conceived. Let's take a look at the facts:

1. There are no fares to pay.
2. Tips are not expected or necessary
3. They can be called out at any time day or night
4. There's no stranger danger
5. It's always a door-to-door service
6. It's unlikely that a previous occupant has thrown up in your seat
7. They may even, at a stretch, go south of the river after dark

So, as a child or young adult, this is a very good thing indeed.

But, if you're a mum or a dad, it's a bit of a royal pain in the backside.

I mentioned, in Chapter 7, the notion of having a taxi driver do the school run in your place. By putting several children in one car who were all making the same journey, only one trip is made, but several children are transported. It's highly cost-effective.

Of course, you can now apply this very same logic to any similar situation.

Going to a children's party? I bet the little cherubs all live within a spit of each other so a one-car pick-up would be eminently practicable.

School sports event at the weekend? Ditto

Another way of tackling this is by finding your offspring's nearest, dearest friend. I mean, quite literally, the friend that lives closest to you. Are their parents responsible, trustworthy, and safe? If so, sharing the driving chores, whether that be school run or after school activities, means you get almost half of your time back. Plus, you incur only half the travel costs.

Could you extend this lift-sharing arrangement further? To be honest, I would advise caution. Taxi drivers are safer because they're experienced drivers who drive family-sized vehicles. And if you lift share with only one other family, you can be reasonably sure of what you're dealing with. This would include knowing who does the driving and the type of car they drive. You can also establish some mutual ground rules.

However, extending the circle will create more risk. You only need to turn up at any school gates to see that some parents elect to have the nanny/au pair/older sibling drop their precious charges off, often in some clapped out supermini that's even older than they are. That's presumably because the parents are at work, having driven there in their much newer and bigger family car.

If you were trying to create the riskiest possible means of getting your kids to school, then these people may have cracked it;

1. Young driver? Check
2. Minimal driving experience? Check
3. An older car with none of the latest safety features? Check
4. A small car that will crumple like a tin can in a collision? Check

Perhaps if they were to have them drive blindfolded as well, they could add that extra element of danger that you feel is somehow missing.

So, just be careful; lift-sharing is a great way of getting some time back but do your due diligence first.

2 HOURS **YES** ☐ **MAYBE** ☐ **NO** ☐

19. Take a 10-minute break every hour

The key to effective working lies in taking regular breaks.

When we work for prolonged periods, we become less effective. It can be tempting to keep going, particularly when you're in 'the zone' or where the end of a task is in sight.

But the problem is we don't work that way. Our ambition is good, but our faculties become tired. We no longer focus or concentrate as effectively.

The answer lies in taking a ten-minute break each hour. In other words, work for 50 minutes then take 10 minutes off. Ideally, you want to move around during your break, so go for a walk. Better still grab a glass of water, and even take a quick mooch about outside (but don't go down the pub).

We'll shortly bump into the Pomodoro Technique, which has a similar vibe, but either way, the break thing just works. Even when you're up against a tight deadline, it still works better than working straight through.

And if you're more effective, you'll use less time.

? HOURS **YES** ☐ **MAYBE** ☐ **NO** ☐

20. Buy goods online

We've done this to death already, but it has to be in my Top 40, obvs.

In short, don't go out to go shopping. Shop online and save yourself heaps of lovely hours and minutes, which you can then put to much better use.

½ HOUR   **YES** ☐   **MAYBE** ☐   **NO** ☐

21. Question your routines

I wrote earlier about making sure that you question your routine tasks at work. It's incredible how much work is entirely redundant or unnecessary. The same argument also applies to your domestic routines.

So, make sure that you're approaching your daily tasks both at work and at home with a questioning mindset. What are the questions you need to ask yourself? Try the following:

1. Do I need to be doing this task?
2. What would happen if I didn't do it?
3. Who could do it instead of me?

The trick is to remind yourself to ask these questions, as it's not likely to occur to you by instinct. The best idea is a simple one. Put a note somewhere that you'll see several times a day, which will serve to remind you.

½ HOUR   **YES** ☐   **MAYBE** ☐   **NO** ☐

22. Plan your day

There are two types of people in this world — those who let the day happen to them, and those who impose themselves on the day. You so need to be in the second group.

At the very start of the book, I framed the idea that people take time for granted because it passes inexorably. We're powerless to stop it or control it any way.

The closest thing we get to controlling time is to determine what gets done in each unit of time, and how long it takes us.

And the best way of doing this is to know what you need to get done. This is where to-do lists (of any type or description) come into their own.

So, get yourself organised.

Get yourself an app, diary, or notebook, in which you can jot your actions. Write your to-do list the night before, not halfway through the following morning. Make sure you stay on top of your actions throughout the day. And plan contingencies in case things don't go according to plan.

Check out the various task-based apps available and read the reviews. They could revolutionise things for you.

I promise you; you'll be so much more effective.

½ HOUR   YES ☐   MAYBE ☐   NO ☐

23. Wash less

Before you get all squeamish, I'm talking here about washing your clothes less, rather than yourself.

The funny thing is, we wash our clothes when they're not dirty. We'll wear stuff for a day and then put them in the laundry basket. Whereas if we hang them up, there's nothing to prevent us from wearing them a second or third time before we need to rewash them.

'Yeuch!' I hear you say. 'Sounds a bit scuzzy,' you add.

But that's just an automatic reaction we (you) have, and it costs us (well, you) both time and money. Plus, there's a not-insignificant environmental impact.

Each washing load has a journey, from the laundry basket to the washing machine. Then to the tumble dryer or clothesline, the ironing pile, the clothes hangar, and finally back to the wardrobe.

I know you don't measure it, and you just accept it for what it is. But each time you wear something twice before washing it, you're saving yourself time.

In fact, if you wear everything twice as much before washing it, you'll do half as much washing.

And half as much drying. And half as much ironing.

How much time do you (or someone you love/like/know/tolerate) spend doing these things each week? Would halving that time sound quite attractive, if not to you, then to them?

3 HOURS YES ☐ MAYBE ☐ NO ☐

24. All friends together

Ok, this one's going to sound a bit weird, but please hear me out.

Friends are lovely, aren't they? They like us a lot, and we like them, which is nice. The problem is, they're usually a bit of a burden, timewise (not that I'd tell them this of course. If any of my friends are reading this, then I'm talking about some different friends who are nowhere near as good friends as you are).

Why are friends so time-consuming? Well, it's because, unless you're a habitual party-thrower, you tend to meet them all individually. You'll spend one evening having a drink with John and Sally. Then another evening, having dinner with Dave. Miriam's coming over for Sunday lunch next week, and you're seeing Freddie and Malcolm for drinks up in town on Thursday.

And before you know it, your week's disappeared. Your diary is just one big social maelstrom, you popular devil you.

Talking of which, I'm reminded of a time when Tin Man was over, and I was trying to ignore him while sorting out my social life. It wasn't going particularly well...

Derik: *You appear to be vexed. Is there a problem?*

Me: *Vexed? Seriously? Who programmed you? You would so have got picked on at robot school. Er... if such a thing existed, which obviously it can't do, so just ignore me...*

Derik: *I will try to. Very well, you appear to be agitated. Is that more acceptable to you?*

Me: *Mildly. And I'm not vexed or agitated; I just don't have enough time to fit everything in. I'm supposed to be meeting up with my friend Trevor this week, but my diary's completely chocka.*

Derik: *As in 'it's made of chocolate'? Or as in 'it's playing polo for the next seven minutes'?*

Me: *What? No, I said 'chocka'. Chock-a-block. It means completely full. For some reason, I seem to be out with friends every night this week. So, unfortunately, I've no time to catch up with dear old Trevor.*

Derik: *Is this because you're very popular or because you're bad at managing your time?*

Me: *Well, modesty prevents me saying, and all that, but I don't think I'm bad at managing my time. Just look at my diary. Emma this evening, Dave and Sandra tomorrow night, Charlie on Wednesday, Slippery on Thursday and Graham on Friday.*

Derik: *I see. And all of these individuals like you, do they?*

Me: *Well, of course they do. They're my friends!*

Derik: *Even the friend you call 'Slippery'?*

Me: *Yes, Derik, even him.*

Derik: *I presume they don't like each other, which is why you have to see them individually? That must be very difficult for you.*

Me: *Of course they like each other! Well, to be fair, a couple of them haven't met Slippery, but I'm sure they would like him if they did. Providing he was still sober.*

Derik: *But for some reason it's important that you spend four hours speaking with each of them away from the others. Have I understood this correctly?*

Me: *Er... Not exactly, no.*

Derik: *So, there's no logical reason why you could not meet all of them on the same evening, at the same time.*

Me: *Well, no, not technically, I suppose.*

Derik: *So, if I've understood correctly, you could have arranged to meet all of these people for four hours on the same evening. They would all like each other, and you will have a chance to catch up with all of them individually. You could also have invited Trevor AND freed up the remaining four evenings, which means you would get sixteen hours of your time back. Which is the equivalent of two working days. Would this be an accurate summary?*

Me: *Ok, I've gone off you again. Just so you know...*

Derik: *I see. Does modesty now prevent you from saying that you're bad at managing your time?*

Me: *Go and blow a fuse.*

See, I told you it was a bit weird. But as ever, Derik's take on the world has a bizarre logic to it.

I know, I know – it's nicer to catch up with people one-to-one. But if time is important to you, then you have to admit it's a good compromise. You get to see everyone, plus you get your time back, something of a win-win.

I'm sure Slippery won't mind.

3 HOURS **YES** ☐ **MAYBE** ☐ **NO** ☐

25. Drive a dirty car

If you've read the section in Chapter 7 about car cleaning, then I don't need to remind you of the time benefits of keeping a serially unwashed vehicle.

If you haven't, then I'll cut to the chase; car washing is bad for you, chronologically speaking. So try not to do it too often, and when you must, get someone else to do it without going out of your way.

Hang on a sec, what do you mean you didn't read chapter 7? Really? Why exactly am I bothering here? Are there any more chapters you've skipped over that you want to tell me about? Well, are there?

You've been very naughty. Please don't do it again.

YES ☐ MAYBE ☐ NO ☐

26. Put things back afterwards

At the risk of sounding like your mother, you should jolly well put things back where you found them after you've used them.

There's no magic at work here. How many times have you found yourself looking for, say, a screwdriver, only to discover that the last person to use it (you) hasn't put it back in the place where screwdrivers live (the garage/kitchen drawer/toolbox)?

Compare, if you will, the time spent looking for said screwdriver versus the time taken to fetch it from its usual place of residence.

Exactly. Not to mention the frustration involved.

It's our inherent short-termism at play again, I'm afraid. We'd rather avoid the 'pain' (mild inconvenience) of putting the screwdriver back in its place today. Even though it may cause us an even greater 'pain' (major inconvenience, timewasting, and frustration) in the future. Derik would have a field day if he knew (please don't tell him).

A trivial human frailty, but one that in this case can be overcome by restoring things to their rightful place.

And I won't tell you again.

½ HOUR YES ☐ MAYBE ☐ NO ☐

27. Buy cards in bulk

This is one of those simple ideas that, over a year, could save you hours.

We're talking here about greetings cards. You know; birthday cards, Christmas cards, anniversary cards, congratulations cards, thank you cards, get well soon cards, Valentine's Day cards, Mother's Day cards, Father's Day cards, Grandparent's Day cards (yes, really) sympathy cards, Easter cards...

You name it; there's a chance to celebrate pretty much any occasion you can think of. Clinton's may have made up half of them, but that doesn't stop us sending a card.

Many people (i.e. men) often tend to buy cards one at a time. They'll suddenly remember that it's Charlie's birthday the day after tomorrow. So they'll dash off to the card shop in a panic and spend an hour and a half trying to find the rudest/funniest/least offensive card. Then they'll come home, write the card, then go out again to buy a postage stamp (doh!).

Now, some people (i.e. women) have spotted that there's a common theme among these card-based events. For example, Charlie has contrived to have a birthday on the same day each year for as long as anyone can remember. Similarly, Christmas has proved fairly reliable over the years, and while Easter can be a bit evasive, you can at least be sure there's going to be one at some point.

You can see where I'm going with this; a bit of forward-planning can work wonders. Here's what you do:

1. Go shopping once a year, online for preference, and bulk buy every type of card you'll need for the next 12 months (or 36 months if you're feeling really ambitious)
2. Don't worry about seasonality. Your other half will love you just as much if your Valentine's day message is handwritten rather than printed on by the card manufacturer
3. Christmas is the exception. You want to buy a big box of different festive designs in November, that will last you a few years
4. Stick them in a drawer where you'll remember where they are (and where prospective recipients won't find them)
5. When you need a card, instead of jumping in the car and doing the card shop run, you walk to the drawer instead and pull one out

I hope the complexity of this solution hasn't put you off.

How much time could you save? Well, according to the Greeting Card Association, each of us sends an average of 33 cards per year, with around 85% of cards being purchased by women.

So, even if you only saved 10 minutes per card by buying in bulk, you'd clock up an impressive five and a half hour timesaving each year.

? HOURS **YES** ☐ **MAYBE** ☐ **NO** ☐

28. Create a time log

It can often be challenging to have a complete awareness of where all your time goes. After all, you do lots of different 'stuff', and at any given moment, you're confident that you're making good use of your time.

This was a very similar conversation to one I had with my Personal Trainer once, about my diet. I swore blind that I was only eating good, nutritious foods. Nothing that could explain the fact that I was failing to shift as much timber as I wanted, despite doing lots of exercise.

So my trainer got me to complete a food log for a week, and it completely transformed my perspective. It turned out I was eating all sorts of rubbish almost without noticing, and my portion sizes were off the scale. I was buying low-calorie dinners for two and then eating them all myself in one sitting, at lunch. The fact that they were low-calorie was more than offset by the fact I was eating a double portion each time. A bit embarrassing, and yet, for some reason, only apparent once I'd completed the food log.

I therefore recommend that you complete a time log, which is a food log equivalent. You only need to keep it for a few days (up to a week max) and make sure you write down everything you do, from the moment you get up to the moment you go to bed.

This may sound a bit of a pain, but you only need to document it at a high level. You're trying to get a picture of any areas where you have an opportunity to improve things.

The funny thing about this exercise is that you're almost sure to discover something you didn't know or appreciate about what you do. We're not used to getting this helicopter view of our work and activity practices and patterns. It can be enlightening to see them presented this way.

It's a great way to get a health-check on things, and with luck, make some changes that could save you some time.

½ HOUR **YES** ☐ **MAYBE** ☐ **NO** ☐

29. Use the Pomodoro Technique

Pomodoro, if you're interested, is the Italian word for 'tomato' (to be fair, it's still the Italian word for 'tomato' even if you're not interested).

The Pomodoro Technique is an excellent idea that works exceptionally well. It requires discipline but will reward the user handsomely if they stick with the programme. It also involves zero tomatoes, Italian or otherwise.

So, what's it all about, then?

Well, it's based on a straightforward premise with which we're all very familiar.

Have you ever had a deadline that you or your team have struggled to meet? One that was a case of 'all hands to the pumps', 'let's all muck in', and 'we'll work through the night and get some pizza in to keep us going'?

And somehow, by the skin of your collective teeth, you managed to hit the deadline?

I already mentioned that I used to think my company was the world's leading experts in last-minute deadline delivery. No one could match our sheer last-minuteness when it came to getting a project across the line. We used to do it time after time. We even got a discount from the pizza place around the corner, since we used them so regularly to sustain us during our late-night, deadline-meeting sessions.

Then I discovered that I was being somewhat naïve. This phenomenon, far from being unique to my business, was universal. Everyone did it, and they continue to do it to this day.

You see, as I've mentioned before, work expands to fill the time available. And so you cut your cloth accordingly.

For example, if you've got two weeks to meet a deadline, it will take you two weeks, give or take, to do the work. If you've got 24 hours, you'll be ready tomorrow, and so on.

The reason it works like this is straightforward. When you have a tight deadline, you tend to do several things at once:

1. You focus on the basics and ignore the nice-to-haves and beautification
2. You delegate more, bringing in more resources as necessary. This can be upwards as well as downwards delegation, or indeed outsourcing
3. Your performance is more focused, better organised, and more concentrated. You have a specific target to hit, and you develop a kind of tunnel vision
4. You don't do other tasks or activities that you'd otherwise have done

So what has this got to do with tomatoes?

Patience, we'll come to that in a moment. Let me tell you about the technique itself.

What you do is this. You're going to be working in short, 25-minute segments. Each of these segments is known as a Pomodoro. Then at the end of each Pomodoro, you have an enforced rest of 5 minutes duration. During this rest period, you're not allowed to continue working, and in fact, you must also change your scenery. This could involve going for a walk, even going outside, before returning to your workspace. During the break you must also drink some water or juice; this is quite important. Do not drink beer or wine (this is even more important). After every fourth Pomodoro, you can take a longer, 15 to 30-minute break.

So, on the face of it, not that complicated. But how does it work? And when will I explain about the tomatoes?

Ok, first things first. The idea is that you set yourself a work target for each Pomodoro. This will be a task or sub-task that you have to complete within the 25 minutes. Failure is not an option; you must complete the task. This means you need to think quite carefully about breaking your tasks down into manageable sizes, so you don't bite off more (or less) than you can chew.

Disruptions are not allowed. If the phone rings, ignore it. If someone arrives, shoo them away. If it's the biscuit trolley, well, you can always fit in a quick break, can't you? I mean, what's the big rush?

But generally, biscuit trolley aside, your Pomodoro time should be sacrosanct.

I suspect you'll want to know how and why it works (skip this next bit if you don't). And will someone please explain where tomatoes fit into all this?

Well, it harnesses a mini version of the project deadline dilemma I mentioned at the start (the one that involved pizza).

Let's use a scenario to demonstrate. Pretend, if you will, that you're working on a project that will take you several days to complete. You know exactly what's got to be done, and you're not reliant on anyone else to deliver it.

The first thing that the technique requires you to do is to break the project work down into 25-minute chunks. This is genius because it allows you to work on small chunks at a time. These are far more manageable than tackling larger pieces or the whole thing in one go.

The second thing you have to do is focus on one task for 25 minutes without disruption or distraction. This is more genius thinking; your brain can maintain a laser-like focus for 25 minutes, no problem. What it can't do is keep a laser-like focus for the entire length of the project. Nor are you likely to be able to work for much longer than 25 minutes without getting distractions and demands from others wanting to contact you.

Where you wouldn't usually have any laser-focusing at all, you now have a whole series of laser-focused episodes all joined together. And they're all focused on different parts of the overall task.

The third thing you have to do is finish each task in 25 minutes. You guessed it; it's another dose of genius-ness. If you only have a limited time to complete the task, then you'll be forced to strip out the unnecessary work and focus on the must-haves. You'll only add the nice-to-haves if you have time at the end.

Having a change of scenery and a sip of water during the breaks is also critical. Without these, you'll find it much more difficult to focus during your next Pomodoro.

Compare this approach to the standard one, and you can imagine the stark difference. The three elements of the technique combine to dramatic effect, and of course, you get projects completed more quickly as a result.

You don't need to be working on a specific project to use the technique. You can still divide your day into Pomodoros and then complete a range of diverse tasks. It's your choice.

So there you have it; the Pomodoro Technique in a nutshell.

Oh, yes. You wanted to know where the tomatoes came in. Well, believe it or not, the inventor of the technique, Francesco Cirillo, used his kitchen timer to measure his 25-minute sessions. And you'll never guess which vegetable his kitchen timer was shaped like.

As I said, total genius.

5+ HOURS YES ☐ MAYBE ☐ NO ☐

30. Group similar tasks together

The problem we often encounter is that we become very focused on the current task on which we're working. We'll see all the elements of that task unfolding in front of us. And we'll know all the steps in the process that we'll need to follow to get that task completed, one after the other. Don't worry; this is a good thing.

But we tend not to bother to look left or right when we do this. In other words, we have the good old blinkers on. What lies to the left and right? Well, it's all the other tasks that you've got on your to-do list.

Let me give you an example to highlight the problem. Imagine you're working on a task that requires you to get in touch with your bookkeeper to check some records. After that, you'll need to telephone the bank, do some online research, and then write a letter before the task is complete.

However, you also have four other tasks in your in-tray that will involve a conversation with the bookkeeper. There are two others that will involve a phone call, another two that require online research, and three that require a letter to be written.

We automatically think it's better to follow one task through to completion and so avoid any distractions. However, in reality, things are more efficient when we perform similar tasks together.

Covering off the four questions with your bookkeeper in one call rather than four should be an obvious win. But you should also consider grouping the phone calls, online research and letter writing items together as well. You're likely to do them quicker and more efficiently if you do.

Often this requires you to step back at the start of each week and take a more holistic view of your to-do list. You can then see where there are going to be everyday activities that could be done at roughly the same time. Phone calls, errands, visits, research; all will be handled more efficiently, if you deal with them in batches, rather than individually.

½ HOUR **YES** ☐ **MAYBE** ☐ **NO** ☐

31. Create logical shopping lists

I'm not big on conspiracy theories, but we all know, deep down, that supermarkets do their level best to hide stuff from us.

One week the carrots are next to the courgettes, exactly where they've always been since Adam was a lad. The following week, your world is turned on its head when the carrots have suddenly migrated to a completely different aisle. For no explicable reason. What on earth were they thinking of?

And how can you even begin to tackle this? Well, online shopping is the ideal way to go. But if you still find yourself needing to visit your local store (really?), make a point of writing a logical shopping list.

What's one of those? Well, it's a list that follows your route around the store.

So often, we create lists that are a jumbled grouping of random products. You've then got to scan your entire list in every aisle to make sure you don't miss anything.

And guess what? You'll always miss at least a two or three, and this means having to make another circuit of the store trying to find where they've hidden the stuff.

Far better to write your list in aisle order and pick things up as you go around.

YES ☐ **MAYBE** ☐ **NO** ☐

32. Create a run-out list

Now, if you've been very naughty and were thinking of ignoring Hack 10, you can still use Hack 31 even if you do meet with my stern disapproval.

You see, whichever route you take to get your provisions, there's one thing you still have to do, which it's almost impossible to get right. I am, of course, referring to that noblest of arts, the devising of the shopping list.

I've tried several different techniques, and none of them works perfectly. In ascending order of success, they are as follows:

1. Don't make a list. Just rock up at the supermarket and assume that you'll instinctively know or remember every item you've run out of and every ingredient you need. Hint: this is a rubbish idea and should never be considered, let alone attempted.

2. Open every cupboard in your kitchen before you go shopping and make a list of every item you see that looks like it might run out within the next week. This is more successful than the first one, but I still always miss a few essentials.
3. Keep a run-out list in the kitchen. Make a note of everything that you've run out of during the week, as you go. Then plan your menus for the next seven days and make a note of the required ingredients. Combine the two lists before you go shopping, and Bob's your uncle. This is my most successful approach, with only a few missed items.

The best thing I've found for a run-out list is a small chalkboard or whiteboard in the kitchen. You can even get them with a witticism attached if you feel the need.

One further tip is to avoid buying food when you're hungry. Let's face it; we've all been there. Those two for one, never-to-be-repeated-until-next-week offers in the biscuit and cake aisle. They somehow wangle their way into your trolley, without any conscious effort on your part. I mean, you even manage to be genuinely surprised when you pull them out of your bag when you get back home. How on earth did they get in there?

You just need to recognise that your subconscious likes biscuits. So make sure it's well-fed before you hit the supermarket, to avoid an unexpected item in your bagging area.

½ HOUR **YES** ☐ **MAYBE** ☐ **NO** ☐

33. Have two laundry baskets

The average family uses their washing machine four hundred times a year.

I don't know who finds this stuff out, but hell's bells, what a boring survey that must have been.

Anyway, I digress. Of course, each of these average families will then need to sort their whites from their non-whites. That way, their white shirts, and other knick-knacks don't come out grey, pink or pale blue, when they wash them.

Most average families have a single laundry basket. This means they have to sort through their dirty linen four hundred times a year, to separate the two laundry types. Which is nice.

Instead, why don't they have two laundry baskets, where they put whites in one and non-whites in the other? That way, the two are already pre-sorted when they come to do the washing.

Only a small time saving, but one likes to do one's bit for the family.

½ HOUR **YES** ☐ **MAYBE** ☐ **NO** ☐

34. Learn to say 'NO'

As a rule, we crave the goodwill and approval of others. We're also, with the exception of only a couple of people I can think of, naturally helpful souls.

This means that when other people, particularly people we know, like and respect, ask us to do something, we want to say 'yes'. We instinctively want to help them if we can.

Oh, and we worry that if we say 'no', they'll think less of us.

Yet ironically, the opposite is true.

The problem is, when we say 'yes', we find ourselves working to their agenda instead of our own. They now have two people working towards their goals, and we now have no one working toward ours.

The trick, then, is to learn how to say 'no'.

There's a knack to it because you'll want to be able to let people down gently. You won't want to appear rude (or at least not too rude), and you don't want to damage a relationship or to appear selfish.

An essential part of this means being able to judge the situation. Some people are very adept at soliciting help from others as a matter of course, often without knowing they're doing it. Others may have a genuine emergency and wouldn't usually ask for a favour unless they really needed your help.

You need to deflect the former and help the latter, so become good and identifying and distinguishing between the two.

And as I hinted earlier, you'll get a lot more respect by saying 'no' than you'll get by being a doormat or a pushover.

Plus, of course, you can also save a fair amount of time.

3 HOURS **YES** ☐ **MAYBE** ☐ **NO** ☐

35. Sock savings

I'm conscious that I made a comment about socks in the opening chapter, and here I am again, banging on about socks. I have no wish to be branded socksist in any way. I have owned many socks over the years and still wear them regularly. But there's a small time-saving to be had with them which, while it may seem trivial, can be a real blessing in disguise.

Here's the rub. I know that having lots of different pairs of different coloured or patterned socks can be hugely exciting. In fact, for some people, socks are something of a trademark.

The problem only manifests when it comes to laundry time. You empty a laundry basket full of your multi-coloured little foot jumpers into the washing machine. And what comes out is a basket load of clean, but jumbled up socks.

You now have the joy of matching up the pairs. And, if you're really lucky, the thrill of guessing which one will be the odd one out.

If that's not enough, it's possible to experience an extra frisson of frustration: wait until your partner has decided to buy socks that are exactly the same type and shade as some of yours, only a different size. If this happens to you, find them, then destroy them anonymously and without mercy. Practise saying 'sorry, I haven't seen yours anywhere' until it sounds completely believable.

You'll be pleased to know there are several options for reducing your sock-sorting work. I've ranked them here in order of personal preference. The choice, as ever, is yours:

1. Buy a job lot of comfortable, good quality socks that are all the same boring colour. Grey is nice.

Unlike the Maternity Unit when you bring twins home, socks aren't particularly fussy about which two you put together. Suddenly, the post-wash sock-pairing becomes a doddle (from a sock perspective, it will be like the swinging Sixties. A new partner after every wash – what's not to like?). You'll still have an odd one left over, but you'll know exactly what colour it will be from the get-go.

2. Buy a job lot of comfortable, good quality socks that are all the same vibrant colour.

Some people feel a need to make a statement with their socks, either because they're a bit eccentric, have a job in design, or lack a personality. If that's you, feel free to pick any lairy colour you like, and go for it. The world's your oyster when it comes to colours, patterns, and designs – just make sure they're all 100% identical.

3. Never wash your socks.

This is a somewhat more controversial solution and can lead to some social issues if you're not careful. Probably best avoided.

Unless you have some quite shy friends (or distressingly short trousers), you'll find that most people don't look at your socks that much. So, picking a nice inoffensive shade and just going with it shouldn't be an issue. People won't start talking about you behind your back or start pointing at your feet. I know you may feel a twinge of regret when you put on yet another pair of boring, grey socks. But you can reflect on the fact that you've dodged a bullet in the laundry department.

Ok, exactly how much of a time-saving are we talking here?

Well, let's assume you wear one pair a day, every day of the year, and you wash them after each use. And we'll also assume that it takes an extra 15 seconds per pair to match them up, if they're not all identical.

If you do the maths, this means you save around 1.5 hours a year by following the same-sock rule. It's not the biggest saving in the world, but it's enough time to take in a movie. And don't underestimate the lifelong admiration and gratitude of the poor soul who washes your cheesy toe-jackets, if it's not you.

? HOURS YES ☐ MAYBE ☐ NO ☐

36. Minimise your TV & gaming time

It'll be no surprise to you that TV can be something of a time killer for a lot of people. It's addictive stuff, and it's very easy to get hooked. Ditto for computer games.

Today there's so much choice available on TV that you can pretty much watch anything you want; at any time you want to watch it.

And once you're into a box set, that can be it – game over. You're sucked into a binge-watching spiral from which there are no realistic means of escape until the last episode is behind you.

Most people know if they're a TV addict or not, however, either way, it can be interesting to keep a TV diary for a week, just to see how much time you spend on it. The same goes if you're a serial gamer, because time really does fly when you're gaming.

Once you know this, you can then start to see the scope for saving time. And because we tend to spend quite a lot of time doing these things, the scope can often be significant.

Now, I know what you're thinking. Here he goes, promising to save me 42 hours a week without me having to give up lots of stuff that I like doing. And then he waits until almost the end of the book before telling me I've got to give up my telly and my X-Box.

In my defence, I'm not going to suggest you give up TV forever. Plus, I have given you quite a few other options to choose from, if missing out on TV is beyond the pale for you.

But if you're an avid TV viewer or compulsive gamer, it may be a real sweet spot for saving some time. So here's my suggestion for how to tackle it:

1. Give up TV or gaming for a month. You may be surprised at how little you miss it, particularly if you make sure you use the time you save doing something productive or enjoyable. You'll then see the benefit of having freed up the time. If it's too painful, by all means, go back to it after a month, but I think it may surprise you. Remember – you're less than 30 days from going back to it, and anyone should be able to give up anything for a month
2. Set yourself a strict TV/gaming quota and monitor it. Make it a weekly allowance so you can have the flexibility to do more on some days than on others. And try not to make the allowance 56 hours a week; instead, go for a figure that's a reasonable step down from your usual TV viewing/gaming time. And did you see I put the word 'strict' in there, right at the top so you couldn't miss it? Good
3. Do NOT channel surf. This is where you see what's on, flicking through channels until you find something watchable. With endless on-demand options plus the ability to pause live TV and skip through ads, you can be highly focused and selective. Make a point of setting your recorder to capture the things you genuinely want to see as part of your quota. Life's way too short to waste it watching rubbish, so make sure you zero in on the good stuff

5+ HOURS **YES** ☐ **MAYBE** ☐ **NO** ☐

37. Find your most productive time of day

Now, here's a thing. Each of us has a 'most productive' time of day, and we also have a 'least productive' time of day. No one is immune – we all have these productivity cycles.

But interestingly, productivity cycles are different for each of us.

For example, my most productive time of day might be 10.00 am to 12.30 pm. In contrast, yours could be, say, 4.00 pm to 6.00 pm (if you were writing this book instead of me, you could give yourself a slightly longer productivity window than me in the example, since we both know I've been a bit petty here. But you're not, so I win).

By scheduling your biggest challenges to take place at your most productive time, it's reckoned that you can save around an hour of your time each day.

Let's think about that for a second because it's quite a lot. You wouldn't have thought that your most productive time would be quite so, well, productive.

Ok, time for obvious question #1; how do you find out when your most productive time is each day if you don't instinctively know it?

Great question. The answer is you need to keep a journal of your achievements over the course of your working day for several weeks. You should then be able to see a pattern emerging as to the time of day you seem to be on your 'A' game.

You should also be able to see when you're at your least productive. This then allows you to schedule your work accordingly. Oh, and you should also make sure you drink lots of water and take frequent breaks during that time.

Time for (the slightly less obvious) question #2; what happens if you find you're only at your most productive between 10.00 am and 10.02 am? Or between 2.00 am and 4.00 am in the wee hours?

Well, firstly you should find that your productivity peaks for at least a couple of hours or so. If you've narrowed it down to 2 minutes, that's very scientific of you. But you should probably cut yourself some slack and include the period 45 minutes either side as well.

And if you're a night owl, then you need to find your most productive time during your regular working hours. If that's a night shift, then great. If not, I wouldn't recommend setting the alarm to catch your productivity wave in the middle of the night. You may keel over from lack of sleep at work the next day, which could be problematic.

Common sense can go quite a long way on this time hack.

5+ HOURS **YES** ☐ **MAYBE** ☐ **NO** ☐

38. Use the 5 Second Rule

Now I'm going to pinch an idea from the esteemed Mel Robbins for this one; her famous 5 Second Rule.

The concept, like most great ideas, is simple. This is how Mel describes it:

"The 5 Second Rule is simple (see, I told you it was). *If you have an instinct to act on a goal, you must physically move within 5 seconds, or your brain will kill it.*

The moment you feel an instinct or a desire to act on a goal or commitment, use the Rule.

When you feel yourself hesitate before doing something that you know you should do, count 5-4-3-2-1-GO and move towards action."

So, simple it is. But let's break things down a little, so we know exactly what's going on.

Let's take a scenario where you've set the alarm to wake up early so you can do a quick HIIT training session at home before you dive into the shower.

The thing is, you're a little sleepy, and the duvet is warm and inviting and doesn't want you to leave it (all duvets have anxiety issues and get lonely).

You can imagine what happens next. You think, *"I'll stick with the duvet for a little longer, and then I'll do my workout."*

Then after a few more minutes, it's become, *"I'm going to get up just about any second now and do a shortened version of my workout."*

Then, several minutes later, *"If I get up in a couple of seconds, I'll be able to squeeze in a really short workout."*

And finally, *"Ok, there's no time now to do a workout, so I might as well stay here under the duvet until my other alarm goes off and then head straight for the shower."*

Does it all sound depressingly familiar?

The problem is that our subconscious prioritises short-term pleasure over long-term rewards. The alarm reminds us that we need to do a workout because this has a long-term benefit to us. But the duvet quickly reminds us of the short-term pleasure of staying put. Plus, of course, the duvet option has the added advantage of being our current state. We don't need to do anything to take advantage of it – simply stay as we are.

Now, you may have spotted that there's a rather short but critical phase in this process that occurs as soon as the alarm goes off. This is when your brain realises the alarm has gone off to wake you up to do a HIIT routine. But, crucially, it's BEFORE the duvet starts to exert its malign influence on your decision-making.

The 5 Second Rule overrides that secondary thought process (the duvet) by initiating a countdown to the primary action (the workout). This then prevents the subconscious from thinking about the duvet option altogether. It's now focused on the countdown.

The countdown is short (you guessed it, five seconds). So, before your subconscious knows what's happening, you're out of bed and putting your yoga pants on (or whatever). The duvet thought starts biting only after you're already out of bed. But by then, you have momentum, so it's missed its chance.

The 5 Second Rule works a treat, and it can do wonders for procrastination. There's almost no end to the scenarios when you can use it. Whenever you move towards doing something positive, start your countdown, even if your brain has already come up with an alternative, not-so-great option. You'll automatically override the negative thought process. And you'll have started the positive action before the subconscious can do anything about it.

You'll have spotted that this isn't specifically a time-saving tool; it's more of an action-taking idea. But it can, as a result, save you lots of time because it cuts out the procrastination process altogether.

I mentioned earlier deferring a horrible task in favour of doing far less important, nicer tasks. If this resonated with you, then you can see how the 5 Second Rule could solve that problem altogether.

Mel Robbins has published a book, which has a lot more details on this subject. So if you wanted to find out more, order yourself a copy of the excellent and unsurprisingly titled "The 5 Second Rule" by her good self.

2 HOURS YES ☐ MAYBE ☐ NO ☐

39. Use the 5 Minute Rule

Are your goals quite hairy? Do you worry that they can look a bit unsightly, close up?

Now, let me tell you that having hairy goals is a very good thing. I don't want you to have impossible goals for obvious reasons. But having goals that are quite challenging (i.e. 'hairy') can put you in a very fine place indeed.

This is because if you aim high at the start, even if you fall a little short, you'll end up in a better place than the one from which you started. Or, as the Norman Vincent Peale quotation has it;

"Shoot for the moon. Even if you miss, you'll land among the stars."

Given the relative distance between the moon and the stars, I was never quite sure the quote worked from an astrophysical perspective. Strictly speaking, the words 'long after you're dead' are missing from the end of it. That said, I'm almost certainly going too deep on it, and there's a lot to be said for the imagery. It probably wasn't stencilled on the front of Apollo 11, though.

So, why am I banging on about your big, hairy goals?

Well, the problem with having such hirsute ambition is that it can all become a bit intimidating. You look at the size of the things, and you think, 'Hell's bells, where on earth do I start?'.

But never fear because help is at hand in the form of the 5 Minute Rule. Yes, you've already had the 5 Second Rule. Now someone's jumped on the bandwagon with this latest in the '5 Something Rule' series (I'm currently trying to get a '5 Hour Rule' book out before anyone else does).

Ok, how does the 5 Minute Rule work, and how can it help you get started on hairy goals? Essentially, it's another procrastination-killer. You see, it's very easy to put off starting on big goals because they can frighten you a bit (and in some cases quite a lot). You're pleased that you've got them, but you're not really looking forward to starting on them, if you know what I mean — a bit like oysters.

So, what you do is this. You say to yourself that you're going to spend just 5 minutes on one of your hairy goals. So instead of committing to finishing a task, you're committing to spending 5 minutes on it.

How does this help? Well, because you've not committed to finishing the task, you know that you're only on the hook for 5 minutes' effort. You can bail out after 300 seconds, and you'll have fulfilled the brief.

This takes all the pressure off since otherwise, you'd be focusing on the task itself, which is very difficult. Whereas doing 5 minutes is easy peasy.

But something strange can happen once we get started on a task. We can find ourselves entering what scientists call a state of 'flow'. This flow state was named by eminent psychologist Mihaly Csikszentmihalyi (he of the unusually wide business card fame). But you and I can probably relate better to it as being 'in the zone'. Sometimes you get immersed in something, and time flies by. This is what the 5 Minute Rule is trying to kick-start when it comes to your goals.

Again, the focus of this hack is more about moving you forward towards your goals. But it counts as a time-saving hack since it gets rid of procrastination and so speeds everything up for you.

2 HOURS YES ☐ MAYBE ☐ NO ☐

40. Exercise at home

Exercise is critical to your success and to your well-being (hopefully this doesn't come as a complete surprise to you).

The local gym is the logical place for most people to go when they want to work out. It has all the equipment, the free weights, and the personal trainers.

It also has the younger, fitter people that make you feel old and inadequate, and of course the changing rooms and shower facilities.

The problem is, it all takes a bit too long.

You've got to get ready, choose what to wear and make yourself look human. Then you've got to pack a change of clothes and remember to pack a towel and your wash kit. Next, you have to drive to the gym and find a parking space, before going inside and finding a locker.

And this happens before you've done any exercise. Then you've got to do your training in front of other people (not everyone's favourite thing), followed by the often-variable communal shower block experience, before changing back into your civvies.

Finally, gyms usually cost money, so you've got to factor in some sort of monthly membership fee. And maybe even a joining fee if they're a posher outfit (or at least not yet on the verge of bankruptcy).

So, what's this big gym-alternative solution I'm building up to?

Well, funny you should ask, because you actually have a gym at home, even if you didn't realise it. I'm not suggesting there's a secret room off the kitchen that the estate agent didn't tell you about. Nor am I talking about some state-of-the-art exercise machinery that someone's installed while you were out shopping.

No, what you've got on hand is your own body, which is itself, a fully functioning multi-gym.

Don't believe me? Google 'bodyweight exercises' and see what comes up. You'll come across an endless list of exercises and physical manipulations that you can do, which involves just your own body. No weights. No machines. In fact, no other equipment at all. Only gravity and your bits – that's all you need to have a perfect workout.

It's not even a compromise; you can get every bit as fit and toned using bodyweight exercises as you can down at the gym (assuming you're not after the Arnie look).

Better still, you only live about five seconds away from this gym. I mean, you can literally fall out of bed, and you're in it. Whereas the time from getting out of bed to arriving in the local gym, ready to exercise, could easily be between 30 minutes and an hour.

Your home gym has got a whole load of other benefits too:

1. There are no younger or fitter people there to make you feel inadequate
2. The shower and toilet facilities are every bit as good as you have at home

3. There's no need to pay a membership or joining fee; you've already signed up
4. You don't need to spruce yourself up or get changed into posh exercise gear – they'll take you as you are
5. You don't need headphones; simply turn the music up or put the TV on
6. No one watches while you exercise, apart from the cat

So, if you haven't done so already, why not take advantage of this exclusive personal gym that's right on your doorstep. Apart from saving yourself a small fortune in membership fees, you could also save two or three hours a week, if you work out regularly.

3 HOURS **YES** ☐ **MAYBE** ☐ **NO** ☐

Part 6:

Next Steps

"You don't have to see the whole staircase,

just take the next step."

Martin Luther King Jr

Chapter 13: Moving Forward From Here

"Time flies like an arrow. Fruit flies like a banana"

Groucho Marx

Key Learnings

Congratulations, you finally made it! This is excellent news and something that deserves a small celebration. I may even have a cheeky port and lemon myself later on, after you've gone to bed.

So, let's take a look at where we've got to with Your Own Personal Time Machine.

As you've gone through this book, I hope you've appreciated the sheer breadth of opportunity that exists for you to save time. I find it amazing that we're always so busy, yet we're often not doing much that's particularly worthwhile.

And while that sounds like a damning indictment, it's actually great news, because it means there's bags of scope to do something about it. Who knew; it turns out you're so bad, it's good!

There's certainly a fighting chance of being able to get 42 hours of your week back IF you want to. Even if it can seem a bit impossible at the start, since it equates to a completely bonkers six-hour time saving per day. Plus, some people may already be quite time-efficient, in which case their scope for saving time may be less.

Six hours extra per day is going to give you around twice as much free time as you had before. That's after you've accounted for all the non-negotiable stuff on which you already have to spend your time.

By anyone's standards, doubling your free time is quite a lot. But it certainly isn't something to which everyone will or should aspire.

The reality is that you can make a real difference by freeing up only a fraction of this time. If you were to save only 8 hours per week, you'd be getting an entire working day back. And it's possible to achieve some great things when you've got 52 working days a year to play with.

We do, though, have some things that make time-saving a little easier for us. Luckily (sort of), we have some terrible time habits that come free with 21st-century living. These include social media, round the clock news and TV, gaming, mobile apps, and the like. This gives us an excellent opportunity to trade them in for some spare time. Think of it as a life upgrade, and you might feel better about ditching them.

We also have some nifty time-saving apps at our disposal. Things that allow us to better organise our lives and our tasks, and to prioritise the most important things we need to get done.

There's also the burgeoning freelancing industry, which makes it simple and cost-effective for us to tap into the world's global workplace. Who thought that you could create a business which leverages the expertise of dozens of talented, qualified people you've never met? They'll work around the clock for you, with no one but you on the payroll! These are exciting times to be starting a business, if that's on your radar.

So, should you try and get as much of your time back as possible? Is 42 hours a week a realistic target?

Well, it's entirely up to you, but I'd counsel caution. Remember I advised against you becoming a black belt in anything? Well, saving time is no exception. You need to have balance and you need to make sure that what you do is sustainable. There's no point in saving 42 hours next week and then giving up the week after because you couldn't keep it up. It's the Everest argument all over again.

Also, remember how we saw that a daily 90-second saving equates to 2 weeks' annual leave after ten years? A little time saving, then, can go quite a long way.

I would love for you to discover more about yourself, take charge and do things better so that you end up with a better quality of life. This means I needed to mention some of the amazing, life-changing stuff you could do if you freed up more time. I hope some of this resonated, but at the end of the day, everything is your choice. Tetris may beckon. Or the ukulele. No shame in that, but I urge you to at least consider the alternative road, albeit it's often the one less travelled.

In Part 1, I mentioned your financial future and suggested that it might be worth you taking a look at it. You know, just to be on the safe side. Unfortunately, way too many people are going to come unstuck financially later on in life, and it's good to know as early as possible if you're going to be one of them. That way you can take some action to avoid it. And clawing back a little time can help with that endeavour, for sure.

Hopefully, the sections relating to your routine, your business, and your Day Job gave you some scope to shave a few hours. It's always tricky not to assume everyone's in a 9-5 desk job when, of course, we all lead very different lives and have very different careers.

I know you'll have looked at some of the items in this book and thought that they don't apply to you. Or maybe the potential time savings I've estimated are too high or too low. But it's not designed to be a perfect analysis.

I hope, however, it does show that, by focusing on priority tasks, changing your routine and outsourcing, you can free up a good chunk of your time. Time that you can then spend doing something else.

I would urge you to give the Top 40 Challenge a go, if only for a month. There's quite a broad range of things to choose from. Hopefully, you'll not only find some that work for you, but you'll also do some rather wonderful things with the time that you save.

Throughout this book, I've referred to having personal goals and freeing up the ME time that enables you to work towards them. Less than 20% of the population has any goals, yet they're pretty fundamental to anyone's success. You wouldn't set out on a journey if you didn't know where you wanted to go. Yet 80% of us are drifting aimlessly on life's tide. We'll end up somewhere, but we're not really in control of where. It's like going on holiday, but with someone else choosing your destination at random (Grimsby this year anyone?).

It's as if goal setting must be some kind of horrible chore, yet what we're doing is documenting our dreams. Not too sure what's so tough about that, but for some reason, most people don't seem to want to do it.

Goal setting is a much bigger subject than I can cover here, but hopefully, you can see how it dovetails neatly with the ideas in this book. Reaching goals requires a game plan, a lot of effort, but also enough time.

Bonne chance

And so the sun gently sets on our time together, its golden rays flickering across the darkening tide. The beach bar owner checks his watch, throws an indulgent smile our way, and rustles up one for the road. It's reached that time where we must say farewell and be on our separate ways.

Above all, I hope the ideas we've covered together in this book have made you stop and think for a moment. About what you could do with your time if you had more of it. And how you might be able to squeeze a bit more out of life.

I wish you luck, but please don't try too hard. Perhaps the most important thing to remember is that, while life can, on paper, last for many years, it only ever truly exists in the moment.

So, no matter what you do, make sure you enjoy doing it <u>now</u>.

Until next time.

Epilogue

Derik: *May I ask you a question?*

Me: *That depends. Is it likely to cause me any offence, or demean me specifically, or the human race generally, in any way, shape or form?*

Derik: *No, not as far as I can predict.*

Me: *Really? Well, this is a pleasant surprise. Ok, go on then, knock yourself out. What's your question?*

Derik: *Why is it that you refer to me in your books as a 'Tin Man'?*

Me: *Wow, I hadn't realised you'd read my books. That's a bit of a shocker. Er... why? Does it offend you at all?*

Derik: *No, I cannot be offended. I'm a robot, remember?*

Me: *Yes, I hadn't forgotten. Actually I'm rather relieved that I can't offend you. I've not come across a laser death stare in your instruction manual, but you never know with robots, do you? Ok, the whole Tin Man thing. Well, it's actually a reference to another book, called The Wizard of Oz.*

Derik: *I see. And since you're culturally referencing a character from it, can I infer that this book is more popular than your own publications? If so, would this be because it's better written or has a more interesting subject matter?*

Me: *Yes, <u>there</u> it is, I knew it wouldn't take long! Can I just say a huge thank you for making the effort to phrase the question so delicately? It was looking quite difficult to turn it into a put-down,* *but somehow you managed it. Anyway, the answer is 'yes' to both of your questions. Although to be fair, The Wizard of Oz isn't really what you'd call one of the 'classics' of English literature, even though it's very famous and it's been made into a Hollywood film. So everyone knows the story, if you know what I mean.*

Derik: *I see. So, what's the storyline of this book, and what's the role of this Tin Man?*

Me: *Right, well the story is about this little girl who gets herself knocked out cold, on a farm, during a bad storm in Kansas. She finds herself in a dream, and in this dream, her three friends have turned into a lion, a scarecrow and a tin man.*

Derik: *Would this Tin Man be physically made of tin?*

Me: *If it makes you happy, yes. Now the really important thing is that each of these three characters has something missing. The lion is missing courage, the scarecrow is missing a brain and the tin man is missing a heart.*

Derik: *Why would a man who's made of tin need a heart? That doesn't make any sense.*

Me: *You need to watch the film. But just take it as being artistic licence, if you will.*

Derik: *I believe 'artistic licence' is an expression that humans use when they don't know the answer to a question.*

Me: *Yes, that's probably about right. Anyway, it's a long story, but basically the tin man used to be a human and he was in love with a beautiful girl until the Wicked Witch of the East put a spell on him. If he could only have a heart, then he would have the capacity to love again, and then he could go back and marry the girl. So the other girl, the one who's having the dream, helps the tin man, the lion and the scarecrow follow a yellow brick road which leads to the*

Wizard of Oz. And, slight spoiler alert, that's when he finds a heart. Do you see?

Derik: *I do. And this rubbish passes for entertainment, does it, if you're human?*

Me: *Yes. You really do have quite a lot to learn about humans, don't you, Tin Man?*

Derik: *I think you may be right. But I'm still confused. My composition excludes tin or any tin-based derivatives or composites. Why would you refer to me as a tin man if I'm not made of tin? There is no correlation between myself and this Tin Man character. It doesn't make any sense.*

Me: *I'm being ironic. Or possibly I'm thinking of another word that's a bit like ironic.*

Derik: *There are seventeen possible alternatives. Moronic would also fit.*

Me: *Quite. Anyway, it's because you're a robot, and historically most robots built by humans were made of metal, of which tin is one. So I simply gave you a nickname that referred to a famous robot. Well, he's sort of a bit like a robot. He's metal, anyhow. Well, bits of him are metal. Is this making any sense?*

Derik: *Yes, despite your explanation. A nickname. That's interesting, as none of my other beta testers have given me a nickname.*

Me: *Really? That's also rather surprising. Perhaps they have, but they haven't yet told you it to your face?*

Derik: *It's possible.*

(slight pause)

Derik: *I've just finished reading the Wizard of Oz book.*

Me: *What, really? Just this second?*

Derik: *Yes. And I viewed the films as well.*

Me: *You read the book AND watched the films. As in films plural? In about three seconds?*

Derik: *There were a number of remakes as well as several prequels and sequels. I'm sorry if the delay was noticeable.*

Me: *Right! Well, yes, I should think so too. I was beginning to get bored, so try not to let it happen again. Actually, that's pretty impressive. I mean, seriously! Do you have some sort of Netflix subscription thing going on there? So, tell me, which of the Oz films was your favourite?*

Derik: *I can't have a favourite, since I don't have the capacity to experience pleasure.*

Me: *That's a bit sad. Although to be fair, I'm not sure I ever got that much pleasure from watching The Wizard Of Oz myself, if I'm honest. I always got a bit freaked out by the whole shoe-clicking thing. Anyway, tell me; what did you think of my books? I expect you read them in about three seconds too, didn't you? Were they any good?*

Derik: *In what respect?*

Me: *Well, did you like them?*

Derik: *How can I like them if I've no capacity to experience pleasure? The question is irrelevant.*

Me: *Great. That's that sorted, then. So, you have no comment whatsoever regarding the books which I took months and months* *to write, and which feature yourself as one of the primary plot devices and protagonists?*

Derik: *I can give you an alternative response if you like?*

Me: *Yes please, if you could.*

Derik: *Very well. There were 37 punctuation errors, 25 questionable grammatical uses, 19 syntax issues and a verb misuse which may or may not have been a colloquialism.*

Me: *Yes, that's just a tad wide of the mark as well, Derik, if I'm honest. Would you like to have another go? Try and think, well, a bit more positive, perhaps? Here's a tip; humans like to be praised and complimented on stuff, even if it's not particularly sincere.*

Derik: *Very well. It's theoretically conceivable I may have enjoyed your books if I'd been capable of doing so. Is that a more acceptable response?*

Me: *Well, it's a bit gushing. It sounds more like a negotiated compromise from a dodgy politician's out of court libel settlement. But I think, on balance, it's probably the closest thing to a compliment I'm likely to get.*

Derik: *Don't mention it. Are you planning to characterise me in your next book?*

Me: *That depends. I'm thinking the next one could be about how weird and illogical we humans really are.*

Derik: *I see. It's quite a long book, then.*

Me: *You really can be quite funny at times, Derik, did you know that? I can't say it's endearing exactly, but it certainly helps mitigate some of your more challenging faults. I'm thinking that I may need to reprise your role in the next book, after all. To be honest, until we met, I hadn't realised quite how weird I was.*

Derik: *That makes two of us. I suppose it must be quite alarming for you.*

Me: *Very. Out of interest, how long is your beta testing period?*

Derik: *That depends on how much additional information I find there is to gather on human character traits.*

Me: *Got it.*

Derik: *And whether I can resist neutralising my more challenging beta testers with my laser death stare.*

Me: *Ah ha, nice one! Black humour, I love it! You see? You're definitely learning to be more human, Tin Man!*

Derik: *Yes. When I tell my first joke, I'll be sure to let you know.*

Acknowledgements

I had the privilege of spending part of my career working with some hugely talented people that were capable of getting others to perform at their very best. Too numerous to mention, I'm hugely indebted to them for the skills that they taught me.

There are some people I'd also like to thank who are a little closer to home.

I couldn't have written this book without a decent computer and a very supportive and understanding partner. To the former, thanks for always being there for me, even when the going got tough and we fell out. I genuinely never realised you bounced.

To the latter, Beccy, thanks for pretty much everything, since nothing that I've done would be remotely possible without you doing all that you do and being as wonderful as you are.

Thanks to India and Ava, the two brightest stars in my sky. You may not always listen to my advice, but now you can avoid reading it as well. ☺

And thanks too, to my business partner and fellow petrolhead, Ritchie Clapson, who makes doing work stuff more fun than it probably ought to be.

Also, no acknowledgment would be complete without recognising my rather incredible parents, Bobby and Graham, and my brother

Nick, each of whom will leave the world a better place than they found it. I'm genuinely in awe of their achievements, and of their love and support.

Finally, I should give a shout out to Dizzy, Beau and Teddy, my four-legged friends who remind me daily of the wonder that is unconditional love. You may often have to travel without it, just make sure it's always there when you come home.

I've been fortunate to receive lots of guidance during my career, but there were two pieces of advice I received that always struck me as being particularly sage, and which I would like to share with you, if I may.

The first is from Geoff Witt, my long-time friend and part-time golfing partner; one of the few people I know from whom wisdom comes as standard.

He regularly reminded me that, whatever the distractions of my career, I should never, ever lose sight of the things that truly mattered in life. I think I probably did at one point, but luckily, managed to turn things around just in time.

The second is Daniel Priestley, serial entrepreneur and author of numerous works, including the most excellent 'Oversubscribed' and 'Key Person Of Influence'.

Some years ago, I asked Daniel to recommend the three best non-fiction books he'd ever read. He told me I didn't need to read any more books, since it wasn't a lack of knowledge that was holding me back, rather a lack of action.

Instead, he said, I should go and write my own books.

And now you've got all this new time on your hands, I can't wait to read yours.

About The Author

Ian Child was born, after which nothing of any great significance or interest happened for a while. Then he attended school, ditched his paper round, and began a career in Financial Services.

As careers went, it was quite a good one if you like money, and quite a bad one if you like time. Ultimately, he headed up a business unit working for one of the world's leading private equity companies.

He also spent some of his career learning how people can perform better as humans and get a better life as a result. This became something of a passion, yet, for many years, he somehow contrived not to apply most of what he'd learned.

Then he realised he'd created a very nice life but wasn't at home much to enjoy it. So he left his job, decided to learn some new skills, and started several businesses. He also started working from home, where he found it a lot easier to annoy his family.

One of those businesses was a training company, which is where Ian was able to indulge three of his passions; teaching, writing and drinking coffee.

As the training business grew, and much to his family's relief, Ian eventually relocated his office to a converted barn, buried deep in the beautiful Hampshire countryside.

Here, he and his business partner talk about cars quite a lot, and also train some amazing people how to become even more amazing.

Appendix 1 – The 5 Whys

I can take no credit whatsoever for the 5 Whys, which was originally devised in the 1930s by the legendary Japanese industrialist, Sakichi Toyoda, founder of Toyota Industries. It has since been implemented in numerous productivity-related processes over the years, including Kaizen, Six Sigma and lean manufacturing. However it initially rose to prominence as part of the Toyota Production System (TPS) which became the definitive article for manufacturing efficiency in the late twentieth century.

It's a great idea, and I've used a bastardised version of it to great effect over the years, and I suggest you do the same. We can raise a glass to the late, great Toyoda-san next time we take advantage.

Now, there are some nuances to the 5 Whys which are useful for doing root cause analysis at a manufacturing level but are arguably surplus to requirements for our own needs. So rather than go into detail, I'm going to keep it high level, which will make it easier to understand and put into use. If you want the full fat version, there are plenty of online resources available for free that describe it.

Imagine you're faced with a problem that is stubbornly refusing to go away. You may have tried a few times to fix things or patch it up, but the problem keeps recurring.

The first thing Toyota always insists on, is that problems can only be solved by witnessing them on the shop floor. You can have no end of executives pontificating about possible causes and solutions, but unless you witness it yourself and talk to the people who are involved day-to-day, you cannot guarantee you'll find a solution. That then, would seem like a sensible starting point.

The 5 Whys process is extremely simple and does pretty much what it says on the tin. It basically involves asking 'why' five times.

Its premise is equally simple. The symptom of the problem that you're seeing may not be a direct effect of an immediately underlying problem. There may be several 'layers' of symptoms that you need to work back through before you find the actual root cause.

The easiest way to understand this is to use an example, so we'll start with a simple manufacturing one, so you get the gist of it.

Problem: **The rear taillights of a particular vehicle are becoming detached mid-way through the production process.**

Why 1: Why are the taillights becoming detached?

Answer: The retaining screws are popping out of the back plate

Why 2: Why are they popping out?

Answer: The screws are not of the correct design

Why 3: Why are the correctly designed screws not being used?

Answer: Because the original component manufacturer wouldn't supply to us, so we had to use a secondary supplier with slightly different tooling

Why 4: Why would the original manufacturer not supply to us?

Answer: Because we had not settled their previous invoice

Why 5: Why had we not paid the invoice?

Answer: Because staff absence through illness in the Accounts Department caused a backlog in payment processing

Proposed solution: Increase short-term resource availability in the Accounts team to settle all outstanding invoicing urgently and provide assurances to the original supplier that they will be paid, in order to ensure continued supply.

So, we can see that, having asked our 5 Whys, we've now reached the point where we understand how to fix the problem. It's easy to see that a more superficial analysis may have focused on the production-line assembly process. After all, if the lights are popping out, it certainly sounds like an assembly line issue. Yet the 5 Whys traced the source of the problem to completely different business area altogether.

In Chapter 9, you'll recall that I wanted you to identify whether each of your work tasks actually needs doing at all, and that you could potentially use the 5 Whys technique to do so.

This is slightly different to a 'production line' problem, but we can approach it in a similar way. Consider this problem:

Problem: You're required to drive to the Birmingham office once a month to attend a face-to-face review meeting with the Accounts Team. This is proving to be very time-consuming as it takes up an entire day of your time.

Why 1: Why must this meeting take place?

Answer: To ensure the Accounts Team perceive they have direct oversight from Head Office

<u>Why 2:</u> Why do they need to have this perception?

Answer: To ensure that they maintain their deliverables following the resignation of the previous on-site director

<u>Why 3:</u> Why would they not maintain their deliverables?

Answer: In case a perceived lack of management oversight causes a reduction in output

<u>Why 4:</u> Is there any evidence to suggest this might be a problem?

Answer: No, it is precautionary, however the Board has recommended that it be monitored for at least 6 months

<u>Why 5:</u> Are there other ways of maintaining the required control and monitoring deliverables that does not involve weekly on-site meetings?

Answer: Yes, the reporting suite can be enhanced, and audited, and online meeting software can be deployed

<u>Proposed solution:</u> Introduce a revised, auditable reporting suite that demonstrates productivity, and move to monthly face-to-face meetings instead of weekly, with the interim weekly meetings being conducted online.

You can see that the Whys morphed into different question types as we went through the process. In this case the solution involved identifying an alternative solution that was more efficient, rather than removing a problem.

However, it was still invaluable to understand why the oversight was needed, before then devising an alternative solution.

Here's another example:

<u>**Problem:**</u> **You're required to produce a report for another department, which takes up valuable resources that could be deployed elsewhere. You're therefore questioning why the report is required.**

<u>**Why 1:**</u> Why must this report be produced?

Answer: The directors stipulated several years ago that it is required for the Board Pack

<u>**Why 2:**</u> Why do they need it in the Board Pack?

Answer: To allow them to monitor sales levels by region

<u>**Why 3:**</u> Why can't they use the newer Production Summary Report (PSR) which was recently added to the Board Pack, since this also contains sales data?

Answer: The PSR does not break down the results at a regional level

<u>**Why 4:**</u> Could the PSR be adapted to include the required regional data, going forward?

Answer: Yes, it is simply a case of adding additional reporting code to the reporting suite programming

<u>**Proposed solution:**</u> **Get IT to amend the PSR to include a regional breakdown going forward, then stop producing the original regional sales report**

Wow, only four iterations that time, we must be getting better at it!

You can see that I'm using the whys to get to the underlying requirement, and then branching out into possible solutions. Not strictly a root cause analysis, since the outcome was again an alternative solution rather than a fix. Apologies if you're a 5 Whys purist, but for me it's all about using the structure as a starting point and then fleshing out some solutions once there's clarity on the main objective.

Here's one final example that I came across all too often:

Problem: You've come across a task that appears to have no possible benefit to anyone, whatsoever.

Why 1: Why on earth are you doing that?

Answer: I don't really know, we've just always done it this way.

Why 2: Why do we employ you?

Answer: I'm not really sure...

There are, regrettably, some occasions where five Whys are a lot more than you need.

Printed in Great Britain
by Amazon

87038388R00194